LEGENDS OF BASEBALL

Legends of Baseball

*An Oral History of
The Game's Golden Age*

WALTER M. LANGFORD

DIAMOND COMMUNICATIONS, INC.
SOUTH BEND, INDIANA

1987

LEGENDS OF BASEBALL
Copyright © 1987 by Diamond Communications, Inc.

Manufactured in the United States of America

Diamond Communications, Inc.
Post Office Box 88
South Bend, Indiana 46624
(219) 287-5008

Library of Congress Cataloging-in-Publication Data

Langford, Walter M.
  Legends of baseball.

  1. Baseball players—United States—Biography.
2. Baseball—United States—History. I. Title.
GV865.A1L35 1987   796.357'092'2 [B]   87-5354
ISBN 0-912083-25-5
ISBN 0-912083-20-4 (pbk.)

To Mary, my wife,
whose daily prodding turned this
project into reality.

Contents

Preface

It has long been popular among those who delve into baseball's past to conjecture and argue over how the sport originated and who gets the credit for starting it. But it matters little whether baseball evolved from the British games of rounders or cricket, or whether Alexander Cartwright or Abner Doubleday deserves to be called the father of the game. The simple historical fact is that baseball in the last quarter of the 19th century became the first American sport to capture the public fancy on both the professional and amateur levels.

Then, professional baseball burst upon the 20th century American scene as a rowdy and boisterous teenager. Regarded with suspicion and some contempt by many in the upper levels of society—and even some not so upper—its appeal was distinctly limited for some time. Lots of old-time ballplayers relate how their parents vigorously opposed their becoming involved in baseball as a profession.

During the first year of the new century the monopoly of the established National League was challenged by a group of upstart promoters headed by Ban Johnson. They succeeded in putting together the American League and, with the grudging consent of the older League, thus created what has ever since been known as the major leagues, or big leagues.

In the eight decades and more since that time the organizational structure of major league baseball has not changed drastically. Only once was the hegemony of the two leagues put in doubt, that coming with the short-lived but upsetting appearance of the Federal League in 1914-15. Luring several dozen players away from their American and National League clubs, including a few standouts and some fading stars, the Feds put on two rousing pennant races but were to lose out both at the box office and in the courts.

The disappearance of the Federal League left two notable items in its wake. Charlie Weeghman, owner of the Federal team in Chicago, was allowed to buy the Chicago Cubs, with his new Federal League park later becoming the famous Wrigley Field. And Judge Kenesaw Mountain Landis, who presided over the court proceedings and the eventual settlement with the Federal League, was installed in 1920 as baseball's first commissioner, following the Black Sox scandal of the 1919 World Series.

After a couple of franchise shifts in the American League (Milwaukee to St. Louis in 1902 and Baltimore to New York in 1903), the eight-team leagues remained unchanged until the Boston Braves decamped from Beantown for Milwaukee in 1953. In subsequent years other teams were moved, most notably in 1958 when the Dodgers went from Brooklyn to Los Angeles and the Giants from New York to San Francisco. Later came the gradual expansion of the two leagues from 16 teams to the present total of 26. And of course all of the original franchises, and several of the newer ones, have changed owners once or oftener.

So, the structural changes in the big leagues have been relatively few given the length of time involved. But in other respects the differences in baseball between 1901 and 1987 are many and rather important. For one thing, the players in the early years of the century, in contrast with today, were a rough bunch whose drinking and fighting made them unwelcome at the better hotels and night clubs.

Yet there were admirable figures to be found in the game from the beginning. Christy Mathewson, for instance, came to the Giants in 1900 after graduating from Bowdoin College to become what some say was the first college graduate in the majors. This background, plus his All-American appearance and fantastic skill, allowed Christy to exert a strong influence for the best in baseball and to carve a niche as one of the game's most superlative pitchers.

Connie Mack was there too in 1901 as manager of the Philadelphia Athletics, a post he would retain (as well as becoming the owner in later years) until 1950. Connie's influence on the game was for good, and through five decades he stood forth as a respected and admired beacon.

And there were other fine figures in the game even in the first decade of the century, yet enough of the players were rowdies that baseball had a rather bad name for a while. Still, the sport grew steadily in attendance and public support; it was the first professional sport played widely in our country. In the era prior to U.S. entrance into World War I in 1917, when there still was no radio nor TV, baseball came to be a major form of entertainment. It commanded growing attention in the sports pages of the major newspapers and public interest began to surge.

In the epoch from 1901 through World War I the major leagues were dominated by a small group of the most successful clubs. They were the New York Giants under John McGraw, Connie Mack's Philadelphia Athletics, the Chicago Cubs led by Frank Chance, the Boston Red Sox, the Pittsburgh Pirates, the Detroit Tigers, and the Chicago White Sox. With only three exceptions every one of the 36 league championships in the years 1901-18 was claimed by these seven clubs. The exceptions were the Boston Braves in 1914, the Philadelphia Phillies in 1915, and the Brooklyn Dodgers in 1916.

By 1919 baseball had grown up and matured. It had won the support of the public and it was becoming known as the national pastime. With the victorious end of WW I it appeared headed for unprecedented success. But in 1919 came the scandal of the World Series in which eight of the White Sox conspired with gamblers to throw the Series to the Cincinnati Reds. Baseball was shaken to its roots and many predicted that the public would turn its back on the sport, perhaps permanently.

Two things saved baseball and allowed it to regain its popularity. One was the naming of Judge Landis as Commissioner of Baseball with truly broad power to police the sport. He gave baseball integrity such as it had not known even before the Black Sox. The other saving occurrence was the eruption of Babe Ruth, who pounded the livelier ball introduced in 1920 for 54 home runs, an unbelievable total shattering his own record of 29 set just the year before. Babe Ruth's bat and charisma revolutionized the game on the field and cemented the sport as The National Pastime.

The period between the two World Wars can only be labelled the Golden Age of Baseball. After 1920 crowds ballooned, interest sky-rocketed, radio carried the games to the urban centers and across the countryside, salaries increased in

Ruth's wake, great and colorful stars multiplied as never before. Baseball became a bigger business, though of course not the BIG business of the '70s and '80s fueled primarily by TV revenues.

The preparation of this book responds to a twofold motivation. For one thing, I feel the need to emphasize further the greatness of the pre-1950 period in the development of baseball by having some of the representative figures of that epoch recount many of their memories and experiences. Besides this, there is the intention to reveal in some detail the numerous differences in the playing conditions and circumstances of that era in contrast to the present.

All of this should give the younger fans of today the opportunity to listen in on reminiscences of real stars of the past. Also it should afford the American public, particularly the older generations, the chance to indulge the current nostalgic appetite for things and periods out of our past.

As a boy I became enamoured of the game of baseball. I played it to the hilt in high school, college, and with the semi-pros. Any further ambitions were done in by the curveball, those shoals upon which countless young dreamers of baseball greatness have crashed.

The collapse of a dream does not imply, however, that interest vanishes. Quite the contrary. My attention shifted avidly to those fortunate enough to realize their dreams. Now, after a lifetime of following teams and players and pennant races and World Series and statistics and the history of the game, it seems the right thing to do to put together a book relating the careers and experiences of some of the fine players I have long admired and, yes, envied.

On launching this project I stepped into the footprints of Larry Ritter and Bill Honig, who plowed part of this field before me. It was 1966 when Ritter gave us his memorable *The Glory of Their Times*, and nine years later his good friend Honig followed up with *Baseball When the Grass Was Real*, another fascinating volume.

Each of these works gave true baseball fans deep pleasure through skillful presentation of the reminiscences of many old ballplayers. The ones Ritter featured were from the early years of this century and few are still alive today. Honig dealt with a later generation. Nearly all of his players were contemporaries of the ones presented in this collection.

Having made the decision to extend the work of Ritter and Honig, I contacted a number of old-time stars. Finding enough of them willing to cooperate, I set forth with tape recorder in hand to visit them where they live across the land. We talked for hours on baseball in general and their own experiences and memories in particular. The chapters which follow are distilled from the absorbing conversations we enjoyed.

I say enjoyed because that's how it was. Obviously I figured to enjoy it, but the exciting part was to see how these old-time ballplayers warmed to the subject. From a calm and casual start their enthusiasm gathered momentum which carried on to the end of the conversation. No surprise in this. They were reliving in memory and word some of their finest moments and most cherished recollections. So, in every case we began talking as strangers and parted as friends.

My conversations were with players whose careers fell almost entirely between 1920 and 1950. It turned out that one of them, Charlie Grimm, first reached the majors in 1916, and Dutch Leonard, Johnny Vander Meer, and Marty Marion played into the early '50s. When I talked with them (between '82 and '85), they ranged in age from 68 to 84.

In view of their age it is not surprising that death has taken some of them since we had our conversations. They are Glenn Wright, Dutch Leonard, Charlie Grimm, George Uhle, Larry French, and Luke Sewell.

When we were talking the conversations were far-ranging, and only a portion of what was said can be included here. But when the ballplayers are being quoted in these pages, the words are theirs just as I have them recorded on tape. Occasionally I have rearranged some of their comments to provide a better sequence to their narrative.

While the emphasis in each conversation was on baseball as it was in the old days and each player's experiences and recollections, we also touched briefly on their thoughts about baseball today. There was agreement that the playing conditions and equipment are different and better today. None of them played on artificial surfaces and it is their opinion that the hard surface changes the game considerably. Its only advantages, in their eyes, are that it assures truer bounces and fewer rainouts.

Few of these old-timers played much night ball. They feel that baseball was meant to be played under the sun, though they readily admit that playing under the lights makes possible larger crowds. They are almost unanimous in being opposed to the designated hitter. For them, the DH is not a complete player and his presence changes the game unnecessarily.

To a man they say the hitters today can't begin to compare with the hitters of yesteryear. They don't blame the players of this era for using their union and free agency to command today's outsized salaries (incredible in their eyes), but they regard the players of today as being pampered and spoiled. And they're certain that ballplayers nowadays don't have a fraction of the fun they did back in the old days.

One thing which disturbs these old-timers is the matter of baseball's pension plan. What rankles is that all but a few of them were left out, by vote of the active players, when the plan was instituted in the late '40s. It seems that when the older players protested their exclusion, sometimes they were asked, "What did you ever do for us?"

To anyone who gives thought to the course of baseball history, it is at once obvious what the pre-1950 players did for the game itself and thus for the players of a later time. They molded and refined the game as it was passed on to them from the 19th century. Like workmen of every description in their time, they bent every effort to produce their best.

They made baseball so competitive and interesting that the sporting public embraced it and cherished it more than any other sport. And they did it under rugged conditions. No pampering of any kind. Moreover, all but a few did it for pay that any self-respecting groundskeeper of today would turn away from in scorn.

So what did the old-timers do for the modern ballplayers? To put it briefly, hundreds upon hundreds of skilled and hardworking players of the earlier generations of baseball handed down to the more recent ones a legacy, a tradition, a sport which they had raised to its peak and which the American public took to its heart. Today's players, though they may not take the time to recognize and consider it, are more indebted to baseball's old-timers than they will ever be able to repay.

I am indebted to Diamond Communications for their encouragement, patience, and direct support at all times. To Bob Broeg of the *St. Louis Post-Dispatch* I am especially grateful for his advice and valued assistance. And to the many friends who constantly urged me on to complete this manuscript, I express appreciation and the hope they find pleasure in the finished product.

To the major league stars of the past who are highlighted in this book I especially acknowledge a very deep gratitude for their willingness to share with me—and with all readers of these pages—many moments and recollections of their baseball careers. The book belongs to them. It is their story. It was my pleasure to put it together. Some may feel it was a labor of love. It was.

1

Baseball's Golden Age

Each of the old-time ballplayers highlighted in the chapters which follow performed during part or all of their careers in the period labelled by many observers as the Golden Age of baseball. This was the time between the 20th century's two World Wars, roughly from 1918 to 1941, with a little leeway on each side.

Not only did baseball truly come of age in that period but it also produced during that time far more superstars than ever before or since.

Two main factors contributed to the maturing of baseball and its broad acceptance by the public after 1920. One was the naming of Judge Landis as Commissioner. This inspired confidence and insured the integrity of the sport. The other was the effect of Babe Ruth's home run prowess. It revolutionized the game in a manner that greatly appealed to the public. Still other factors were the growth of baseball's farm system (Branch Rickey's brain child of the '20s), the gradual emergence and importance of relief specialists in the bullpen, and higher salaries stemming partly from Ruth's success.

As for the fabulous collection of superstars in that epoch, consider for a moment this array of baseball talent which wrote indelible chapters in the annals of baseball history:

* Walter Johnson   * Hack Wilson   * Jimmy Foxx
* Tris Speaker   * George Sisler   * Eddie Collins
* Lou Gehrig   * Rogers Hornsby   * Frankie Frisch

1

* Al Simmons
* Dizzy Dean
* Harry Heilmann
* Joe DiMaggio
* Gabby Hartnett
* Lefty Gomez
* Paul Waner
* Bill Terry
* Casey Stengel
* Earl Averill
* Dazzy Vance
* Red Faber
* Waite Hoyt
* Max Carey
  Carl Mays
* Bucky Harris
* Eppa Rixey
* Al Lopez
  Art Nehf
  Charlie Grimm
  Glenn Wright
  Babe Herman
* Rick Ferrell
  Paul Derringer
* Sam Rice
* Arky Vaughan
* Ty Cobb
* Babe Ruth

* Lefty Grove
* Ted Williams
* Ducky Medwick
* Bill Dickey
* Hank Greenberg
* Joe Cronin
* Charlie
    Gehringer
* Jim Bottomley
* Stan Coveleski
* Heinie Manush
* Ted Lyons
  Lefty O'Doul
* Kiki Cuyler
* Fred Lindstrom
* Joe Sewell
* Travis Jackson
  Mel Harder
* Johnny Mize
  Lon Warneke
* Lloyd Waner
* Dave Bancroft
* Rabbit
    Maranville
  Wes Ferrell
* George Kelly
* Grover
    Cleveland
    Alexander

* Burleigh Grimes
* Mickey
    Cochrane
* Carl Hubbell
* Bob Feller
* Pie Traynor
* Mel Ott
* Edd Roush
* Luke Appling
* Zack Wheat
* Red Ruffing
* Goose Goslin
* Billy Herman
* Chick Hafey
* Herb Pennock
* Rube Marquard
* Chuck Klein
  George Uhle
  Bucky Walters
* Jesse Haines
  Freddie
    Fitzsimmons
  Dixie Walker
* Earl Combs
  Tony Lazzeri
* Ernie Lombardi
  Urban Shocker

* Denotes Hall of Fame member

Add the rest of the players spotlighted in this book plus a lot of others and it is not hard to see that the period of which we are speaking was clearly the most talent-laden in the history of baseball. For good measure add the fact that the sport was enlivened in those days as never since by colorful figures galore and great characters whose deeds and antics are legendary.

In Baseball's Golden Age great hitters were plentiful. Batting averages were amazingly higher than now, even though great pitchers abounded in that era too. Consider some examples of their hitting prowess:

Item: In 1985 the Boston Red Sox led the majors in team batting with an average of .282. Not one of the other 25 teams averaged as high as .270. Contrast that with the 1930 season, when nine of the 16 major league clubs had team batting averages over .300, and the poorest hitting team of them all averaged .264. The New York Giants led with .319 but even the last-place Phillies hit .315 as a team. Indeed, in 1930 the entire National League (regulars, pitchers, pinch hitters, and utility players on all eight ball clubs) had a combined batting average of .303!

Item: In 1985 only 11 players in the National League and seven in the American League who qualified for the batting title hit .300 or better. A total of 18. Ponder for a moment the fact that in 1930 the .300 average was attained by a total of 73 batters, 42 in the National League and 31 in the American. Lest one think that 1930 was a weird exception, three other years chosen at random during that era show 69 .300 batters in 1921, 59 in 1925, and 51 in 1936.

Item: Of the 50 players with the highest all-time career batting averages, only two (Rod Carew and Roberto Clemente) played their entire careers after the Golden Age. Fourteen others finished playing prior to 1920. Stan Musial had barely reached the majors as our Golden epoch ended. Ted Williams had the bulk of his career later but in 1941 belted the ball at a .406 clip. And Joe DiMaggio's time in the majors was about evenly split between the Golden Age and later. So, 31 of the top 50 belong completely to that golden time and two others enhanced it considerably.

Item: In the modern history of baseball beginning in 1901 the magic batting average of .400 has been achieved a total of 13 times. Ty Cobb and Rogers Hornsby each did it three times and George Sisler twice. The others were Nap Lajoie, Joe Jackson, Harry Heilmann, Bill Terry, and Ted Williams. And every one of them did it in the Golden Age or earlier!

Item: One more area in which the old-timers put the modern hitters to shame is in the matter of strikeouts. A comparison of 1985 statistics with those of

1920 reveals that the batters in the earlier year struck out just a little more than half as often as they do nowadays. In 1985, 29 major league hitters struck out more than 100 times, led by Steve Balboni with 166 whiffs. Nobody fanned 100 times in 1920, when George Kelly's 92 was high in the majors. *The Baseball Encyclopedia* lists the 35 major leaguers with the most strikeouts per at bat, and not a single one of them played in the pre-1950 era. On the list of players with the fewest strikeouts per at bat, the only post-1950 hitters are Nellie Fox and Don Mueller. Joe Sewell of course is the all-time champion at not striking out. He had two seasons with a total of just three strikeouts and three others with only four and he averaged one strikeout for every 62 times at bat.

Item: The number of runs batted in during a season is one of the most important indicators of a batter's power and value. A statistic which goes beyond the RBI figure is that of "Runs Produced," which is calculated by adding RBIs and runs scored and then deducting the number of home runs (because a home run is tallied in both of those categories). In the history of major league baseball the total of 250 runs produced in a season has been reached only 29 times. In only three instances was this feat accomplished in years outside of the Golden Age—by Nap Lajoie (256) in 1901, Ty Cobb (263) in 1911, and Ted Williams (266) in 1949. The significant thing is that nobody has produced as many as 250 runs in a single season since 1949.

Lou Gehrig is the all-time RP champ with 301 in 1931, Babe Ruth ranks second with 289 in 1921, and Chuck Klein third with 288 in 1930. Both Gehrig and Ruth produced 250 runs or more in five different seasons, and the following hitters did it twice: Jimmy Foxx, Hank Greenberg, Al Simmons, Klein, Hack Wilson, and Rogers Hornsby. The only others to reach 250 or better (besides Lajoie, Cobb and Williams) were Kiki Cuyler, Joe DiMaggio, and Charlie Gehringer. Hank Aaron's best in this category was 207 in 1963, and Stan Musial reached 227 in 1948. The highest Willie Mays got was 223 in 1962. And of today's active players, Don Baylor compiled the best total of 223 in 1979.

The difference in pitching between the Golden Age and later is not so great. Among the 300-game winners, there were three in the golden years (Walter Johnson, Grover Alexander, and Lefty Grove) and seven since then (Warren Spahn, Early Wynn, Gaylord Perry, Steve Carlton, Tom Seaver, Phil Niekro, and Don Sutton). When we come to career shutouts we find Johnson and Alexander are far ahead of the field (with 113 and 90 respectively), but in the short list of those with 50 or more shutouts the modern period prevails with the likes of Spahn, Bob Gibson, Don Sutton, Tom Seaver, Jim Palmer, Steve Carlton, Juan Marichal, Perry, and Nolan Ryan. Walter Johnson was the all-time strikeout king with 3,508 from 1927 until the 1983 season, when first Ryan, then Carlton and Perry and finally Seaver overtook him. In complete games and innings pitched, the old-timers again have an edge, but when it comes to relief pitchers the leaders are all from the post-1950 era.

Numerous differences exist between old-time baseball and the game as played today which do not concern performance on the field but rather other aspects of the overall baseball operation in the major leagues. Here are some of those differences:

— In those days there were only 16 teams, eight in each league.
— The schedules called mostly for four-game series. Since fewer trips were made to each city during the season, postponements caused more five-game series and doubleheaders.
— Travel was by train almost completely.
— There was no night ball in the majors until 1935. Each team was limited to seven night games per year for a while. The number was raised to 14 after World War II, and later nearly all limits were removed.
— There were only two umpires, one at home plate and one for the bases. The plate umpire had to rule on balls hit down the foul lines and also on home runs hit near the foul lines. There were no foul poles and so home runs were allowed only if the ball landed fair rather than if it left the playing field in fair territory. If one umpire had to leave the

game through injury or somehow didn't ever get to the ball park, the two teams would have to agree on a player or a coach from one team to act as the base umpire.

— The strike zone was larger, the pitching mound was higher, gloves and mitts were laughably smaller and flimsier.

— Infielders and outfielders, when they retired the other team and came in to bat, threw their gloves on the grass of the playing field, thus creating a certain hazard for fielders and even for the batted ball.

— Until around 1930 there were a few instances in which a team would allow a pinch runner for a slightly disabled player on the other team, with the player permitted to continue thereafter in the game.

— Batters wore no batting helmets nor batting gloves, and hitters were much more commonly brushed back or knocked down by pitches.

— Players wore no numbers or names on their uniforms, which gave real meaning to the old cry, "You can't tell the players without a scorecard." Note that it was just a scorecard and not a fancy program as is sold in all parks today.

— No electronic scoreboards. The simple scoreboards then in service were hand-operated and gave the score by innings of the game in progress as well as the batteries and scores of other games in the same league.

— The outfield walls were not padded and there were no warning tracks (except that in Fenway Park the outfielder went up a rather steep incline as he neared the wall). The outfield walls carried a number of signs advertising various products and companies.

— Photographers were allowed on the field and moved in close to the action when a crucial play was developing, sometimes interfering with players.

— There were no artificial surfaces.

— No TV, of course, until after World War II. Radio broadcasts came into popularity in the 1920s.

— Games were played in much less time than it now takes. Complete games in an hour or so were fairly common.
— The players thought, talked, and lived baseball infinitely more than most of them do now, especially on trains and in hotel lobbies.
— Relief pitchers as such came into the picture only after the performance of Fred Marberry in that role in 1924.
— No minimum salary, and players' salaries were but a faint fraction of what they are today. Rookies now get more than many great stars earned at their peak.
— There were no guaranteed, no-trade, or multiple-year contracts.
— No free agency after a few years. Indeed, no free agency, period.
— No pension plan, either then or now, for these old-time players.
— No players' agents, no players' union, no strikes. (Actually, the Detroit Tigers went on strike for one day in 1912 to protest the suspension of Ty Cobb by the league president for assaulting an abusive fan.)
— The old ball parks were more individualized and more cozy, with the fans closer to the action. Varying more in capacity and dimensions than all the new parks, they also had their distinctive characteristics in terms of outfield walls, angles, distances, etc. An outfielder had to learn to play the angles in each different park. The only old ball parks still in use today are Comiskey and Wrigley in Chicago, Fenway in Boston, and Tiger Stadium in Detroit. Yankee Stadium dates from 1923 but has been considerably remodeled in recent times.
— Not only were ballplayers paid very little in those days but also on road trips their daily allowance for meals was scant, hardly enough to buy a Big Mac these days. Moreover, endorsement of products by ballplayers was quite rare back then. Indeed, their opportunities for outside income were few and far between.

— Players (usually bench warmers) were often put to work as coaches at first or third base, because teams generally had only a couple of coaches on their staff.

— There were no public address systems, and so the lineups and other announcements (pinch hitters, relief pitchers, substitutions, etc.) were given through megaphones.

— The playing fields (all grass and dirt, of course) were not given the same manicuring and professional attention they receive today. Consequently, bad bounces were a part of the game and to be expected at any given moment.

— The same ball was left in play as long as it was not fouled into the stands or hit out of the park. Even with this obvious advantage, the pitchers were unable to keep the great batters of those days from achieving all the accomplishments detailed earlier.

All the foregoing having been said, it is now time to let some of the Golden Age stars of the diamond speak for themselves and tell us how it was in their day.

So, sit back and begin a nostalgic journey into baseball's past.

2

Joe Sewell

Tragedy stunned the baseball world on August 16, 1920. In a game at the Polo Grounds in New York, Yankee pitcher Carl Mays threw a ball which struck the Cleveland Indians' shortstop, Ray Chapman, in the head. This was, of course, a few decades before batting helmets came into use. Chapman never regained consciousness and died the next day.

This fatal accident, the only one of its kind in major league history, was a terrible blow to the Cleveland team. Chapman, in his ninth big league season, was a sparkplug and the Indians had no suitable replacement. At the time of his death Chapman was batting .303 and was one of the top-rated shortstops in the American League.

For about three weeks the Indians used Harry Lunte at short. Harry's previous major league experience consisted of 26 games with Cleveland in 1919. He hit .195 that year and was hardly punishing the ball at .197 in 1920 when he pulled a hamstring and went out of action.

In desperation Tris Speaker, the Cleveland manager, called on a utility outfielder, Joe Evans, to take over at shortstop until something else could be arranged. The dilemma of the Indians is underscored by the fact that they were in a dogfight for the American League pennant with the Chicago White Sox and the New York Yankees.

In 1919 the White Sox won the flag but were upset in the World Series by the Cincinnati Reds, five games to three. Even before the Series ended, rumors were rampant that some of the Sox players had conspired with New York gamblers to "throw" the Series. These rumors jelled in the last month of the 1920

9

Little Joe Sewell, the best "contact" hitter in baseball history. Sewell, with Cleveland and the Yankees from 1920 through '33, played two full seasons in which he struck out only four times each. (Another year, he fanned only three times in 109 games.) Despite a defensive attitude at the plate, shortstop-third baseman Sewell averaged .312 lifetime and twice (1923-24) drove in 100 runs a season. In 1977 he was inducted into the Baseball Hall of Fame.

season when a grand jury in Chicago indicted eight Sox players after hearing the confessions of two of them. Owner Charles Comiskey at once suspended all eight. The loss of the "Black Sox" ruined Chicago's chance to repeat as American League champs. Eventually they finished two games back of Cleveland, with the Yankees another game behind.

Cleveland had a working agreement with the New Orleans Pelicans of the Southern Association, and at this juncture they brought up a 21-year-old Alabama lad only three months out of college. His name was Joe Sewell.

Few players had entered the majors in a more dramatic situation. And very few with so little experience have ever made it so big once they got their chance. Joe batted .329 in the last 22 games of that 1920 season. With Sewell filling the vacuum at short Cleveland went on to win the pennant and then took the World Series five games to two over the Brooklyn Dodgers.

Joe Sewell was no temporary phenom. He played in the majors through 14 seasons (the last three with the New York Yankees) and hit over .300 in 10 of those years. His career batting average of .312 places him 66th among all the thousands of hitters in both major leagues. Besides the 1920 Series with the Indians, Joe also played with the winning Yankees in the 1932 Series clash against the Chicago Cubs. Joe's career was crowned in 1977 with his induction into the Baseball Hall of Fame.

"Joe, how did you get started in baseball?"

"I was born and raised in Titus, Alabama, down in Elmore County. My father was a country doctor and he practiced medicine in the country for 40 years in the horse and buggy days. I had three brothers and two sisters and we were all athletes.

"My brothers Luke and Tommy went to the major leagues like I did. But Tommy didn't stay long. I thought my oldest brother was the best athlete in the family. He played on the University of Alabama team but then he went into World War I, and after that he studied medicine.

"As I said, my father was a doctor, and he saw the value of education. He educated every one of us children. My older brother came to the University of Alabama and Luke and Tommy and I followed him.

"When I came to the University it was the best break I ever had in my life. We had a football coach who came in here from Cleveland named Zinn Scott. He also wrote for *The Cleveland Plain Dealer*. He recommended me and Luke and Riggs Stephenson to the Cleveland Indians. There were seven of us from our baseball team that went off to the major leagues and made it.

"At that time New Orleans was a farm club that worked with the Indians. I signed a contract with the Pelicans in the spring of 1920, after our season was over at Alabama. I went to New Orleans and stayed with them part of the summer, until after Ray Chapman got killed.

"Now mind you, I had never seen a major league ball game. I didn't know anything about it. Well, they called me to the office not long after Chapman had passed away. They said to me, 'Joe, how would you like to go to the major leagues?'

" 'I don't want to go,' I said. 'I never saw a major league game. I don't know whether I could play up there or not.'

"At that moment Larry Gilbert, our centerfielder, came in. Larry had played on the 1914 Boston Braves 'miracle team.' And he said to me, 'Joe, you could play shortstop up there.' So Larry was the fellow who talked me into going to Cleveland.

"I was brought up, just in time to see the last of a four-game series in Cleveland with the Yankees. Babe Ruth hit two home runs that day. I remember sitting way down at one end of the bench and watching.

"Doc Johnston was playing first base for Cleveland and he got five hits in five times up, and also stole home. Elmer Smith was in right field and he went to right-center and jumped as high as he could and caught a line drive that was like a shot out of a cannon. Every time something happened I'd scrunch down deeper and deeper on the bench. I said to myself, 'I ain't supposed to be up here.'

"So the next day our manager, Tris Speaker, came over to me in the clubhouse before we were dressing and said, 'Joe, you're playing shortstop today.' I said to myself, 'Oh, my God!' But there was nothing for me to do but get ready.

"We were playing the Philadelphia Athletics and old Scott Perry was pitching. I'll never forget old Scott. I ought to send him a Christmas card. Well, Tillie Walker was playing center field and the first time up I hit a ball to left-center like a shot. Old Tillie just coasted over there and got it.

"The next time up—I'll never forget it—old Scott threw me a little old curve. It came in on the outside of the plate and

I hit that thing over the third baseman's head and away down there in the corner for three bases.

"Boy, I went around those bases just like I was flying. Not even my toes seemed to touch the ground. When I got to third base I said to myself, 'Shucks, this ain't so tough up here.' And from that day on I was never nervous again."

Later in the game Joe got another hit, a single, scored once, and was the pivot man on Cleveland's only double play. He also committed two harmless bobbles in the field which, given the excitement of the moment, one can easily forgive and forget.

It is safe to say that Cleveland would not have won the American League pennant in 1920 if Joe Sewell had not plugged the gap at shortstop and if the Indians hadn't brought up a left-handed pitcher named Walter "Duster" Mails a few weeks before Joe arrived. Sewell was a surprisingly suitable replacement for poor Chapman, but Mails was nothing short of a sensation. He started eight games, completed six of them, won seven and lost none, threw two shutouts, and had an ERA of 1.86.

The Indians went on to whip Brooklyn in the World Series, five games to two. This was the second Series in a three-year experiment with a maximum of nine games instead of seven. Though the 1920 Series was not memorable in terms of the competition, there was no lack of highlights and "firsts." Stan Coveleski, a spitballer, became the eighth of the 12 pitchers who have won three games in a World Series, allowing the Dodgers just five hits in each of his complete game victories.

But it was the fifth game which produced three World Series firsts. In the very first inning Cleveland rightfielder Elmer Smith blasted a pitch over the right-field fence and screen for the first Series grand slam. Then the Indians' pitcher, Jim Bagby (who had 31 wins that season), hit a three-run shot in the fourth to become the first pitcher in Series history to hit a home run.

The most unusual first—still unequalled in Series play— came as the Dodgers batted in the fifth inning. The first two batters singled and then pitcher Clarence Mitchell slashed a wicked liner toward right. Bill Wambsganss, the Indians' second baseman, leaped high to spear the ball, stepped on second for the second out and then tagged the runner coming from first to complete the unassisted triple play.

Joe Sewell was neither hero nor goat in the 1920 Series. He didn't hit much and made a few errors in the field, yet his shortstopping contributed nicely to the Cleveland triumph. Duster Mails, on the other hand, kept right on his sensational pace. After six and two thirds innings of shutout relief pitching in the third game, he came back in game six to throw a three-hit 1-0 shutout. Joe Sewell likes to tell about that game:

"Let me tell you a story about Walter Mails. You could say I was just breaking in at that time, and all this stuff was new and exciting to me. But Mails went out to warm up that day of the sixth Series game, and when he came in and sat down with a towel wiping himself, he said (and he always talked loud anyway): 'Well, boys, if you'll get me one run today we'll win.' I said to myself, 'Gee whiz, what a thing to say.' But I never said a word out loud. But one run was all we got and all he needed. In the sixth inning Tris Speaker singled and George Burns doubled to drive him home."

Heroes don't always, however, go on in the same vein. Duster Mails' glory was rather shortlived. After a 14-8 season in 1921 he developed arm trouble and soon was gone from the majors, having won a total of 32 games. Joe Sewell, on the other hand, was to enjoy 13 more seasons of outstanding performance which would lead to the Hall of Fame.

Joe also has lots of other things to say about that 1920 Series and about the Cleveland ball club of those years.

"Sherry Smith of the Dodgers was one of the toughest pitchers I saw. He came over later and pitched for Cleveland. I'm going to tell you something about Sherry Smith. If he were up there right now with those boys stealing all those bases, he'd pick every one of them off. He had the greatest move to first base I ever saw.

"Did I ever tell you how we beat old Burleigh Grimes in that '20 Series? The Dodgers had a little second baseman named Pete Kilduff. And Burleigh was throwing that spitter so good it looked like the batters were swatting flies. But every time Burleigh was going to throw the spitter, Pete Kilduff would reach down and get himself some sand to make sure that his throwing hand was dry.

"We picked that up and just watched Kilduff. If he didn't pick up the sand we knew it was a fastball or a curveball and we could jump on it. And that's the way we beat him. Burleigh came over to the Yankees after I got there, and I told him what I've just told you. He said, 'I *thought* you boys were hitting me too good.'

"That old Cleveland team was a mighty good ball club. If we were intact right now in either league we'd have the pennant cinched after about two-thirds of the season. When I first went to Cleveland Larry Gardner at third and Bill Wambsganss at second helped me a lot.

"Doc Johnston and George Burns alternated at first base. In the outfield we had Charlie Jamieson in left, with Speaker of course in center, and Elmer Smith or Joe Wood in right. Joe was a great pitcher until he hurt his arm and came over to us from the Red Sox as an outfielder. He helped us a lot and later went on to coach baseball at Yale. About the only way you could get a hit against our outfield was to hit a line drive.

"And Stan Coveleski was a great spitball pitcher. He was in his prime and to tell the truth it was a pleasure to play behind him. I've seen him start a spitball right at a right-handed batter who would fall down and then watch the ball break right over the plate.

"And we had other pitchers who were mighty good too— Jim Bagby, Ray Caldwell, Mails, Guy Morton, George Uhle. George ought to be in the Hall of Fame.

"Our catching was done by Steve O'Neill. He was smart and he could block the plate better than anyone I ever saw. One day I saw Ty Cobb slide into him. Cobb and the ball got to the plate at the same time and Steve had it blocked. Cobb came into him and his spikes cut big holes in Steve's shin guards. You know what Steve did? He just tagged him and the umpire called Cobb out and Steve walked away. Didn't even rub his shins. But Cobb was still lying there on the ground. His cap had come off and after a bit he reached out to get it and he put it on and then he slowly got up. He barely could make it.

"But our manager and real star was Tris Speaker. Now you put this down as coming from me. I played with Tris for seven years as our centerfielder. I've seen Joe DiMaggio and I've seen Willie Mays and I've seen Sam West, Johnny Mostil, and all the rest. Tris Speaker is the greatest centerfielder I ever saw.

"You know how a shortstop gets down as the pitcher is about to throw the ball? Well, when the ball was hit over my head like a shot, at no time when I turned around did I ever see Speaker make his turn. He had already gone by the time I could get my head around. He would turn with the swing of the bat and go toward the wall with his head down. And he'd go away off out there and when he'd turn the ball would be right there. I asked him a number of times how he did it, and he would reply, 'Instinct. I can't tell you anything more.' And you know, he's got a lifetime batting average way up over .340.

"I'm gonna tell you this. You talk about hitting. Back when we were playing, you know the spitball was legal. And the ball was dead. If they legalized the spitball now and gave some pitchers time to perfect it, some of these .250 hitters would be batting about .150. They can't hit the knuckleball right now, and the spitball broke worse than the knuckler. Coveleski, Grimes, Ed Walsh, Red Faber, old John Picus Quinn, and a lot of those fellows could really throw that spitter. I can't even think of all of them now.

"You know, if Ty Cobb were playing today on artificial surfaces the way he played in his prime, he'd hit closer to .500 than to .400.

"Even as it was, there was one year in Cleveland where for a long time during the season we had 13 guys on our team hitting over .300. In fact, my old Alabama teammate and lifelong friend, Riggs Stephenson, was hitting over .330 and couldn't even break into the lineup except as a substitute."

As soon as Joe Sewell had played a handful of games in the majors it became apparent that he didn't strike out very often. But just how great a contact hitter he was came to light in 1925. In the four previous full seasons he had whiffed 17, 20, 12, and 13 times, respectively. These yearly totals were rather eye-popping, but the baseball world hadn't really seen anything yet.

In 608 official trips to the plate during 155 games in 1925, Joe set a record which still stands—he struck out exactly four times. Later he was to have two more four-strikeout seasons and even two years when he whiffed only three times, though he played fewer games in those seasons. In 1929, between May 17 and September 19, Joe Sewell went 115 consecutive games without striking out!

In his 14-year career embracing 1,902 games and 7,132 official at-bats, Sewell struck out a total of 114 times, or about once in every 62 trips to the plate. These mind-boggling figures leave Joe so far ahead of all competitors in this respect that in truth it may be said he has no competitors. Probably the closest any full-time performer has come is Charlie Hollocher of the Chicago Cubs (1918-24), who in 2,936 at-bats fanned a total of 94 times, or once in every 35 at-bats. In 1921 Hollocher struck out only five times in 592 plate appearances. In 1924 he whiffed on only four occasions, but he made only 286 trips to the plate.

"Joe, how could you make contact with the ball so consistently?"

"I can't remember a time, when I was a boy back in Titus, when I couldn't throw up a Coca-Cola top or a rock and hit it with a broom handle or stick. All that time I was developing reflexes, coordination, and I've always had good eyes. I followed the ball. And when I reached the major leagues I didn't look at the pitcher. I'd pick up that ball and I'd follow it right up to when it hit the bat. Of course, I had to learn the strike zone and make sure the ball was in it, and then I could see that ball leave my bat.

"And I can tell you that in the two years when I struck out four times, I took the called third strike three of the four times. I only swung at one third strike and missed it."

"Joe, could the umpire have been wrong on some of those called third strikes?"

"One time I know he was wrong because he came out the next day and apologized. That was old Bill McGowan and the ball was right at my cap bill. He said, 'Strike three, you're out. Oh, my God, I missed it, Joe.' But I didn't say a word. I just walked back to the bench. And the next day he came out and apologized and I said, 'Bill, don't worry about it. You were trying and honest about it.'

"And, you know, about my strikeout record, I can take it down to the bank and I can't borrow a nickel on it."

For many years after he retired Joe Sewell ranked third on the list of players who had appeared in the most consecutive games, behind Lou Gehrig's 2,130 straight games and Everett Scott's 1,307. Joe had a string of 1,103 games. Then, in the early 1970s Billy Williams inched ahead of Joe with 1,117. And at the tag end of the 1982 season Steve Garvey also caught up with Joe and passed him. In the 11th game of the 1983 season Steve broke Williams' National League record. However, but for a heel injury that sidelined Sewell for one game, Joe would be firmly ensconced in second place.

"I played in 460 or so consecutive games and we were playing the St. Louis Browns in Cleveland. I hit a ball down to first base and the pitcher Van Gilder came across to cover, but I beat him to the bag. And he stepped on my heel with his front spike. They took four stitches. Well, the next day I couldn't walk and so I missed that ball game. We worked on that heel and soaked it in epsom salts and everything, and the next day I cut my shoe open a little and played. And then I went on to appear in 1,103 straight ball games. And I must have played almost a month with that shoe cut open before I was back to normal. But I played."

Joe moved over to the New York Yankees in 1931 and finished out his playing career with three seasons there. He got into his second World Series in 1932 when the Yankees faced the Chicago Cubs in what was perhaps the Series that generated the most bitterness between the opposing teams. Invective and vituperation flowered on both sides, before, during and after the Series.

Much of this feeling was fueled by the vote of the Chicago players to give only a half-share of their World Series money to Mark Koenig, a former Yankee shortstop who had joined the Cubs several weeks prior to the end of the season after their regular shortstop, Billy Jurges, had been sidelined by an injury. Koenig hit .353 for the rest of the season, played well at short, and in the minds of many had made it possible for the Cubs to claim the National League title. The Yankees characterized the Cubs as stingy penny-pinchers, and thus began the feud. Joe recalled the scene:

"Every day before the Series the Yankee resentment just kept building up. Then came the day of the first game, which was played in New York. In Yankee Stadium in those days all the players had to come on to the field through the home team dugout. They had to come right past our bench. Babe Ruth would come and sit right where the Cubs had to come through.

"And when the first Cub came out, you never in your life heard the language that Ruth and all of them let the Cub players have. None of them said a word in return until Gabby Hartnett came by. He stopped after a few feet and turned around and blasted Ruth, and then the two of them really cussed each other out. And everybody in the stands near the dugout could hear it all."

Aside from the bitter feelings between the two teams (and perhaps the fact that the Yankees extended their Series winning streak to 12 games—four game sweeps in 1927, 1928, and 1932), this Series is best remembered for the controversial "called" home run by Babe Ruth in the fifth inning of the third game. The preponderance of opinion seems to be that Ruth really didn't predict his homer, but on the other hand plenty of people swear that he did, and Joe Sewell is definitely one of them. We pick up his recital of the events just as he has made the first out of the inning:

"I went back to the bench and got my drink of water as usual and then sat down. Ruth was up there at the plate clowning around, holding up one finger after a strike and then two fingers after the next one. Then Ruth backed out of the batter's box.

"He was holding the bat in one hand (not with the heavy end resting on the ground like they show it on the plaque in Cooperstown). Looking at Burleigh Grimes and Bob Smith in the Cub dugout, he pointed with those two fingers. And as he pointed I got a mental picture of the ball going out of the ball park.

"Now don't let anybody tell you he didn't point to where he hit it. You've seen golf balls, how they take off, well, that ball just went straight out and through a tree outside the ball park in center field. The tree was loaded with youngsters up there watching the game, and as the ball went through the tree all those kids evaporated. They had all gone after the ball. When Ruth rounded third base, cabbages and oranges and apples and all kinds of mess were thrown out there, and the grounds crew had to come out and clean it up."

And that turned out to be Babe Ruth's last World Series home run. Before he went from the Indians to the Yankees, Joe Sewell had switched from shortstop to third base, where he continued to play through his last five seasons in the majors. He says, "I played shortstop all those years and I know if I'd played third from the beginning I'd have lasted two or three years longer."

"You mean you had slowed down, Joe?"

"Yeah, yeah. You know, there isn't anybody on earth knows better than yourself that you've slowed up, but you don't tell anybody. When a ball is hit over the pitcher, the shortstop is supposed to get in there fast and take care of the thing. When I was young I used to be there waiting for the ball to come down. Then it got to where I was straining to reach those balls. Later I was just missing them by six inches and then by a foot or more. So I moved over to third base. If I was playing today like I was at the end of my career, I could stay on as a designated hitter, for I was still hitting the ball as well as ever."

"Joe, I understand one rule change was made because of you."

"Lou Fonseca and I played together in Cleveland for a while. Lou was a good hitter and led the American League one year. But he had a little old trick bunt down the third-base line that often worked for a hit.

"After I went to the Yankees and he went to the White Sox, I was playing third against them in New York one day, and to keep Lou from working his little bunt I was playing up close. Charlie Ruffing was pitching for us and he got one strike on Fonseca. I moved back just one step, not thinking Lou was aware of it. And as I did he dropped the ball down the third-base line.

"The ball was rolling along just inside the foul line with pretty good momentum. Bill Dickey tried to catch up with the ball but couldn't, and I knew I had no chance to throw Fonseca out. Ruffing came over to pick up the ball, but as he bent over I yelled, 'Let it roll!' And he did.

"I got out in front of that ball with my front spikes and scratched a trench across the foul line at a 45 degree angle. The ball hit that trench and rolled foul, and as soon as it did I grabbed it.

"Fonseca was already at first base, but old Bill Dinneen, the umpire, yelled 'Foul ball!' Donie Bush was managing the White Sox then, and boy did they charge out at old Bill. You never heard such a commotion. I never said a word but just laid back laughing to myself. So they made Lou go back to the plate and then Ruffing struck him out. That was the icing on the cake. Lou threw his bat up in the air and both Dickey and Dinneen had to run to keep from getting hit when it came down. Fonseca turned on me and cussed me out with everything in the book. But I never said a word and just kept laughing.

"Will Harridge was president of the American League and the next day as we were taking batting practice Bill Dinneen came out and called for me. I went over and said, 'Bill, what in heaven's name have I done now?' He said, 'It ain't what you did today, it's what you did yesterday.' I said, 'What was that?' And he replied, 'You know that canyon you dug down the line and made the ball roll out? Well, that's against the rules today.'

"What happened was that Dinneen had called Harridge and they made a temporary rule, and then the following summer the rules committee put it in the rule book. And it's still in the rules book right now."

"What was your best game in the majors, Joe?"

"Well, let me tell you this. One Sunday, I think it was in 1933, the Athletics came to New York and Lefty Grove pitched for them. A big crowd was on hand to see Ruth and Gehrig and Grove and the other big stars. I went to the plate five times that day against Grove and I got five hits, the last one a home run. I hit it up in the right-field stands.

"Grove threw his glove away up in the air and when he caught it he followed me around the bases, cussing me for all he was worth. I always had a real good batting average against Grove.

"When I got around to home plate, Ruth was there waiting to hit next. And he said, 'Well, kid (you know he called everybody kid), they all came out here today to see me hit a home run, and you pick me up.' I got a kick out of that."

"What did you do after hanging up your spikes at the end of the 1933 season?"

"I coached two years for the Yankees, then I came back here to Tuscaloosa in 1936. I was in the hardware business for 17 years. But the government came along with all kinds of regulations, and I like to say they ran me out of business. They didn't really run me out of business but they made it so unpleasant that I decided to get rid of it."

"Can you pick an All-Star American League team for the years when you were playing?"

"First base ain't too hard—Lou Gehrig.

"Second base? Charlie Gehringer. Eddie Collins was a mighty fine second baseman too. But when I was hitting against Detroit with Gehringer on second and Hank Greenberg on first, I always tried to hit through the left side of the infield. I couldn't hit a ball through them unless it was a line drive.

"I'll put Joe Cronin at shortstop and Ossie Bluege at third.

"In the outfield I'll take Ruth, Cobb, and Speaker.

"And it's a tossup between Bill Dickey and Steve O'Neill as catcher. Of course, a lot of persons younger than I would pick Mickey Cochrane. But Mickey couldn't throw with those other two. He was a great hustler, though.

"Grove would be the left-handed pitcher and Walter Johnson the righthander."

Like nearly all old ballplayers, Sewell has quite a repertoire of stories to tell. Somehow Smead Jolley's name was mentioned, provoking this story:

"Like I said, old Smead just hit for exercise. Well, he was playing for the White Sox managed by Jimmy Dykes. In old League Park in Cleveland they had a great big cement wall in right field. Dykes put old Smead up against that wall so he couldn't hurt himself. It had rained a little bit before the game started, which made some balls take a skip when they hit the grass in the outfield.

"Glenn Myatt hit a line drive straight at Smead. When the ball hit the wet grass it scooted right through Smead's legs for error number one. Smead turned around and headed out after the ball as it bounced toward the cement wall. It was hit hard and bounced off that wall and went right back through Smead's legs again. That was error number two.

"By that time we were all out of the dugout just laughing and hollering. Smead was running along like a fellow trying to catch a rabbit, just grabbing at that ball and never getting it. He ran that ball halfway to the infield and when he finally picked it up Myatt was already heading for third. Smead braced himself and cut loose and threw that ball 15 rows up in the stands.

"The fans were screaming and hollering. Smead took his cap off and stretched himself and then hollered so you could hear him all over the park, 'My God, I didn't know I could throw a ball that far.' Neither did we, for he had a mighty poor arm.

"So he wound up making three errors on one play, and I've seen that featured at least twice on Ripley's 'Believe It or Not.' You know, we had a lot of fun. They don't have that kind of fun any more."

Joe Sewell looks back with deep and fond feeling on baseball as it was played in his time. They played then, he asserts warmly, for the love of the game.

"Baseball was *the* sport in our day. Top of the ladder. When I signed a contract with New Orleans, you know what I asked for as a bonus? Nothing! When I got through signing, you know what the fellow gave me? $300. He said, 'Here, take this and go buy yourself some clothes.' I had a little old seersucker suit and a little old straw hat. I didn't ask for any bonus because I just wanted to play.

"And in 1923 I hit .353 for Cleveland and I played every

inning of every ball game and drove in 109 runs. You know what my salary was? $6,000. You know where that contract is now? Up in Cooperstown. I sent it up there for the Hall of Fame.

"And it's like I told them when I was finally inducted there in 1977. My record ain't a bit better today than it was in 1933 when I quit."

Joe Sewell resides now in a large southern-style home in Tuscaloosa, Alabama, with his gracious wife of more than 50 years. Joe reached his 88th birthday on October 9, 1986, but of all the old-time ballplayers interviewed for this book none is livelier or shows more zest than he does. Joe thinks he got a great deal out of playing baseball, and it is clear that he did. But several hours of chatting with him causes one to conclude that he gave even more to it than he took out of it.

JOSEPH WHEELER SEWELL

BL   TR   5'6½"   155 lbs.

Born on October 9, 1898 in Titus, Alabama

Hall of Fame, 1977

YEAR	TEAM	G	AB	R	H	RBI	2B	3B	HR	BB	SO	SB	AVG.
1920	Cleveland AL	22	70	14	23	12	4	1	0	9	4	1	.329
1921	"	154	572	101	182	91	36	12	4	80	17	7	.318
1922	"	153	558	80	167	83	28	7	2	73	20	10	.299
1923	"	153	553	98	195	109	41	10	3	98	12	9	.353
1924	"	153	594	99	188	104	45	5	4	67	13	3	.316
1925	"	155	608	78	204	98	37	7	1	64	4	7	.336
1926	"	154	578	91	187	85	41	5	4	65	6	17	.324
1927	"	153	569	83	180	92	48	5	1	51	7	3	.316
1928	"	155	588	79	190	70	40	2	4	58	9	7	.323
1929	"	152	578	90	182	73	38	3	7	48	4	6	.315
1930	"	109	353	44	102	48	17	6	0	42	3	1	.289
1931	New York AL	130	484	102	146	64	22	1	6	62	8	1	.302
1932	" "	124	503	95	137	68	21	3	11	56	3	0	.272
1933	" "	135	524	87	143	54	18	1	2	71	4	2	.273
	14 yrs.	1902	7132	1141	2226	1051	436	68	49	844	114	74	.312

WORLD SERIES

YEAR	TEAM	G	AB	R	H	RBI	2B	3B	HR	BB	SO	SB	AVG.
1920	Cleveland	7	23	0	4	0	0	0	0	2	1	0	.174
1932	New York	4	15	4	5	3	1	0	0	4	0	0	.333
	2 yrs.	11	38	4	9	3	1	0	0	6	1	0	.237

Glenn Wright was a premier shortstop in the majors from 1924-33, playing five years each with the Pittsburgh Pirates and the Brooklyn Dodgers.
He ended his career in 1935 with the Chicago White Sox. A .300 hitter
four times in his career (.294 lifetime average), Wright four times batted
in more than 100 runs. Coloring his career were two World Series with
Pittsburgh, in 1925 and 1927, and one of baseball's rarities, an unassisted
triple play, in 1925 vs. the St. Louis Cardinals.

3

Glenn Wright

Glenn Wright was one of the many—a majority, really—
old-time ballplayers who came from very small towns
across the land and went on to major league stardom. For the
10-year period between 1924 and 1933 he was one of the premier
shortstops in the big leagues.

Playing five years each for the Pittsburgh Pirates and
Brooklyn Dodgers, Glenn hit for a career average of .294. Four
times he hit over .300 and he enjoyed four seasons of driving
home more than 100 runs. Had it not been for an off-season
shoulder injury his stay in the majors would have been longer
and his productivity even greater.

A pleasant, soft-spoken man, Glenn met with me in his
home in Fresno, California, in the late spring of 1982. We had
a most enjoyable conversation for several hours, after which
he browsed with me through his fascinating collection of me-
mentos and baseball memorabilia. Listen to him now tell of
his early days in baseball:

"Well, I was born in Archie, Missouri, a little town of
about 500 souls some 50 miles south of Kansas City. I had one
brother and one sister, both older than I. My father had a hardware and lumber yard and we all worked there when we got
old enough.

"My brother wasn't athletic. He was a big man over six
feet and weighed over 200 pounds, but he kind of sponsored
the town baseball team by getting the equipment through the
hardware store. Our team was made up of farmers and what
few there were in town who could play. I was the youngest on

the team. Oh, I could throw hard, but no telling where. That's the reason they called me 'Buckshot' later in Kansas City.

"We had a pretty good team and sometimes played teams from Kansas City. That's how some fellow noticed me and recommended me to Kansas City. That's when George Muehlebach owned the Kansas City Blues.

"After finishing high school I went to the University of Missouri, in Columbia. I only went for one year because I had this offer from Kansas City and at a salary way larger than most kids were offered. That was in 1920, I guess. They offered me $250 a month. Most of the young players were offered maybe up to $100 or $125.

"My father left it up to me as to whether I should take the offer. My mother didn't want me to go. And at that time I had never seen a professional game. In college I only played fraternity baseball. I also played some basketball and football. In a pre-season football game between the varsity and the freshmen I happened to catch a pass intended for somebody else and ran about 60 yards for a touchdown. I couldn't help it, really, for everybody was taken out on the play.

"George Sisler, who was already a big star with the St. Louis Browns, was at that game and I met him at a party that night, where he congratulated me. It was really great. And years later he chose me on his All-Star team, and so did Al Lopez.

"I went to spring training with Kansas City and then they sent me to Houston. I believe Ray Blades was managing Houston at the time. But I had to have a lot of dental work done there, and I'm not sure I even put on the uniform. Later Kansas City sent me to Independence, Kansas, in the Southwestern League. I stayed there most of that year, and Kansas City recalled me when our season was over. They played me right away and said they wished they had had me all year. I was still just a big country kid, you know, and everybody played jokes on me.

"Then in 1923 we won the pennant in Kansas City and played Baltimore in the Little World Series. At that time it was a nine-game Series and we finally beat them in nine games. We beat Lefty Grove the last game in Kansas City. And that was quite a team they had. Practically all of them later went up to Connie Mack's Athletics.

"The first ball Lefty Grove threw me went behind me. Like to scare me to death. And years later, sitting in the lobby of a hotel in Oakland during the World Series, I asked him if he remembered that. 'Why yes,' he said, 'I threw behind you but I didn't mean to.' Of course, if I'd known that at the time I would have been more scared than ever.

"Pittsburgh had an option on me and eventually they made a deal where I think they gave Kansas City $40,000 and two players for me. Anyway, I wouldn't sign with Pittsburgh unless they gave me some of the purchase price. Well, Pittsburgh said Kansas City got the money for you and they should give it to you. I said, 'I don't care where I get it as long as I get it.'

"Barney Dreyfuss was the Pittsburgh owner and Bill McKechnie was the manager. So finally Dreyfuss said he would give it to me in cash at the end of spring training when we came back through Kansas City to play them in two or three exhibition games.

"I hopped a train to Paso Robles, California, and sure enough when we got back to Kansas City Barney handed me an envelope with the $7,500 cash in it. A rather odd thing, I left that envelope in my locker overnight. I forgot all about it. But it was still there the next day.

"Anyway, when I got out to Paso Robles, Bill McKechnie said, 'You're my shortstop. I don't care whether you ever pick one up or ever hit one.' Of course, that gave me a lot of confidence. Rabbit Maranville had been the shortstop, but he moved over to second base, and he had a good year too.

"A funny thing comes to my mind. I got a double-play ball hit deep in the hole and I threw it to Rabbit, but he threw it right back at me. He said, 'Don't throw it so damn hard!' Imagine something like that in a regular ball game!

"I remember that my first game in the majors was against Cincinnati and Wilbur Cooper was our pitcher, a lefthander. It seems like I booted one, and he gave me the deuce, too. I took it and then later I happened to hit one that drove in the winning run. I was always fortunate that way. I've made a lot of errors, probably more than other shortstops, but even in Kansas City when I'd pull a booboo it always seemed that eventually we'd win the game and they would forget about it."

"Glenn, your rookie season was a mighty good one, with a .287 batting average and 111 runs driven in."

"Well," replied Glenn, "I know Bill McKechnie used to tell people that if I was at the plate and it didn't mean anything, he'd just as soon have the bat boy up there. Then he would add, 'But if there's a run in scoring position, I'd rather have Glenn than anyone.'

"I think McKechnie was the best manager I ever played for. He got the most out of his team. And I know he always gave me lots of confidence. He was a kindly man. And I didn't hear him swear hardly ever. So, I think overall Bill was the best manager. Wilbert Robinson of the Dodgers was the most lovable.

"When I was traded to Brooklyn, Robinson made me his captain. Of course, I got a little raise. At that time the captain got an extra $500 and got to take the lineup up to the umpire. And the umpires would listen to him a little more in an argument. Maybe my voice didn't carry too well, but I knew all the words and got on plenty of umpires. But all of them were my friends. They got to know that if I kicked I had a right to do so.

"I also played under Donie Bush at Pittsburgh. He was a good manager and a great fellow too. But we had our fights. He was an old shortstop like I was, and although we were good friends we had our arguments. He had played at Detroit and said he used to have his arguments with Ty Cobb too."

We recalled the 1925 World Series between Pittsburgh and the Washington Senators, in which the Pirates were the first team ever to come back and win a Series after being down three games to one.

We shook our heads at how the Senators' shortstop, Roger Peckinpaugh, already voted the American League's MVP, had a horrible Series, committing a record eight errors. And how Stan Coveleski, hero of Cleveland's 1920 Series win, lost two close games to Pittsburgh's Vic Aldridge. Also about the aging Walter Johnson, fairly well battered in Washington's 1924 triumph over the New York Giants, coming back to be as masterful as ever in two games in '25 but unable to hold a big lead in the seventh game. I remarked about the Senators having baseball's first true relief specialist in Firpo Marberry.

"Well," said Glenn, "you mention Firpo Marberry. He came on in relief in the third game. He struck me out so fast it seemed like five miles back to the bench. And I swung at all of them, all high and tight, a pitch I had to learn to lay off of.

"Speaking of Aldridge, with Vic you stood on one foot and then the other. He was 3 and 2 on everybody. He just hated to let a batter hit a strike. You know, we almost thought he was throwing the game when they scored four runs on him in the first inning of that last game. And of course he wasn't. I shouldn't even have said that. As for Coveleski, I know I hit a home run off him that helped us win the second game, 3-2.

"You know, I get requests for autographs even now, maybe 10 or 15 a month. A lot of them ask me my biggest thrill. I tell them it was standing at attention before the first game of the '25 World Series in Pittsburgh. The Pittsburgh Symphony Orchestra was out in center field and some huge Italian lady was singing our national anthem. Both teams were standing along the first and third-base lines. I still think that was my biggest thrill, because cold chills ran up and down me and it was just wonderful to be in America and to be in that spot."

"Glenn, tell me something about pitchers as you saw them back in your days. Spitball pitchers, knockdown pitchers, and so on."

"Burleigh Grimes loved to win," Glenn began. "Like everybody said, he'd knock down his own grandmother if it meant a ball game. And I think he would have. You know, I got hit one time in St. Louis by Vic Keen. He was the one pitcher on their club that didn't knock you down. I don't know whether I didn't see it or whether I froze. It hit me here on this big cheekbone and cracked like a rifle. I was unconscious for 30-some hours.

"I was out about six weeks and when I got back in who was pitching but Burleigh Grimes. And the first pitch knocked me down. I went down but while I was still in the dirt I thought, 'Well, if I can get out of the way of that, I can get out of the way of any pitch.' And I got up and was all right again. If he hadn't done that, I might have stayed scared.

"Naturally, I don't think that's why he threw at me. We really were good friends off the field, but he was tough to hit against. Not real good stuff, but he could break a spitter two or three different ways, and he went to his mouth on every pitch. Sometimes it wasn't a spitter, but you never knew. And when you were in the field and a spitter was hit at you, you had to handle it. I've thrown a lot of spitballs to first base.

"Some pitchers you hit better than others, but I don't ever remember having a 'cousin.' Willie Sherdel, the little lefthander of the Cards, said he was my cousin, yet they were all tough as far as I'm concerned. Alexander was the best pitcher I ever faced, as far as pitching goes. He didn't have the most stuff, like Walter Johnson or Dazzy Vance or Lefty Grove. But old

Pete could thread a needle with every pitch he had. And he had lots of pitches.

"Every once in a while Alexander would have a fit on the bench, and that's what they were, fits. We used to think it was because he was drinking, but he was an epileptic and we didn't know that. And you hear about his drinking before he struck out Lazzeri in the last game of the '26 Series. If it's true he drank a lot it sure didn't bother him on the mound.

"Alexander and Lee Meadows got in a throwing match one day. You know, somebody gets knocked down, the other side retaliates. Pete told Lee, 'You might hurt 'em more when you hit 'em, but I'll hit more of 'em.'

"Pat Malone and Charlie Root of the Cubs used to knock you down, and I mean they could throw hard. I know when McCarthy was their manager they knocked me down twice during one time at bat. His theory was, 'Well, you knock him down once, he'll think it's over, so we'll just floor him the next time too.' But actually I hit those fellows a little better because of that, for while I was ready to go down I was still ready to pull the trigger too."

"How about your trade to the Brooklyn Dodgers after the 1928 season?"

"It was kind of a surprise. It was after one of those arguments with Donie Bush. Anyway, Donie loved Jesse Petty, the lefthander who was with Brooklyn, and Wilbert Robinson wanted me because I always hit pretty good against his team. He loved hitters like Babe Herman, Johnny Frederick, Rube Bressler, and those fellows. Anyway, I was a little surprised. But I had hurt my shoulder that winter. I told Robby about it but he said, 'Well, it doesn't make any difference. I'd rather have you than Petty, anyway.' I loved to hit against Petty. In fact, I loved to hit against all lefthanders.

"I hurt my right shoulder playing handball at the Athletic Club in Kansas City. I went back after a ball against the back wall. It was low and trying to get it I just crashed into the concrete wall.

"I was lucky to be able to come back after that. They had a doctor, a kind of chiropractor, but that didn't help. Then they had me strapped up for a month or two and that didn't work. Finally Dr. Quitman and his son Armitage operated on me. They had to bore holes in the clavicle and the scapula and tie them

together with a dash of muscle covering which they took out
of my left leg.

"And then I was in a cast holding my arm up like that for
about six weeks. I missed nearly all of the '29 season. I could
throw just as hard, that is, I would go through the same motion and everything, but it took the ball longer to get there. But
I did have a good season in 1930."

"In fact, your best one offensively—.321 average, 22 home
runs, 126 RBIs."

"Yeah, but I would have had another homer if I hadn't
passed Babe Herman on the bases after one ball I hit out. I hit
the ball to left-center, and in those days there was a low fence
in left field. I guess no one was sure the ball was going to go
out, though I hit it pretty good. Anyway, when I stepped on
first base I almost spiked Babe's foot, but by then the damage
was done and so I went on around the bases.

"And we were fighting for the pennant then, too. I got to
the bench and I started cussing Robby out about his pet and
everything. Babe came in and I was thinking up all I was going
to say to him, but he beat me to it and said, 'Cap, you always
told me to watch that runner in front of me.' And what could
I say then?

"But Babe was a wonder. He was a lovable guy, and still
is. I still hear from him. Babe was uncanny. He could hit with
his eyes closed, I think. They said he was a poor fielder but he
was a pretty good fielder, and he could run with anybody and
throw with anybody. I don't know why he's not in the Hall of
Fame.

"Babe and Hollis Thurston and I used to sort of run around
together. And Al Lopez was with us too. I think Al was the
best catcher I ever saw. Hollis would call him a lowdown Mexican and Al would say, 'You know I'm a highborn Spaniard.'
Hollis would think up things like that to say, and we were all
the best of friends.

"Dazzy Vance was, I thought, more of a thrower than a
pitcher. You couldn't tell him that, though, because he was big
and strong and could throw hard. He used to wear a kind of
raggedy shirt on his pitching arm until they made him quit that.
Everybody talks about his fastball, but he had one of the best
curves anybody ever had.

"Dazzy got on me one day because I didn't get a ball that

was hit past me. He said, 'If Thurston had been pitching you'd have caught that ball.' And I replied, 'Yes, I probably would because I would have been playing over there, since Hollis throws where he says he's going to. You don't even know yourself where you're going to throw the ball.' But Dazzy was tough to hit, especially in Wrigley Field. He could always strike out a lot of Cubs."

"Tell me about the Waner boys you played with in Pittsburgh."

"Well, Lloyd was the best centerfielder I ever played with. And I helped Paul sign his first contract. I used to hunt with Fred Clarke, who owned part of the Pittsburgh club. In fact, I went with his younger daughter Muriel for a while. I would go to Kansas and hunt with him in quail season and he'd come to Missouri to hunt with me, and we both had good dogs. Fred had a little ranch out of Westfield, Kansas, with about 10 oil wells in the front yard.

"Anyway, I was down there and Paul wanted me to help him with his first contract in 1926. So I invited him over to Fred's place, with Fred's permission, of course. Paul got there in a Dodge coupe which looked pretty beat up. When he got out of the car he had on the purplest suit I ever saw. He had a couple of knocked-around bags, and I could tell one of them had a musical instrument in it.

"After dinner we were sitting around the fireplace and eating popcorn while Muriel played the piano. They had a big fireplace that would hold half a tree. After a while I said, 'Paul, why don't you get your instrument out and play along with Muriel?' He took it out and it was a saxophone and Muriel asked what she should play. 'Oh,' he said 'play anything and I'll just follow along.' So she did and he did, and did a right good job too.

"Well, we got out in the field the next day and the dogs found a bird. I said, 'Paul, this is your bird.' And he said, 'All right.' So we kicked the bird out and Paul up and shot and he didn't have his gun anywhere near his shoulder. Just shot from the hip, you know. But the bird fell deader than a doornail. Fred and I looked at each other and he said, 'We'd better stay behind this kid.'

"The dogs found another bird and I said, 'Paul, you take this one too.' But he said, 'No, this is yours or Mr. Clarke's.' So I told him, 'Well, to tell you the truth, we think that first shot was an accident.' 'Oh,' he said, 'all right.'

"We kicked the bird out and the same thing—gun still down by his hip but the bird didn't even flutter after it fell. He didn't miss a bird all day. He was the best field shot I ever hunted with. Lord, what a shot! Must have learned it where he was raised down in Oklahoma.

"Paul was known to take a drink and sometimes would come out to the ball park after having a few. One time we got to Chicago and Pat Malone was pitching for the Cubs. Paul told him. 'Don't throw too close to me today. I can't see too well.' Pat agreed and then that day Paul only got four straight doubles, all of them blue darters."

"How about Lefty O'Doul and Hack Wilson?"

"Lefty was one in a million, he was. We had him in Brooklyn, though he was with the Phils longer than he was with Brooklyn. He played left field for us and every ball that was hit out there I had to go away out to take his throw, because he had a real weak arm. If I went out far, someone would have to come out to get it from me, for my arm wasn't much better then.

"Lefty couldn't throw but he could run, when he wanted to. And nobody could hit like him. He had an open stance with his back foot in closer to the plate. He could hit to left field sometimes, though not too well.

"Well, there's nobody like Hack, either. You mentioned how thick my bat handle was that I showed you. Well, his was as small as mine was thick. He'd get the smallest handle he could and then shave it off some more. He had little hands but he still had a lot of bat because he used a heavy bat. He was pudgy and had a lot of power in his arms. And he was known to have a drink or two.

"In Chicago we used to get an Elgin watch for a home run, and he saved all of them to have something special made up for his wife. I got several watches there myself; that's a good place to hit home runs. You also got watches in St. Louis in those days.

"I gave all of mine away to relatives, because we still had a series in each of those towns and I thought it was a cinch to get one for myself. And of course we played those two series and I didn't even come close to the wall. That's the way it happens sometimes.

"Hack was a pretty good outfielder too, but he never felt good. Every day when we had him in Brooklyn he would be in front of his locker with his hands on his knees, and then I'd slip up behind him and shake his head and run. And he'd pick up whatever was close and throw it at me.

"One time Hack drank a bottle of gin and a bottle of some kind of whiskey and a case or two of beer and then went out and had a couple of hamburgers. And the next morning he said, 'I'll be damned if I ever eat any more of those hamburgers. Made me sick as a dog.'

"One time I got a questionnaire asking about the greatest feat in baseball, such as DiMaggio's hitting in 56 straight games and Vander Meer's two straight no-hit games. I wrote back saying that Hack Wilson's feat of driving in 190 runs in one season was the greatest. Nowadays they go crazy about a guy that drives in 80 runs or so."

"Did you know Connie Mack and Branch Rickey personally?"

"Oh yes," he replied. "Somehow or other my World Series tickets used to be alongside Connie Mack, and I always enjoyed sitting next to him. And one time I was at a prominent semipro tournament in Wichita and Connie was there, along with such other old-timers as Fred Clarke, George Sisler, and Kid Nichols.

"Fred decided to have a dinner for all of them, a kind of picnic-like dinner outside with beer and lots to eat. He had a couple of dozen balls there for the Hall of Famers to sign— Connie Mack and Sisler and Nichols and maybe somebody else.

"Well, Connie was signing a ball. It took him about a half hour, it seemed like, and I said to him, 'Connie, would you like for me to go ahead and sign the rest of them for you? I can write sort of the way you do and I'll sign them for you.' Connie said, 'Well, that's mighty nice of you, Glenn, but I think they would prefer to know that I signed them.' And I said, 'Oh, I'm sure they would.'

"I knew Rickey too. When I was later the general manager at Spokane we had a working agreement with Brooklyn. I just loved to hear Branch talk, like Franklin Roosevelt and William Jennings Bryan. Branch could talk about anything. It didn't have to be just baseball. And he was a gentleman."

"Baseball meant a lot to you from the time you started until the time you retired, didn't it?"

"Yes, all of it meant a lot. Baseball doesn't owe me anything. But I've still got a connection to it with the Red Sox. I scouted for them for many years, and now I'm supposed to be a consultant. I still go to games when I can, though I don't go out at night."

"Did the old-timers have a greater desire to get into the game and stay in the lineup, even if they had to play when they were hurt?"

"Definitely," said Glenn. "One time a fellow cut my knee open sliding into second. It was bleeding and kind of flabby. The trainer poured a bottle of iodine on it and then pinned it together with a safety pin. And I finished the game. Afterwards a doctor put some new skin on it and stitched it up. Nowadays a player with a hangnail, you might say, wants to sit out a while. We were afraid to get out of the lineup. If we did somebody else might take our job."

"How about the unassisted triple play you made in a game on May 7, 1925?"

"Well, on the day of the unassisted triple play we were playing the St. Louis Cardinals in Pittsburgh. Jimmy Cooney was on second and Hornsby was on first. Jim Bottomley hit a liner to me and all I had to do was catch it, step on second base, and then I started to throw to first, but Hornsby was right there in the way and I went over and tagged him. He said, 'Nice work, kid.'

"Hornsby wasn't too well-liked by baseball people, but he was the best right-handed batter I ever saw. And he helped me a lot, just sitting and talking in hotel lobbies. He would tell me how to hit the curveball, back through the box or to right field.

"But I think the best play I ever made wasn't that triple play. There's another one I like better. In 1925 at the end of the season we were ahead of the Phillies, 2-1, in the ninth inning, and I believe Tom Sheehan was pitching for us in relief. There was one out and a runner on third. Someone hit a pop fly down the left-field line, right on the line and about halfway to the fence.

"I went out and caught it and then threw a strike to the plate. Johnny Gooch was catching and we got the man coming home. And that cinched the pennant for us. The miracle is that I missed the runner with the throw, because he was going down the line and I was right on the line as I threw. To me that was my best play because it cinched the pennant. In that same game we completed six double plays, only one short of the major league record for a nine-inning game."

"Glenn, compare Pie Traynor and Brooks Robinson, and how did you like Forbes Field?"

"Oh, to me Pie was better," he said, "I think he was better than anybody at that position. There wasn't anything he couldn't do, except he couldn't hold a ball and wait for the first baseman to get to the bag. He had to throw it when he caught it. If he held it he would throw it away.

"And Forbes Field, it was my favorite park. You know, they had me come back there when they were tearing it down. They even had a camera out there taking pictures of me where shortstop used to be, among all the rocks and debris. I always loved that park."

To me the simple and evident truth is that Glenn Wright always loved baseball itself and, like so many others of his time, played the game primarily for the love of it.

Only a few months after our good conversation in Fresno, Glenn Wright suffered a stroke and went to live near his son Forrest in Olathe, Kansas. He recovered a bit and was able to enjoy his grandchildren, especially when they were playing baseball. But Glenn died on April 6, 1984, and baseball mourned the loss of another of its more admirable players and personalities.

FORREST GLENN WRIGHT
BR   TR   5'11" 170 lbs.
Born February 6, 1901 in Archie, Missouri
Died April 6, 1984 in Olathe, Kansas

YEAR	TEAM	G	AB	R	H	RBI	2B	3B	HR	BB	SO	SB	AVG.
1924	Pittsburgh NL	153	616	80	177	111	28	18	7	27	52	14	.287
1925	" "	153	614	97	189	121	32	10	18	31	32	3	.308
1926	" "	119	458	73	141	77	15	15	8	19	26	6	.308
1927	" "	143	570	78	160	105	26	4	9	39	46	4	.281
1928	" "	108	407	63	126	66	20	8	8	21	53	3	.310
1929	Brooklyn NL	24	25	4	5	6	0	0	1	3	6	0	.200
1930	" "	135	532	83	171	126	28	12	22	32	70	2	.321
1931	" "	77	268	36	76	32	9	4	9	14	35	1	.284
1932	" "	127	446	50	122	60	31	5	10	12	57	4	.274
1933	" "	71	192	19	49	18	13	0	1	11	24	1	.255
1935	Chicago AL	9	25	1	3	1	1	0	0	0	6	0	.120
	11 yrs.	1119	4153	584	1219	723	203	76	93	209	407	38	.294

WORLD SERIES

YEAR	TEAM	G	AB	R	H	RBI	2B	3B	HR	BB	SO	SB	AVG.
1925	Pittsburgh	7	27	3	5	3	1	0	1	1	4	0	.185
1927	"	4	13	1	2	2	0	0	0	0	0	0	.154
	2 yrs.	11	40	4	7	5	1	0	1	1	4	0	.175

4

Carl Hubbell

One of baseball's greatest pitchers almost never made it to the major leagues. In fact, it's quite possible he wouldn't have were it not for the fact that the Democratic National Convention was held in Houston in 1928. Alfred E. Smith, the presidential nominee of that convention, went on to lose. But this pitcher who got to the big leagues as an indirect result of the Convention made it big, but BIG.

His name was Carl Hubbell and he was to stand out as a giant among major league baseball players for some 15 years. In 1933 and 1936 he was the Most Valuable Player in the National League, the only pitcher in his league to be named MVP twice. In a span of five years (1933-37) Hubbell won 115 games and lost but 50. He strung together the amazing total of 24 straight wins in the '36 and '37 seasons (his last 16 decisions in '36 and the first eight in '37).

On May 8, 1929 Hubbell threw a no-hitter against the Pittsburgh Pirates. In 1933, 10 of his 23 wins were shutouts and his ERA was a league-leading 1.66. He pitched for the National League in five All-Star games between 1933 and 1940. He was the winning pitcher in '36 and gained a save in '40. During the decade of the 1930s Carl Hubbell was, almost without serious challenge, the dominant pitcher in the National League.

But Hubbell is perhaps best remembered for his spectacular feat in the 1934 All-Star game when he struck out in succession five of the finest sluggers the American League has ever known—Babe Ruth, Lou Gehrig, Jimmie Foxx, Al Simmons, and Joe Cronin. Mention Hubbell's name to almost any dyed-in-the-wool baseball fan and the immediate reaction will almost

Carl Hubbell, master of the "butterfly," as they labeled his screwball, the pitch that turned Hub into Bill Terry's "meal ticket" with the New York Giants. King Carl shows here the wrenching clockwise twist of the elbow required to throw a "reverse curve," as best described by Branch Rickey. Hubbell, a 20-game winner for five straight seasons, 1933-37, pitched the Giants to three pennants in that stretch. He was 115-50 over that period, 253-154 overall. Hubbell was a 1947 Hall of Fame inductee.

always be, "Oh yeah. He struck out five guys in a row in an All-Star game." This was brought home to me only recently as I was mailing something to Carl. The postal clerk, a middle-aged fellow, looked at the name on the envelope and his eyes lit up. "Hey," he exclaimed, "that's the one who struck out those five batters in a row in an All-Star game." He then proceeded to name all of them except Joe Cronin.

The other thing most remembered about Hubbell is that he was the greatest screwball pitcher ever to hit the major leagues. Fernando Valenzuela has a long way to go before he can ever replace Carl as the King of the Screwball.

Now we're going to let Carl Hubbell do some talking himself:

"I played for two years in a little Class D league there in Oklahoma, and Oklahoma City was in the Western League, which was a good Class A league at the time, you know. Older players, common in the minors then, with no farm system, no nothing, had nowhere else to go. The clubs in the minors were independent clubs and the majors bought their players.

"My little Class D league broke up before the end of my second season, and the owner or manager of our team talked with Oklahoma City about some of his younger players with promise. So I got over there and I was all eyes and everything else, you know, just getting up to that level.

"Perhaps one of the most fortunate things in my life was that there was an old left-handed pitcher on the club named Lefty Thomas. He'd been up for a cup of coffee several times in the big leagues, didn't quite make it, but he really knew how to pitch.

"For some reason he was the only one who attracted me, even though others on the team threw harder. But he made pitching look easy. He had a kind of sinking fastball. He could go out there and get a runner or two on and nobody out, and he'd just throw that sinker on the outside corner and get little three-hoppers to the shortstop for a double play. He'd get 'em out and walk off without breaking a sweat. He amazed me. It was a damn good thing I had the instinct to know he was the one to learn from.

"I got to pitch a couple of games and won one and lost one before the season ended. All winter long I was thinking about how I was gonna go to spring training and work on turning that ball over and mastering that sinker. So we went down to train in Weatherford, Texas, and man, I started right in.

"Fortunately, I had pretty flexible wrists, which sure helps on the screwball. I found out the more I turned it over the more I'd come up and over the top. Then I could get a much better break on it, you see. And of course the more spin you get on the ball the more it slows it up. When I threw over the top, I turned my arm clear over and let the ball out of the back of my hand.

"Everybody said, 'Oh geez, you're going to tear your arm up throwing the ball like that.' The amazing thing about it, we only trained 30 days and I could get that damn ball over the plate just as well as I could my fastball. The real effectiveness of the screwball wasn't its break at all. It was the speed of the ball! I'd throw it exactly like my fastball, you see, and the hitters all looked just for the last release of the ball. So they couldn't tell if they were getting the fastball or the screwball.

"I did have a fairly good fastball and that just increased the effectiveness of the screwball when I could throw them both with the same motion. And I also had a pretty good curveball. You see, hitters always have to be thinking about protecting themselves against the fastball, figuring they can adjust to the slower stuff. That's how I developed the screwball.

"Let me tell you how it got that name. When we hit Oklahoma City the owner bought an old minor league catcher. He'd been around baseball a long time, and I was warming up with him one day soon after he got there. I threw him a fastball and then a curve and then I wound up and threw him a screwball. He said, 'Throw that thing again.' I threw it again and he said, 'Well, that's the screwiest damn pitch I ever saw.' And it was the screwball after that.

"Before I go on I want to establish something with you right now. I've heard a lot of old ballplayers talking about their recollections and telling great stories, and you know they're stretching things to the point of outright lying. But whatever I tell you, that's it. That year I pitched for Oklahoma City, won 17 and lost 13 and immediately was sold to Detroit. That was a surprise because most of the players out of the Class A Western League were sold to Double A teams in the International League, American Association, or Pacific Coast League. You talk about somebody that was up in the clouds! I couldn't wait until next spring when I'd go into training with Detroit.

"In 1926 we trained in Augusta, to be close to home. Ty Cobb's home! Ty was the manager of the Tigers then. He never said a word to me at any time during training. George McBride was his guy to handle the newcomers and everything else. I started throwing the screwball and McBride said, 'What are you doing?' I told him, 'That's the screwball.' 'For Christ's sake,' he said, 'you're gonna tear your arm up. Don't throw that again!' Well, naturally, you're going to do what they say. If he'd said to stand on my head and throw I would have tried it. There was no Players' Association then. So I gave it up.

"But there was one thing I never figured out. I never pitched one inning of an exhibition game for Detroit in three years! Three years! I pitched batting practice a lot of the time, and they held on to me, farming me out every year.

"First they sent me to Toronto, where they were just opening a new stadium. They had a strong team with a bunch of old major leaguers and some younger guys. They put me in the bullpen and I never did start a game for them. But the Washington Senators, who had won the American League pennant a couple of years in a row and the World Series in 1924, stopped in Toronto for an exhibition game. We were in first place and the manager didn't want to break the rotation of his starting pitchers, so they threw me into the lion's den. I had been told not to use the screwball up there, but before the game I talked with Steve O'Neill, the old American League catcher who was with us in Toronto, and told him I'd just like to try the screwball. And he said sure.

"Well, we just wound up and beat Washington, 5-4. And I pitched the whole game. Then the Yankees with Babe Ruth and Lou Gehrig and all the others came into town for another exhibition, and they threw me in there again and we just wound up and beat them, 5-1. That's the truth. I had those box scores for a long time and I wish I had kept them. Wouldn't you have thought that those two games would have rung a bell somewhere up in Detroit?

"The next season Detroit optioned me out before spring training. The third year I went to training with them and didn't get into any ball games, and I was sent out to Beaumont in the Texas League. That was the only club that wanted me, I guess, after three years. And I didn't expect any scouts ever to come around, because they would think, 'Detroit had him for three years and if he couldn't help them he sure isn't going to help us.'

"Right there is the only time that I questioned myself, you know, asking myself what in hell I was doing. After I had finished high school I worked two years in the Oklahoma oil fields, all of which had baseball teams. I could always go back to them to get a job. But I knew that if I did quit I'd blame myself for the rest of my life. So I said, 'Dammit, I'm going to stick it out some way or other and see if I can't get a chance.'

"We were in last place and Houston was in first place. I'm going to use the phrase 'it just so happened' so many times that you'll be sure I'm making it up. Anyway, the only scout the Giants had was Dick Kinsella, an old guy who was a politician in Illinois and lived in Springfield. He was a dear friend of John McGraw and about the same age. He'd go every time they heard about somebody in Triple A ball (it was only Double A then) and take a look at him.

"Dick Kinsella was a delegate to the Democratic National Convention in Houston in 1928. It just so happened Beaumont was playing in Houston, and it was 100% day baseball in those times. One afternoon there was nothing much going on in the Convention and Kinsella said to himself, 'Hell, I'll just amble out to the ball park and watch a ball game.' And again it so happened I was pitching that day, against Bill Hallahan, a damn good pitcher later with the Cardinals.

"We got tied up in a close one out there and it was all even at 1-1 after nine innings. In about the 11th inning we scored and won, 2-1. And from here on it's Dick Kinsella's story. I just read it in the paper because I didn't know anything about it until later.

"Kinsella hurried to a phone and called John McGraw. He said, 'I saw another Art Nehf today.' McGraw got all excited and asked who and where and was he available and everything else. Kinsella told him, 'Well, I don't know. He's been with Detroit for three years and they sent him down here to Beaumont, so he must be available.' McGraw told him, 'Forget about that damn Convention. You get over there to Beaumont and find out about everything.' And the Giants bought me on July 16, 1928, and in three days or so I was on my way to join the Giants in Chicago. That's the truth, every bit of it. Nobody's going to believe it. You're the only person I ever told that to."

"That's quite a story, Carl," I commented. "Obviously, the screwball helped immensely in making your career so great.

And it didn't wreck your arm right away, like a lot of people said it would. But it must have put some strain on it."

"The only thing it bothered was this. You see, my left arm is crooked. I never had an ache or pain in my shoulder, in a ligament, or nothing. Just the calcium deposits in the elbow from all the pounding. Naturally, you feel it but you can still throw with a bad elbow. But if anything happens in the shoulder area, you think you're going to keep on firing the ball, but you can't. No way in hell you can do it. And I never had an ache or a pain in my upper arm. Actually, my arm started crooking up in 1934, six years after I joined the Giants. And if I'd had it fixed then by a doctor like Bob Kerlan I could have gone right on. Finally, a doctor in Memphis took the chips out. Pretty soon I was just half a pitcher. I'd win 11 or 12 games a year. That's all I could do.

"Looking back, nobody ever mastered the screwball. What they do is throw it. Warren Spahn came up with a pretty good one, and so did that relief pitcher Mike Marshall. But they didn't turn their arm over. It's hard for me to tell if Fernando Valenzuela does or not. You know how he spins and comes right up over the top, but unless you catch him in real slow motion you can't tell. If his fastball was a good bit better, you couldn't beat him. My fastball was about 88-90 miles per hour. Something like that. With the other stuff I had, that was enough. If I didn't have the other stuff, it wouldn't have been."

"What about John McGraw, your manager on the Giants until early in the 1932 season?"

"I can tell you a lot about McGraw. This is something else I've never told. He's a legend in baseball, and a lot of people are going to say, 'Well, here's an old left-handed pitcher talking about a legend in baseball.' I'll tell you, he was something. He played that 'little Napoleon' bit to the very hilt. I mean that was his life. His life! He lived it. He must have dreamed it. The little Napoleon!

"I couldn't understand it. I didn't know what I was going to do. I'd had such a bad experience with Detroit but finally McGraw (we all said 'Mr. McGraw') gave me a chance to pitch in the big leagues. And I appreciated that a hell of a lot.

"But he called every damn pitch, see, and every damn one was a breaking ball. It would be a curveball or a screwball. He didn't think you had enough sense to throw a fastball. The only pitcher he allowed to pitch his own game was Christy

Mathewson. And the only reason for that was that he was the only college graduate pitching in the big leagues at that time. And so he let him pitch his own game and Christy won 30 or more games lots of years. But nobody else! Four years with him and I'm telling you it's a wonder my arm lasted as long as it did.

"Well, there are so many other things about him. The old catcher Roger Bresnahan was the coach when I went up to join the club, and one day I was on the train with him and I started to ask him about John McGraw, how he could be like he was. Bresnahan said, 'Well, you don't understand how it was when he began managing before the turn of the century in Baltimore before he took over as manager of the Giants late in 1902.'

"In those days a regular player made about $2,500 a year, and a fellow like Mathewson probably would make about $5,000. But there was only one Mathewson. Teams couldn't stay in a decent hotel. They would get drunk and get thrown out. So they had to stay in rooming houses down by the railroad tracks. So that's what McGraw had to start with and go along with well up into the 1900s, you see.

"But then Ruth came along and everybody else and the salaries went up and the college players began coming in because the teams then could afford them. They signed Frankie Frisch right out of Fordham. But McGraw didn't change. He was the little Napoleon right straight on through. Why, Frisch quit the club in St. Louis and went home and told Mac what he could do with his ball club. And that's when McGraw traded him for Hornsby.

"McGraw and Hornsby lasted together only one season. At the end of the year, Hornsby went to Boston. Burleigh Grimes quit, saying he'd never pitch another ball for him. And McGraw traded him in 1928 to Pittsburgh for Vic Aldridge. In the '28 season Grimes won 25 for Pittsburgh and Aldridge won four and lost seven for McGraw. That's the way it went with a lot of the trades he made.

"McGraw had Hack Wilson on the Giants and Hack was just running him crazy, so he left him available in the draft and the Cubs drafted Hack for $7,500. McGraw just let him out, he didn't want him. But he said it was through an error in the office.

"Let me say another thing about McGraw. He had the news media so conned with his little Napoleon bit that after every home game he'd go into the little room that was his office.

Nobody interviewed McGraw. Nobody! So he'd get in his little room, and he'd bring in the old sportswriter Bozeman Bulger, who was about as old as McGraw.

"Nobody would say a word but McGraw would write out everything that happened in the ball game. If they had won the game, it was about something he had done, and if they lost, it was about what some dumb ballplayer had done wrong. Bozeman would take the report out and say, 'Well, fellows, here's McGraw's report.' And they would write their stories accordingly. And that's how much he had them conned."

"How about Bill Terry and Mel Ott, the two other managers under whom you played?"

"Terry was a real good baseball manager, and when he took over in 1932 he was just perfect for the ballplayers. Of course, he had been through the McGraw bit. And the following year we won the pennant and the World Series, though we were picked by the majority of writers to finish in fifth place. We had good pitching and defense, but Ott and Terry were the only good hitters we had.

"And that World Series win did a little something for Terry's ego, and after that he got kind of uppity in his managing and everything else, you know. I hate to say that about him because he was so perfect in the beginning. But that winter at the baseball dinner in New York, with Manager Max Carey of the Dodgers present, some of the writers got to talking with Terry about the next season and happened to mention Brooklyn. And Terry said, 'Oh, is Brooklyn still in the league?' Remember that one? Boy, he lived to regret that!

"Mel Ott was too good a guy to be a really effective manager. And Horace Stoneham had a good deal of influence on him, you know. But Horace was a baseball fan and a fan has likes and dislikes, and so his influence wasn't always the wisest."

"Carl, what about your most famous feat, that of striking out those five great hitters in a row in the '34 All-Star game? Did you get them out mostly with the screwball?"

"That's the only thing I got over the plate, yeah. I didn't start off too good. You get all pumped up waiting. Damn, you just want to get started. You wait around, and sit on the bench, and then walk up and down. And you finally get out there and naturally you have nervous energy built up, and you try to throw the ball harder than you usually do.

"Charlie Gehringer was the first hitter and I got behind

him. Then I got one close enough that he singled to center. Then I walked Heinie Manush, the next batter. And now I had Ruth, Gehrig, and Foxx coming up.

"Terry and Frisch and Traynor and Hartnett, all to be Hall of Famers later, gathered around me out at the mound, but none of them could help me a damn bit. It did give me time to get control of my emotions and everything and to realize that I'd beat myself the way I was doing it. I knew I was going to have to start getting the ball over the plate and give myself a chance. I didn't expect to get out of it without some damage, but I did compose myself so I knew what I was doing. And you know the rest. I got all five of them on strikes.

"Of course, All-Star games were new then and you got more worked up about them. You mentioned maybe never again will we see the likes of those five hitters in a row. Well, do you realize that those nine starters for the American League in 1934 all walked right into the Hall of Fame? There's never been anything like that since. Actually, in 1934 they only picked 20 players on each team, or a total of 40, and 26 of them are now in the Hall of Fame."

"Why were there so many great stars in those days in comparison with today?"

"It's very easy to explain, I think. I believe, not just because I played then, but I believe the decade of the '30s was the greatest decade in the history of baseball and probably will always remain so, for the one reason that they were all hungry ballplayers. Not to just get a bite to eat, you understand, but to have a home and family and to raise kids and to have a decent life.

"With the Depression going on, you wouldn't see one of those players saying, 'Oh, I can't play today because I've got this or that.' Hell no, someone else would get in there and he might lose his job. They were just fighting for their jobs all the time. And they played all the time. When they said they were hurt, they were really hurt. You weren't going to get them out of that lineup otherwise.

"Today there are no more farm boys coming into baseball. Boy, there were a lot of them way back then. Of course, now there aren't many farm boys, period. It's all machinery now. I lived 12 miles from where Paul and Lloyd Waner grew up. I played against Lloyd in high school. I'll tell you, a farm boy has got work to do and he gets used to it. And I'll tell you those country boys made pretty good ballplayers."

"What about your teammates on the Giants, players such as Freddie Fitzsimmons, Hal Schumacher, Jo-Jo Moore, Dick Bartell, and Roy Parmelee and the like?"

"Freddie? Oh, he was strictly a knuckleball pitcher, you see. He never had any trouble with McGraw because he only threw knuckleballs anyway. He was a vicious competitor. They called him Fat Freddie but there wasn't an ounce of fat on him. He just had a round body. It just burned him up to be called fat and he was ready to tear somebody apart.

"Terry traded him to Brooklyn in the '37 season because he kind of thought Freddie was washed up and because he had come up with Cliff Melton and Harry Gumbert and didn't feel he needed Freddie. Then Fitzsimmons had that really great 16-2 year with Brooklyn in 1940.

"Schumacher was a different kind of pitcher. He was a terrific competitor too. I don't know what he would have done there with McGraw, though. He was strictly a fastball and sinker pitcher. And his curve was more like a slider.

"Bartell was called Rowdy Richard and was a character. A good competitor. We won two pennants with him at shortstop in '36 and '37. Everybody that slid into second base, he'd say, 'You see that guy try to cut me?' He was kind of paranoid in that respect, that everybody was trying to get him. He was in Philadelphia before we got him, and when I was pitching against him he used to get me teed off. He'd get up there like a little bantam rooster, you know, and he'd get right on the plate. When he's that close you're going to try to pitch him on the inside. And if you came too close to him he'd act like he was going to come out after you. Hell, I wasn't throwing at him, I was just pitching him on the inside of the plate.

"Jo-Jo Moore was a ballplayer's ballplayer. Now I don't know just exactly what that means, but I know what I mean by it and I'm just glad he played on my team. I'm telling you, he was a strange leadoff man. You know, they want the leadoff batter to get on base by walks and hits and anything, but that wasn't for Jo-Jo. He just wanted to get that ball close enough to him so he could swing at it.

"Here's a good story about that. We went into Cincinnati one day and Bill McKechnie was their manager. Joe was leading off for us, you know, and in the game Joe took four swings, every one of them on the first pitch and every one a line drive. Two of them were caught and two were base hits. There was an article in a Cincinnati paper the next morning saying that McKechnie had called a meeting after the game and told all his pitchers, 'If you throw a first pitch to Joe Moore and he swings at it, it's going to cost you $50 every time he swings at it.' And $50 in those days was a pretty good fine. You should have seen what happened out there the next day. Each time the first pitch to Joe was away up in the air and everywhere.

"I saw Joe not too long ago. You see, I've got a little museum in my hometown of Meeker, Oklahoma. Back in my day there weren't too many trophies and honors. The MVP was about it. But anyway, Cooperstown is so out of the way that you are apt never to get there. Its value ought to be greatest for the youngsters, and most youngsters aren't ever going to hear about it, let alone see the Hall of Fame.

"That kind of went against my grain, and so what little stuff I had I donated to the city of Meeker when they built a new city hall and put a little glass cubicle in it for my things. Well, Joe Moore came up for the opening and we had a big time. The people there were just tickled to death to see Joe. You see, Joe was the guy that scored the only run in the 18-inning, 1-0 game I pitched."

Hubbell also told of another sort of epic game he pitched against the Cardinals, only this time he lost, 2-1, in 17 innings.

"Roy Parmelee was a fine physical specimen and we called him Tarzan, but he had a better body than Tarzan did. But emotionally he reminded you of a kid, yet he wouldn't hurt anybody or anything. He could pitch like hell, but if he was leading up around the sixth inning, boy he wanted to hurry up and get that game over with. Harry Danning was catching a lot for us, and Parmelee would just wind up and throw before he ever got the sign. And the catcher really had a time of it back there.

"Anyway, Bill Terry traded Parmelee to St. Louis in the winter of 1935. In our first trip out there in '36 I go out to warm up and there for the Cardinals is Leroy Parmelee doing the same thing. He said, 'This is the greatest mismatch in history,' and he was just laughing like everything.

"Well, we started the game and it gets along to the ninth inning and we're tied at 1-1. Parmelee always walked four or five men in a game, but he was grinning around out there on the mound and not walking anybody. He was so relaxed he was pitching like hell. We went right into the 17th inning still 1-1, and he hadn't walked more than two or three batters yet.

"The game didn't start until 3 P.M. and by this time the sun was down. The photographers were allowed on the field in those days, you know, and they all used flash cameras. Well, in the bottom of the 17th inning somebody hit a ground ball to Bartell and he made a wild throw to Terry, so the runner went on to second. They bunted him over to third. Travis Jackson was playing third and Gus Mancuso was catching. The cameramen were all running out to get the best angle on the upcoming play.

"The next batter hit a high hopper to Jackson right down the line, and the photographers closed in to get the play at the plate. Jackson was going to nail the runner easily at the plate. But just as he threw the ball all the flash bulbs started going off and blinded Mancuso so that he missed the ball and the winning run scored. That sounds like an old story somebody makes up but that's absolutely what happened."

"Carl, you mentioned earlier about playing in the minors with lots of old ballplayers who had spent their time in the majors. I remember that as a very common thing up until World War II. You don't see much of that anymore, do you?"

"No, you sure don't see that now. Why, there were plenty of them playing in the Class D league when I started out. They were there just because they loved to play ball. In those minor league towns they would give the old players a job. They would work in the winter and then play ball in the summer. Some of them even were guys about 30 years old who never did get to the big time. They did it. Hot damn, they just loved to play baseball."

"Who was the hitter you found the toughest to get out?"

"Joe Medwick. All he wanted you to do was get the ball close enough to the plate. I don't think he even knew whether it was a curve or a fastball or what. He just wanted to attack that ball. And the hell of it was, a lot of times when you'd expect him to pull the ball if it was inside and hit it the other way if it was outside, it wouldn't make any difference to him. He'd hit either pitch either way. In the big leagues you pitch 'em one way and play 'em one way, and if you can make 'em hit the way you think they will, then you've got a big advantage. But you couldn't do that with Medwick."

"How about Casey Stengel?"

"Casey managed the Braves and later the Dodgers while I was with the Giants. And I've been at dinners with him where he'd get up and just go on. He was the greatest guy in the world for talking on and on about something and then all at once be off on something entirely different. And lots of times you had to know or guess at what he was saying to understand him. Part of it you just couldn't. There's the story about two guys listening to Casey give a talk, and they're jumping up and down and clapping. And one guy says, 'Wow, what a speaker!' The other says, 'Yeah, but what did he say?' Casey was quite a character."

"How about the Giants' move to San Francisco and the choice of location for Candlestick Park?"

"You can't believe the way it is there in Candlestick. It's the worst. It's like somebody said, 'The coldest winter I ever spent was July and August in Candlestick Park.' Back in my time every baseball park had its own character. Every one of them was separate and different. I just wonder whether it's really as interesting for the players now as it was then."

"So, what's your best memory out of baseball?"

"Oh, I don't know. I never thought about that. Well, naturally, when you get to the big leagues you hope to play in the World Series. That was especially true in my time. You know, back then they didn't play the Star Spangled Banner before each game but only for the All-Star game and the World Series.

"So there I was ready to start the first World Series game in 1933, and of course you know they don't play the national anthem until you get out on the field. I believe that was the most emotional moment of my life. It seemed like it took 30 minutes to play the Star Spangled Banner. I'm telling you things were running up and down my back and my neck and all over. It had to be my most emotional moment. And you have to think about all the really great players with long careers who never got to play in a World Series. Like Ted Lyons and a lot of other guys who had been at it for 20 years or so."

After finishing his active career in 1943 (all of it with the Giants), Carl Hubbell was named supervisor of the Giants' farm club system, a post he held for over 30 years. He still is associated with the Giants as a scout. Since 1977 he has lived in Mesa, Arizona. Hubbell was voted into the Baseball Hall of Fame in 1947, where he is enshrined along with several of his teammates. As long as baseball is played, Carl Hubbell will be remembered and admired as the King of the Screwball.

CARL OWEN HUBBELL
BR TL   6' 170 lbs.
Born on June 22, 1903 in Carthage, Missouri
Hall of Fame, 1947

YEAR	TEAM	W	L	PCT.	ERA	G	GS	CG	IP	H	BB	SO	ShO
1928	New York NL	10	6	.625	2.83	20	14	8	124	117	21	37	1
1929	" " "	18	11	.621	3.69	39	35	19	268	273	67	106	1
1930	" " "	17	12	.586	3.76	37	32	17	241.2	263	58	117	2
1931	" " "	14	12	.538	2.66	36	30	21	247	213	66	156	4
1932	" " "	18	11	.621	2.50	40	32	22	284	260	40	137	0
1933	" " "	23	12	.657	1.66	45	33	22	308.2	256	47	156	10
1934	" " "	21	12	.636	2.30	49	34	23	313	286	37	118	5
1935	" " "	23	12	.657	3.27	42	35	24	302.2	314	49	150	1
1936	" " "	26	6	.813	2.31	42	34	25	304	265	57	123	3
1937	" " "	22	8	.733	3.20	39	32	18	261.2	261	55	159	4
1938	" " "	13	10	.565	3.07	24	22	13	179	171	33	104	1
1939	" " "	11	9	.550	2.75	29	18	10	154	150	24	62	0
1940	" " "	11	12	.478	3.65	31	28	11	214.1	220	59	86	2
1941	" " "	11	9	.550	3.57	26	22	11	164	169	53	75	1
1942	" " "	11	8	.579	3.95	24	20	11	157.1	158	34	61	0
1943	" " "	4	4	.500	4.91	12	11	3	66	87	24	31	0
	16 yrs.	253	154	.622	2.97	535	432	258	3589.1	3463	724	1678	36

WORLD SERIES

YEAR	TEAM	W	L	PCT.	ERA	G	GS	CG	IP	H	BB	SO	ShO
1933	New York NL	2	0	1.000	0.00	2	2	2	20	13	6	15	0
1936	" " "	1	1	.500	2.25	2	2	1	16	15	2	10	0
1937	" " "	1	1	.500	3.77	2	2	1	14.1	12	4	7	0
	3 yrs.	4	2	.667	1.79	6	6	4	50.1	40	12	32	0

Charlie (Jolly Cholly) Grimm was one of baseball's most colorful "characters." Grimm was best known as a player and manager for the Chicago Cubs, having guided the Cubs to three pennants in 1932, 1935, and 1945. In his 20-year playing career, Grimm had a .290 batting average and was recognized as one of the finest fielding first basemen ever to play the game. Baseball was Grimm's passion and his longevity in the game was equalled only by Connie Mack.

5

Charlie Grimm

I n the forefront of best-known names in baseball are those
such as Ty Cobb, Babe Ruth, Christy Mathewson, Walter
Johnson, Ted Williams, Hank Aaron, Joe DiMaggio, and Willie
Mays. But when it comes to choosing the most popular and best-
liked you can start the list with the name of Charlie Grimm.
Charlie might well be the one who got the most fun out of
baseball and gave the fans the most entertainment.

Charlie Grimm first hit the major leagues in 1916. Then
just 18 years old, he played in 12 games with the Philadelphia
Athletics under one of baseball's most revered legends, Connie Mack. After a year in the minors he resurfaced with the
St. Louis Cardinals in 1918 before going the next year to the
Pittsburgh Pirates. He had six fine seasons there and then was
traded to the Chicago Cubs.

It was during his 12 years as an active player with the Cubs
that Charlie forged his image as a folk hero, an image polished
and magnified during his many years as a manager. All told,
Charlie spent most of his adult life in the majors in one capacity
or another—player, manager, executive, public relations man,
and even broadcaster. His was a baseball career equalled in
longevity only by the likes of Connie Mack himself.

"What got you started in baseball, Charlie?"
"I played semipro ball in St. Louis, and when I was about
13 years old I was playing with some pretty big guys. And of
course in those days you went to work when you were 16 years
old. At that time few went to high school; you went until about

53

the fifth or sixth grade. I always said I could have gone to the seventh but I didn't want to pass my father.

"Baseball has been my passion all the way along. I used to sell peanuts and popcorn at the old Robinson Field on Natural Bridge and Van Deventer in St. Louis. That was in the days of Roger Bresnahan, Dan Greiner, Ed Cody, and all those ball-players. They took a liking to me and that's when I began to think it was really a great game. I played semipro ball and was picked up by Ira Thomas of the Philadelphia Athletics in 1916, when I was 18 years old. I went there and finished the season of 1916 with Connie Mack.

"I've never forgotten that Connie sent me up to pinch hit against Walter Johnson twice. I took a brand new bat up there, and not a mark on it when I came back. Connie Mack was a wonderful man. You know, he never called anybody by their first name. Everybody was 'Son.' Even Jimmy Dykes, that hard-nosed ballplayer, was 'Son' to Connie. Everybody wanted to play for Connie. They always said Connie had one ball club sitting in the stands watching the game, one on the field, and one on the train coming in.

"In 1917 our country got into World War I and Connie sent me to Durham, North Carolina, in the old Piedmont League. Naturally, they folded up because of the war. I came home and then played some in 1918 for the St. Louis Cardinals, after getting my release from Connie. The rest of that year I played in the minors at Little Rock. Then the Pittsburgh Pirates bought me in 1919."

"You played with or against some of the great names of baseball in the first quarter of the century."

"Yeah. I was in St. Louis when Rogers Hornsby came out of the Texas League in 1915 to join the Cardinals. Best right-handed hitter I ever saw. When I played for them in 1918 Branch Rickey was the general manager. The next season he took over as manager for several years. At that time their pitching staff was headed by Bill Doak, Lee Meadows, and Red Ames.

"And of course when I was with Connie in Philadelphia I was on the same team with Stuffy McInnis, Nap Lajoie, Amos Strunk, Wally Schang, and Bullet Joe Bush. And I got to see a lot of the great players in the American League at that time, like Walter Johnson, Ty Cobb, Sam Crawford, George Sisler, Eddie Plank, Eddie Collins, Red Faber, and Babe Ruth when he was a great pitcher."

"You had a number of big names as teammates in your years at Pittsburgh, too."

"Oh, you bet. Max Carey was a big name in baseball and the leading base stealer. And Carson Bigbee and Billy Southworth. Glenn Wright was the best throwing shortstop that ever threw a ball to me. He had a great arm and was a fine hitter. And old Rabbit Maranville. He was an eccentric fellow, very colorful, not too much of a hitter but he slapped that ball around. He was a fine shortstop and a great storyteller, too. He played for George Stallings on the Boston Braves' Miracle team of 1914.

"And Pittsburgh always had a good pitching staff—Babe Adams, Wilbur Cooper, Ray Kremer, Lee Meadows, and others. And Pie Traynor at third. Now you're talking about a great third baseman, the best in that time.

"We had a quartet there in Pittsburgh—Cotton Tierney, Clyde Barnhart, Rabbit Maranville, and myself. Barney Dreyfuss, who owned the ball club, loved to hear us sing around the batting cage, but he never told us so. When we'd lose a ball game he'd come down to the clubhouse and say, 'You can't sing your way through this thing.' I loved that guy Barney."

After six good seasons with the Pirates (especially 1923 when he hit .345 and knocked in 99 runs), Charlie Grimm was traded to the Chicago Cubs along with Rabbit Maranville and Wilbur Cooper for George Grantham and Vic Aldridge. He would finish his playing days with 12 more seasons in the uniform of the Cubs. It really was in Chicago that Charlie came into his own as a player, a comic, the favorite of the fans, and finally as manager.

Charlie picked up the nickname of "Jolly Cholly" because of his banjo strumming, his telling delightful stories in a heavy German accent, as well as his genial antics on and off the field, and his relaxed manner that kept everybody loose. It has to be one of the most popular and widely recognized nicknames in baseball lore.

Another thing contributed much to immortalizing Charlie Grimm in the public mind and eye. Norman Rockwell, who capsulized hundreds of typical human aspects of American life in his paintings (especially for the cover of the old *Saturday Evening Post*), was inspired to depict the bench of the Chicago Cubs during one of the lower moments of their long National League history. The scene which Rockwell portrays is set in the season of 1948 when the Cubs were wallowing in the cellar and Jolly Cholly was their manager, though quite evidently not so jolly as he would care to be. Titled simply "The Dugout," the painting depicts in despondent attitudes the batboy (standing at the top of the dugout), Johnny Schmitz (standing in the dugout at the right), and slouched on the bench Bob Rush, Charlie Grimm, and Rube Walker. Behind the dugout are visible the faces of a dozen fans, all of them (as Cub fans always and inexplicably are wont to be) infinitely more alive and enthusiastic than the players. Among the fans Rockwell included his own face.

In 1926, the year after Charlie joined the club, the Cubs brought in Joe McCarthy as manager and they began a steady climb to the top. In '28 they finished third but only four games back of the pennant-winning Cardinals. By the start of the '29 season the club had been so thoroughly rebuilt under McCarthy's leadership that only Grimm, catcher Gabby Hartnett, and pitchers Sheriff Blake and Guy Bush were regular holdovers from the 1925 squad. Rogers Hornsby had been acquired to play second base, Woody English was at shortstop, and Norm McMillan was on third. Kiki Cuyler, Hack Wilson, and Riggs Stephenson made up a slugging outfield which between them drove in 372 runs to go along with Hornsby's 149. Blake and Bush were joined by Charlie Root, Pat Malone, Hal Carlson, old Art Nehf, and others.

The only problem spot turned out to be in the catching department. Gabby Hartnett, a great one, was almost completely immobilized by a sore shoulder that hardly let him throw the ball back to the pitcher. Five replacement catchers were tried during the season, ranging from aging Mike Gonzalez (38 years old) to rookie Earl Grace, age 22. No one of the five was even a pale shadow of a healthy Hartnett.

Propelled by a team batting average of .303 and a corps of strong-armed pitchers, the Cubs breezed into the 1929 World Series. Opposing them were Connie Mack's Athletics, another awesome bunch featuring Al Simmons, Jimmie Foxx, Mickey Cochrane, and such hurlers as George Earnshaw, Lefty Grove, and Rube Walberg. It gave every promise of being an exciting Series, and it was.

Connie Mack, the canny Irishman, threw the Cubs off balance in the first game and kept them that way through all five games by his use of the pitching staff. For the opener he reached away back in his bag of tricks and brought forth Howard Ehmke, a 35-year-old veteran well past his prime who had been used only rarely in fashioning his 7-2 season record.

This so discombobulated the Cubs that they succumbed quietly, 3-1. In fact, Ehmke, who averaged about three and a half strikeouts per nine innings through his whole career, whiffed 13 of the Cub batters, setting a World Series record up to that time. This turned out to be Ehmke's last win in the major leagues.

Connie started George Earnshaw in the second game but, when the Cubs touched him for five straight hits and three runs in the fifth inning, Lefty Grove was summoned. Lefty shut down the Cubs and the Athletics went on to win, 9-3. Guy Bush pitched the Cubs to a 3-1 win in the third game, in which Connie brought Earnshaw back after only one day's rest.

The following day Charlie Root and the Cubs held a lead of 8-0 as the bottom of the seventh inning rolled around. But before the side was retired in that historic inning four Cub pitchers had been mauled for 10 runs, a record tied only one other time in World Series play. Again Lefty Grove, who was not to start even once in the Series, came on in relief to throttle the Cubs in the final two innings.

Much the same thing on a smaller scale occurred the next day. Pat Malone had the Cubs in front, 2-0, until the bottom of the ninth inning, when the Athletics again erupted to take the game, 3-2, and the Series, 4-1.

In the five games a total of 50 Cubs struck out, a Series record which stood until 1958 when 56 Milwaukee Braves whiffed, though in a seven-game Series. There really weren't too many bright spots in that '29 Series for the Cubs, but one of the few was found in the performance of Charlie Grimm. He batted .389, hit a homer, drove in four runs in the five games and wound up receiving a $500 prize from the *Chicago Tribune* for having been the Cubs' most valuable player in the Series.

The 1930 season found the Cubs finishing second, two games behind the Cardinals. Second place, it turned out, was not good enough to satisfy the Cub bosses, who fired Joe McCarthy as manager with four games left in the season. As his replacement they named the man most people regard as the best right-handed hitter in baseball history—Rogers Hornsby. Rogers had guided the St. Louis Cardinals to their dramatic World Series triumph over the New York Yankees in 1926, but that was far and away the best managerial success he enjoyed in 13 years of trying with five different clubs in both leagues.

Hornsby's Cubs dropped to third place in 1931, 17 games off the pace set by the Cardinals. About two-thirds of the way through the 1932 schedule the Cubs were contending for the top spot with the Pirates and Hornsby was abruptly fired because of profound differences on policy matters with Cub president William Veeck (whose son Bill in more recent decades left a deep mark on major league baseball).

Named to succeed Hornsby was none other than Jolly Cholly. There were some who wondered if the easy-going Grimm could control his players suitably. The fears were ill-founded. The Cubs responded happily to Charlie's leadership and came to the wire four games in front of Pittsburgh.

The jubilation, alas, was short-lived. The Yankees, as was their wont in those years, swept the World Series in four games. More than that, the '32 Series engendered the bitterest feelings between the opposing teams of any Fall Classic. This was covered in the chapter on Joe Sewell, and it seems unnecessary to dissect the feud further.

Charlie Grimm does, however, deny vigorously that Babe Ruth called his shot on the famous home run he hit in the fifth inning of the third game. Charlie insists that Ruth, reacting to fierce needling from the Cub bench (especially the pitcher Guy Bush), pointed to the mound and hollered to Bush something like "You'll be out there tomorrow and then you'll get yours." Which indeed is what happened. Bush lasted one third of the first inning in the fourth game, though he was not the loser in the wild 13-6 contest.

The Cubs under Grimm's leadership slipped to third place in 1933 and remained there the following year. But 1935 saw more glory days at Wrigley Field. Trailing the Giants and the Cardinals most of the year, the Cubs put on a blazing finish in September, clinching the flag with a string of 21 consecutive wins. In this super season they posted 100 wins, led the league in batting with a .288 team average, and boasted six workhorse pitchers who combined for 96 wins and the best ERA in the league at 3.26.

Favored slightly to cop the Series with the Detroit Tigers, the Cubs, jinxed in Series play ever since their two wins over these same Tigers back in 1907 and 1908, went down to another defeat though this time only after six closely contested games.

Jolly Cholly's team finished second both in '36 and '37. In midseason of 1938, with the Cubs performing at less than championship pace, the reins of management were handed over to Gabby Hartnett. Just as had happened when Charlie was given control during the 1932 season, the team picked up steam to catch and pass the Pittsburgh Pirates in the last days of the season, highlighted by Gabby's dramatic "homer in the gloaming" which vaulted the Cubs past the Pirates. But in the ensuing World Series the Yankees once again took the Cubs apart in four straight games.

After serving as a Cubs' front office man for several years, Grimm again took over the helm of the club just 11 games into the 1944 season. That year the Cubs came in fifth but in 1945 Charlie once more brought them to the league title—their 10th and to date their last. World War II had just ground to a bloody close and all major league teams were weakened by the loss of star players to military service. In fact, as the Cubs approached the Series with the Detroit Tigers, famed sportswriter Warren Brown was moved to say, "This is a Series neither team can possibly win."

Well, one team did win, and it wasn't the Cubs. Detroit finally prevailed in seven games. As in 1932 a midseason Cub pickup of a former Yankee propelled them to the pennant. In '32 it had been shortstop Mark Koenig; this time it was pitcher Hank Borowy, whose record was 11-2 after he joined the Cubs. He added two wins in the Series but was not up to capping it off with another victory in the final game.

Charlie Grimm credits the key acquisitions of Koenig and Borowy to Jim Gallagher, Charlie's nominee as the best general manager in Cubs' history. It seems that Gallagher watched the waiver lists like a hawk, and he claimed Borowy when someone in the Yankee office neglected to recall him from the list.

The fortunes of the Cubs went into decline after 1945— third place in 1946, sixth in 1947, and dead last in 1948 and 1949. After 50 games in the latter year Charlie was mercifully relieved of his thankless task. Frankie Frisch, Stan Hack, Phil Cavarretta, Bob Scheffing, and a string of other managers struggled unavailing for years to revive the proud tradition of the Cubs.

Meanwhile, the Boston Braves beckoned to Jolly Cholly early in the '52 season to come to Beantown as manager. He went, to finish the year in seventh place, and then moved with the Braves the next year to Milwaukee. That season they placed second and then finished third and second in '54 and '55. Still, very early in the 1956 season, Braves owner Lou Perini turned the handling of the team over to Fred Haney, who was to reap the fruit of the rebuilding in National League championships in 1957 and 1958, to which a World Series title was added in '57.

The Cubs, after more than a decade of dismal performances, called Grimm back to the helm for another try in 1960. Then, in the third week of the season, P. K. Wrigley pulled a switch unprecedented in major league history. Manager Charlie Grimm and Cubs radio announcer Lou Boudreau exchanged positions. Lou didn't survive beyond the end of that year and Charlie's reaction to the switch is clearly expressed in this comment: "I didn't want to sit up there. I was the most lonesome man in the world up in that broadcasting booth."

After that Charlie performed public relations work in the Cub organization for some time before going to the southwest to settle in Scottsdale, Arizona with his gracious and talented wife, the former singer/actress Marion Murray. He openly enjoys talking about his long life in baseball, and no book could hold all his memories and stories.

"Charlie, I see in the record book that you played one game at third base when you were with the St. Louis Cardinals."

"It was second base, Walter."

"Well, either second or third is a little more than unusual for a lefthander."

"Oh, a lefthander will try anything to stay in the game."

"Okay, Charlie. Now, how did Joe McCarthy and Rogers Hornsby get along?"

"Hornsby came over in '29 and was in the Series with us. He was Mr. W. W. Wrigley's ballplayer."

"Are you saying that McCarthy didn't particularly want him or need him?"

"No, McCarthy didn't like him."

"Well, he had to like him a little bit, for Roger hit .380 that year."

"Oh, he could play on my team with a bat in his hand any time. But he wasn't a second baseman like Frankie Frisch or Hughie Critz or fellows like that, though he played it adequately. But his job was to hit that ball."

"All right. In that nightmare 10-run inning of the Athletics in the fourth game of the '29 Series, a couple of balls landed near Hack Wilson in center field that he might have caught. Did he lose those balls in the sun or what?"

"I don't know. That sun was sitting right over the edge of the stands, and the glare just got in his eyes. I felt sorry for the guy because he was out there every day giving you 100%."

"And in those years he was really slugging that ball. Nobody has broken his RBI mark of 190 set in 1930."

"I don't think anybody ever will beat that. And don't forget, he did that in 154 games."

"Charlie, was Burleigh Grimes really a mean pitcher?"

"Yeah. He threw at Johnny Gooch, our catcher, one day when I was with Pittsburgh. Burleigh would dust you off with a spitball, you know. He wouldn't throw his fastball at you, but he'd knock you down with a spitball. And Gooch says, 'I'm gonna get him one day. If he hits me I'm gonna get him under the stands.'

"So, on a particular day we're playing in Brooklyn at Ebbets Field and Burleigh went through all his motions and threw it right under Gooch's chin. And Gooch yelled at him. He didn't run out like they do now with the bat, so someone has to grab the bat, but he went out to Grimes and Burleigh said to him: 'Lookit. Pitching is my bread and butter. When I knock you down with a runner on third base that could beat me, I'm buttering my bread.' "

"How about Guy Bush, who pitched your only win in the '29 Series?"

"Guy Bush, the Mississippi mudcat! Well, Guy was a showman, you know, and he dropped to his knees when he made a pitch and he'd fall all over the mound. I don't think he ever fielded a ground ball through the box in his life, but he could pitch. And he was a tough competitor and a great guy."

"And Riggs Stephenson?"

"Riggs, the Old Hoss. Stephenson was a great clutch hitter. I always said he never left a man in scoring position that I know of."

"Phil Cavarretta?"

"Phil came right out of Lane Tech High School there in Chicago, and he only spent one year in Peoria. He came up and they wanted to make a pitcher out of him. I said no. He had to play every day because he already was a good hitter when he joined our club. And I knew I was over the hill; and that was '35, my 19th season in the majors. I said, 'I'm going to put this kid at first base and he's going to stay there. Don't worry about that position; he'll do the job.' Later, when Phil Wrigley asked me about making Cavarretta the manager, I went 100% for it. But from what I heard he started bulldozing the guys he'd been running around with. That was one of the few regrets I had out of baseball. I could have sworn he'd make a good manager."

"Augie Galan?"

"Augie was almost—just almost—a complete ballplayer. He could run, he could hit, a good outfielder, and he could throw good. But he just wasn't quite the guy that you could say has got it all, like Willie Mays. But I'll tell you what, he'd give you 100%. And one year he only hit into one double play!"

"Now, Stan Hack."

"Stan was a helluva third baseman, much on the type of Pie Traynor. His arm wasn't good like a lot of third basemen, but he had the knack that when the ball hit in his glove it was on its way. Real quick hands. And he was one of the best leadoff men ever to play baseball. And a good hitter too."

"In 1937 you picked up Dizzy Dean from the Cards."

"Yep. Gave five ballplayers to get him. Plus $165,000 of Wrigley's money. And we pitched him on Sundays and filled the ball park every Sunday. He pitched a helluva ball game in the '38 Series.

"Diz never complained at all about anything. He was always ready to pitch. As a matter of fact, if he was sitting on the bench and our pitcher got in a jam he'd get up and go down to the bullpen. And was he a terrific character! He kept that ball club alive on the bench. And there weren't many of that kind around even then. There aren't any now."

"Why didn't Lou Novikoff make it in the majors?"

"He was like a lot of ballplayers who are great minor league players. Particularly pitchers, who pitch like hell in the minors for any ball club, and the minute they get to the major leagues— boom, they're gone. But Novikoff was the most colorful ballplayer of all.

"I'll tell you a good story about Novikoff. In 1950 Bill Veeck and I bought the old Milwaukee Brewers of the Triple A American Association. I was the manager and Lou Novikoff was our star. He was also a great alibi artist. One day he was on second base and Hal Peck was on third, with Ted Gullic at bat. Hal would be the tying run and Novikoff the winning run.

Gullic was a good hitter and in that bandbox we played in he could hit home run after home run. All I was looking for was a single.

"On the mound for Indianapolis was a big lefthander who had a heck of a good move in picking off runners. I wanted to remind Novikoff not to get very far off second base, so I whistled to him and went through all the motions telling him to watch out. And Novikoff signaled me as if to say, 'I've got everything under control, Skip, don't you worry about it.'

"And I turned around to see what Gullic was going to do, and I heard a thump at third base. Novikoff was stealing third with Hal Peck standing on it! In my nonchalant way I went over after the dust cleared, and I said to Lou, 'Where in the world do you think you're going?' And very pitifully he said to me, 'Back to second, if I can make it.' Novikoff was the kind of guy people would come out to see do something wrong. A ball would go through his legs or he'd get hit in the head by a ball in the outfield, or something."

"How was Claude Passeau as a pitcher?"

"He was a good pitcher. We got him from Philadelphia. He had a bad finger and it helped him. They accused him of throwing spitters. And if he hadn't got another finger hurt in that '45 Series against Detroit, after he had thrown a one-hitter at them, he would have pitched that last game. And Detroit didn't want any part of him."

"Bob Rush, another pitcher you had?"

"I couldn't see why he didn't make a great pitcher. Some said he couldn't really bear down in the clutch, but every time I saw him pitch he threw his heart into every pitch he made. Maybe he was trying too hard to get the ball in certain spots. My feeling is that all he had to do was wind up and let that thing loose and see where it would go."

"Charlie, tell me about Clyde McCullough."

"Aw, he was a good catcher. You know, the funny thing is that he was great for a ball club because with him everything and everybody was the greatest. 'I'm the greatest, he's the greatest, that's the greatest, etc.' When we traded him to Pittsburgh someone over there asked him, 'What are you doing here? You're the greatest.' And Clyde said, 'Oh, that has nothing to do with it. I just quit laughing at Grimm's jokes.' "

"And Roy Smalley, the father of today's Roy Smalley?"

"Roy threw the ball in the stands or anywhere. Everybody

was jumping and going like this. I thought he was going to be a great shortstop. Great arm but no accuracy at all. Where it was going nobody knew. Kids used to sit behind first base with gloves."

"Did you know John McGraw well?"

"Yeah. He was tough and had a heart as big as this room. Everybody thought he was a lion, but I spent a lot of time with him when we played in New York. I came to realize that when he had that baseball uniform on he *was* a lion. If you met him on the street corner he was just like you or me. And a great baseball man. And he had some tough guys to manage. That catcher Earl Smith and Jack Scott, the pitcher, for example.

"One time McGraw called a team meeting because he had learned that Scott and Smith and others were fond of going to a little nearby pub after each home game and spending a few hours there. 'I know you're stopping at this pub,' McGraw told them, 'and it's all right to take one or maybe two, but don't sit around the joint forever because that ginger ale or whatever you're drinking along with your booze doesn't go with me. And the first one I catch hanging around there too long, it's going to cost him his job.' At this point Scott got up and started out the door. 'Where you going, Scott?' demanded McGraw. 'Aw, you don't need me in this meeting,' replied Scott. 'I drink the damn stuff straight.' "

"What was train travel like in your day?"

"It was beautiful. You could call the porter and have him set up a table for pinochle or gin or whatever. And you had your ballplayers together all the time during trips. Now they leave a city after a night game and fly until four or five in the morning and have to try to sleep during the day. The manager doesn't see his ballplayers until about 4 o'clock in the afternoon."

"What's the most memorable game you were involved in, Charlie?"

"Well, I'd have to pick that World Series game in '29, the 10-run inning. That was the most brutal inning I ever lived through. And I'd hit a home run off Jack Quinn and I'd already written a telegram to send to my folks. It was something to stand there at first base and watch the fellows going around me. It looked like a white picket fence."

"Your greatest thrill in baseball?"

"Well, there were many thrills. I think the biggest one I had was in Milwaukee. Of course, I wasn't playing then but managing. When we came back from Florida to Milwaukee for the first season after the move from Boston, they had a ticker tape parade for us. That was the doggonest thing. I never thought I'd be in one of those. And, you know, in 10 years there owner Lou Perini saw the team draw 22 million people. And just because he only drew about 900,000 the last year he moved off to Atlanta. I think he knew later that he was wrong."

"And your best memory?"

"Best memory. Well, the best memory I have was when I reported to Connie Mack in Philadelphia. I was 18 years old and to meet a man like Connie and to be in the majors. Of course, I had been around major leaguers for a good while selling peanuts and popcorn in St. Louis but here I was with the same uniform on they had. That was a real thrill."

"How did veterans treat rookies when you came up to the majors?"

"I never got in the batting cage," Charlie replied. 'Get out there and shag.' That's what they would tell us."

Charlie Grimm looked back on his life in baseball with satisfaction. And well he might. Twenty years as a player in the majors. Lifetime batting average of .290 and uniformly regarded as a standout first baseman. Played in 2,164 games, exactly the same number as Lou Gehrig. Even if he didn't appear in 2,130 consecutive games, as Gehrig did. Manager for 19 years, with three National League pennants and four second place finishes.

In all of Chicagoland there is no question that Jolly Cholly and Ernie Banks stand as the most popular and best-remembered Cubs ever to perform in beautiful Wrigley Field. Few big league teams have had players who meant as much over so long a period as Charlie and Ernie meant to the Cubs. They brought happiness to millions of fans.

I visited and talked with Charlie Grimm in Scottsdale on several occasions. I found him to be as fine a gentleman as he had been a ballplayer. Along with all the baseball public, I mourned his loss when the national press reported his death on November 15, 1983 following a long and valiant struggle against cancer. In accordance with Charlie's wishes, his ashes were scattered across Wrigley Field. Nothing could be more fitting, for his spirit already wanders the confines of that historic site—and always will.

CHARLES JOHN GRIMM
BL   TL   5'11½"   173 lbs.
Born on August 28, 1898 in St. Louis, Missouri
Died November 15, 1983 in Scottsdale, Arizona

YEAR	TEAM	G	AB	R	H	RBI	2B	3B	HR	BB	SO	SB	AVG.
1916	Philadelphia AL	12	22	0	2	0	0	0	0	2	4	0	.091
1918	St. Louis NL	50	141	11	31	12	7	0	0	6	15	2	.220
1919	Pittsburgh NL	12	44	6	14	6	1	3	0	2	4	1	.318
1920	" "	148	533	38	121	54	13	7	2	30	40	7	.227
1921	" "	151	562	62	154	71	21	17	7	31	38	6	.274
1922	" "	154	593	64	173	76	28	13	0	43	15	6	.292
1923	" "	152	563	78	194	99	29	13	7	41	43	6	.345
1924	" "	151	542	53	156	63	25	12	2	37	22	3	.288
1925	Chicago NL	141	519	73	159	76	29	5	10	38	25	4	.306
1926	" "	147	524	58	145	82	30	6	8	49	25	3	.277
1927	" "	147	543	68	169	74	29	6	2	45	21	3	.311
1928	" "	147	547	67	161	62	25	5	5	39	20	7	.294
1929	" "	120	463	66	138	91	28	3	10	42	25	3	.298
1930	" "	114	429	58	124	66	27	2	6	41	26	1	.289
1931	" "	146	531	65	176	66	33	11	4	53	29	1	.331
1932	" "	149	570	66	175	80	42	2	7	35	22	2	.307
1933	" "	107	384	38	95	37	15	2	3	23	15	1	.247
1934	" "	75	267	24	79	47	8	1	5	16	12	1	.296
1935	" "	2	8	0	0	0	0	0	0	0	1	0	.000
1936	" "	39	132	13	33	16	4	0	1	5	8	0	.303
	20 yrs.	2164	7917	908	2299	1078	394	108	79	578	410	57	.290

WORLD SERIES

YEAR	TEAM	G	AB	R	H	RBI	2B	3B	HR	BB	SO	SB	AVG.
1929	Chicago NL	5	18	2	7	4	0	0	1	1	2	0	.389
1932	" "	4	15	2	5	1	2	0	0	2	2	0	.333
	2 yrs.	9	33	4	12	5	2	0	1	3	4	0	.364

CHARLIE GRIMM AS MANAGER

YEAR	TEAM	G	W	L	PCT.	FINISH
1932	Chicago NL	57	37	20	.649	1
1933	" "	154	86	68	.558	3
1934	" "	152	86	65	.570	3
1935	" "	154	100	54	.649	1
1936	" "	154	87	67	.565	2
1937	" "	154	93	61	.604	2
1938	" "	81	45	36	.556	3
1944	" "	146	74	69	.517	4
1945	" "	155	98	56	.636	1
1946	" "	155	82	71	.536	3
1947	" "	155	69	85	.448	6
1948	" "	155	64	90	.416	8
1949	" "	50	19	31	.380	8
1952	Boston NL	120	51	67	.432	7
1953	Milwaukee NL	157	92	62	.597	2
1954	" "	154	89	65	.578	3
1955	" "	154	85	69	.552	2
1956	" "	46	24	22	.522	5
1960	Chicago NL	17	6	11	.353	8
	19 yrs.	2370	1287	1069	.546	

WORLD SERIES

YEAR	TEAM	G	W	L	PCT.
1932	Chicago NL	4	0	4	.000
1935	" "	6	2	4	.333
1945	" "	7	3	4	.429
	3 yrs.	17	5	12	.294

6

Mel Harder

W hen mention is made of the 1934 All-Star game, any true baseball fan will recall Carl Hubbell's astounding exploit of fanning Ruth, Gehrig, Foxx, Simmons, and Cronin one right after the other. And, this feat well deserves the renown it has achieved.

Yet baseball is above all a team game and the bottom line focuses on the winner. In the 1934 mid-season extravaganza between the two leagues, it was the American League which prevailed by a final tally of 9-7. After Hubbell's three scoreless innings the American contingent fell upon the offerings of Lon Warneke, Van Mungo, and Dizzy Dean to push all their runs across in the next three frames.

The winning pitcher and, at least the co-hero with Hubbell, was Mel Harder. Mel came on in the fifth inning with no one out and shut down the National League sluggers the rest of the way on one hit and no runs to become the winning pitcher. It was one of the better performances ever turned in by a pitcher in the All-Star battles which have been going on for more than 50 years.

I first talked with Mel Harder in mid-June of 1982 at his home in Sun City, Arizona. He and his wife Sandy have since moved back to Ohio to be closer to children and grandchildren.

"How did you get started in baseball, Mel?"
"Well, I started in Omaha. We moved there when I was two years old, and I began playing ball in grade school and went on through high school, then into amateur ball and later professional ball with Omaha. I was always a pitcher. Never played

Righthander Mel Harder spent his entire 20-year playing career (1928-47) with the Cleveland Indians, winning a total of 223 games. He is one of only 65 pitchers to work more than 3,000 innings with an ERA of under 4.00. Harder pitched in four straight All-Star games, 1934-37; he reached the World Series not as a player, but as a Cleveland coach in 1948 and 1954.

any other position. It just seemed natural for me to get out there and throw it.

"I started in organized ball with Omaha in the Western League. I signed with them in 1927 and went to my first spring training with them in Yoakum, Texas. I was with Omaha at the beginning of the season and along about the latter part of April they sent me over to Dubuque, Iowa, in the Mississippi Valley League, which was a non-option league. No one was supposed to option players to its teams. All players were supposed to be owned by the individual clubs.

"Well, of course, Omaha had a claim on me and other clubs found that out, with the result that they threw out all my games. On July 1 I had won 13 and lost eight, so they threw out those 13 games and sent me back to Omaha. And I was sold to Cleveland about August 15 of that year.

"I joined Cleveland in the spring of 1928 and stayed with them all year. In 1929 I began the season with the Indians and was there until about the middle of August. At that time New Orleans was in a pennant race and needed a pitcher, so Cleveland sent me down there for six weeks. In New Orleans I won seven and lost two and then went right back to Cleveland and spent the rest of my active career with them.

"In '28 and '29 I was used almost entirely as a relief pitcher. Our manager, Roger Peckinpaugh, would put me in around the seventh inning or later. I got quite a bit of experience that way. When I got there I was only 18 years old and as green as they make 'em. I had a good arm and a good sinker but I hadn't developed a curve yet. It took me a couple of years to get a good curve, but once I got it by 1930 I started to win some ball games.

"I think the first appearance in the major leagues is a stand-out memory for any young player. I remember that in my first game I pitched three and two third innings in relief against the St. Louis Browns. And then the second time out I got my first loss. It was a game in Cleveland against the Detroit Tigers. We went into the ninth inning a run behind but we tied it up. Peckinpaugh surprised me by putting me in at the start of the 10th inning. I got through the 10th all right, but in the 11th they got a man on and he stole second base on me and then they got a base hit to score the run."

"Mel, tell me about the different managers you played for."

"Actually, I played for or worked under 13 managers in all my years as pitcher and coach for Cleveland. They were all real baseball men, but they all had different personalities. As for their managing, it depended on the type of club we had.

"I always admired Roger Peckinpaugh because he was my first manager. He carried me along for a couple of years there at the beginning and taught me quite a bit. Walter Johnson was a fine manager, but he had trouble in handling a couple of players and that snowballed on him. Steve O'Neill was one of my best friends in baseball. I admired Al Lopez a lot as a manager. He had what it takes and he never overmanaged.

"In 1940 Oscar Vitt was our manager and he lost the respect of the players. It all started with the way he operated. He would pat you on the back one minute and then criticize you the next minute to somebody else. It was a two-faced way of doing things and finally it got to some of the players. We had a good ball club—Bob Feller, Hal Trosky, Jeff Heath, and a lot more—and they all thought we had a good chance to win the pennant. But they didn't feel we could do it with Vitt managing.

"Johnny Allen and I tried to calm the thing down. The players wanted to go to Mr. Bradley, the owner, right away. We tried to talk them out of it. Johnny and I wanted to go to Bradley just by ourselves, since this wouldn't cause any publicity. Nobody would know about it.

"The way it finally happened was that the whole ball club went down there. Well, everybody who saw the club walk into Mr. Bradley's office knew that there was something going on. So that's how it started. But Vitt was kept on and we wound up losing the pennant to Detroit by one game.

"In 1941 Roger Peckinpaugh was brought back for one year before Lou Boudreau took over in '42. Lou was a good manager. He had some of his best playing years as a manager and that helped considerably. He had the respect of all the ballplayers and he was a good leader."

"Did you have a sore arm in 1941, Mel? You had only nine decisions, five wins and four losses."

"Well, my troubles with the arm started in 1936. I had a real good season going, with 12 victories and three defeats by All-Star time early in July, and I pitched in the All-Star game in Boston. Then we went to Philadelphia and I had three days before I pitched again. Along about the fifth inning I felt a twinge in my shoulder and I knew something had happened. I went ahead and finished that game, but by the next day I couldn't raise my arm to comb my hair or do anything.

"From that day on I had trouble with my arm. It really bothered me all through the 1941 season. We decided on an operation and I had some chips removed from the elbow after that season. Once I got those chips out I rested the arm over the winter, and when I went to spring training in '42 the arm started coming around again after it got stronger."

"Mel, you retired one year before the Indians won the World Series in 1948."

"That's right. But I was happy to be involved in two Series—'48 and '54—as a coach for the Indians. That kind of took some of the sting out of not making it in my playing days."

"In the first game of that '48 Series, when Johnny Sain beat Feller, 1-0, was Phil Masi out on the controversial pickoff play at second base just before he scored the only run?"

"Oh, yes. I've got some still shots that show it well. Lou tagged him on the arm as he tried to get back. He was out! We really had a good pickoff play. That wasn't the first time we used it. Boudreau used to tell the umpire to watch for it."

"A while ago you mentioned Johnny Allen. In 1937 he was 15-0 until the last game of the season and then he lost a tough one."

"Yeah," Mel replied, "1-0. Detroit scored a run on a little ground ball to Sammy Hale at third. Sammy probably would have handled the ball a hundred times in a row, but it just took a last little bad hop and rolled over his glove. That scored the run and broke Johnny's streak.

"Allen was a tough pitcher, I'll tell you. I used to pitch against him when he was with the Yankees, and he was one pitcher I didn't like to hit against. He was rough out on that mound. He'd come with a sidearm delivery that made it tough to see the ball. And he'd push batters back."

"You also had quite a career as a coach."

"Well, I was with Cleveland from 1948 through 1963, then I went with the New York Mets and Casey Stengel in 1964. New York just didn't agree with me, though Casey did. Bob Kennedy, who had played for us several years in Cleveland and was then managing the Cubs, asked me to come to Chicago in '65 and I did. But Bob was let out and Durocher came in as manager and brought his own coaches, so I went from there to the Cincinnati Reds for three seasons. Then I finished up with Joe Gordon in Kansas City when the Royals started out as an expansion team in 1969. So, in all I was in major league baseball for a total of 42 seasons."

"How about Casey Stengel?"

"Ah, the one and only Casey. I found out he was as smart a manager as he was made out to be. I was surprised because when he was with the Yankees I used to think anybody could do it with the players he had. But he made moves that worked out because he knew the history of each player against each team and each pitcher. Casey was like an elephant. He always remembered what every player did and he could capitalize on it.

"I used to stay up all night listening to Casey talk. I really enjoyed being with him. He treated me and all his coaches good, and his ballplayers too. He worried about all his players. He really worried about those kids. I was much surprised.

"He was a wonder, and nearly everybody liked Casey. A few of the writers got on him now and then, and one of them was Howard Cosell. A lot of people thought Casey was a kind of clown, but he worried about everybody and really knew what was going on. A great human being. And in all the years he managed the Yankees they really wore the league down. In Cleveland we usually would hold our own for a few months going into maybe June or July, but they had too much. They just kept going. The only time we beat them out was in '54."

"Mel, as pitching coach in Cleveland you had a number of mighty fine pitchers under your tutelage—Feller, Bob Lemon, Early Wynn, Mike Garcia, Herb Score, and a lot of others, including Satchel Paige."

"Yep. Old Satchel. He was a wonder. In his first complete game in the majors he shut out the White Sox in Comiskey Park in 1948. I used to get a kick out of Satch. On the sidelines when he'd loosen up, he had an act he'd put on. He would take a match stick and lay it in front of the catcher to serve as the plate and throw a strike right over it. Then he'd say, 'Turn it the other way, so it's facing me.' And he'd throw it right over that thin match. He pulled that all the time."

"Bill Veeck gave Paige a chance to pitch in the majors at an age when everybody else thought he was washed up."

"Yes," Harder replied, "and Veeck also was one of the first to use a pitching coach. During my active career they didn't have pitching coaches. At the end of the '47 season Veeck gave me a job as pitching coach for the entire Cleveland organization. I went to the major league camp in spring training and when they broke camp I went to the minor league camp in Florida. I worked with their minor league teams for a while and then went back to the Indians and stayed there."

"Do pitching coaches get as much credit as they deserve?"

"Well, I think pitching coaches have a good deal to offer a manager in matters of strategy and everything. And there are so many pitchers who lack just one or two things to become outstanding. Control or maybe a breaking pitch, a slider or a change of pace. So a pitching coach can help considerably there. He has time to work with the pitchers.

"When Bob Lemon first started to pitch he had the idea that he had to throw the ball by the batter all the time. Lem had one of the best sinkers I've ever seen, and the harder he threw it the less it would sink. It took Lem a while to realize that and to believe that he didn't have to throw so hard to get a ball by a batter. Watching Bob Lemon develop from a third baseman/outfielder to a pitcher was a source of much satisfaction.

"And I remember Early Wynn coming over to us from Washington. All Early had then was a fastball and a knuckleball and a dinky curve that was more like a slider. So Early and I worked together and developed a pretty good curveball, a good change of pace, and a hard slider. And he learned how to pitch.

"Early didn't think he could pitch that way, you know. He was a hard thrower and used his knuckleball and that was it. He finally started changing speed and didn't give in to hitters.

"Early was a high ball pitcher. He'd throw a ball just above the strike zone, and it would be called a ball. Then he'd throw another one real close to that same area. The batter would take it, and it would be a strike. So pretty soon the batter would swing at pitches like the one called a strike, and then he would start swinging at pitches a little bit higher. Early had them in between all the time, and he was changing speeds all the time. The batter was off stride and didn't get the good swing."

"Mention a couple of your best games, Mel."

"Oh, I can recall some good ones. Like the opener at the Cleveland Stadium in '32 when Lefty Grove beat me, 1-0. And one of the best games I recall pitching was after my arm operation, probably in 1942, against the Yankees in Cleveland. I beat the Yankees that night, 5-3, and I struck out Joe DiMaggio three times. And of course the All-Star game in 1934."

"Any good memories as a hitter?"

"Well, I got my hits and drove in some runs now and then. While I only had four home runs, two of them came in the same game in 1935, so I remember that pretty well. That was against the White Sox."

"Your biggest thrill in baseball?"

"Well, I think the greatest feeling I ever had was when we won the pennant in '48. Although I was then a coach rather than a player, I got a real thrill out of that. We had to go to Boston for a playoff game with the Red Sox before we won it, and that added to it. The first few games of the World Series were actually kind of like an anticlimax, after the playoff."

"What effect did your sore arm have on your career, Mel?"

"You know, just the other day I was telling my wife Sandy that it's amazing how Gaylord Perry can pitch so many years and never have a sore arm. After I started having my arm trouble in '36, I was still able to pitch another 11 seasons. But if I could have gone through without arm trouble I know I could have added another 40 or 50 wins. But I really struggled the last 10 years I pitched. I had some pretty good seasons in '38 and '39, but it was always a struggle."

"Where did your family live during your 42 years in baseball?"

"Well the first year or so we went back to Omaha in the off season. After our first daughter was born in 1936 we made the trip back to Omaha one more time. By then we were tired of loading things into the car and going back and forth, so we bought our first house in Cleveland. In the years I was coach with other teams my wife would come now and then and stay with me while the team was playing at home.

"I have to give the baseball wives a world of credit for carrying the burden of family life much of the time. And it's even worse now with night ball. Even during a home stand the husband probably leaves the house about three or four in the afternoon and doesn't get back until close to midnight. It's pretty tough on the wives and you sure have to give them a lot of credit."

"Who were some of the best American League sluggers during your time?"

"Well, Ruth and Gehrig were in a class by themselves. Ruth was dangerous all the time. When you were behind Babe on the count, you couldn't throw your fastball in there and hope to get away with it. You had to come in with something different. Gehrig was a different kind of hitter. He could hit to left or right with equal power. He and Gehringer were the two hitters who always gave me the most trouble.

"I thought Jimmy Foxx was one of the most powerful hitters in the game. He had tremendous wrist action. In a game in Cleveland one time I thought I threw him a pretty good curveball and he hit a low line drive in the Stadium that landed about 15 rows up in the farthest section.

"While Foxx hit longer home runs, Al Simmons hit to all fields and with power. They both hit for mighty good average. Hank Greenberg could hit for power and distance with either of those two.

"Ted Williams was a different type of hitter. He had an awfully good eye. It got to the point where, if Williams took a pitch real close to the corner of the plate, the umpires would mostly call it a ball. Joe DiMaggio rates with all those hitters we've been talking about. Joe could do it all, a great player.

"While I was coaching in the National League I got to see a lot of another player who, like DiMaggio, could do it all. That was Roberto Clemente. He was one of the most outstanding ballplayers I've ever seen. I admired him.

"As for some of my teammates at Cleveland, Wes Ferrell and I came up together in 1928. They sent Wes to Terre Haute in 1928 and kept me with the club. In 1929 Wes stayed with the Indians and proceeded to win 20 games for four consecutive years.

"By the time I got there Joe Sewell was slowing up a bit and they soon shifted him to third base. But he was still a mighty good hitter. And tough to strike out. He didn't overswing. All he did was try to meet the ball. You couldn't hardly throw a ball by him.

"Earl Averill joined the Indians in 1929, and boy he was a good hitter. He used one of the heaviest bats in the league— it was over 40 ounces. He could hit the long ball and also for average.

"Charlie Jamieson was probably one of the best leftfielders that Cleveland ever had. And he also was a good hitter, not so much for power, but he'd hit for the average all the time. I know that in 1928 he was one of the most popular ballplayers on the Indians.

"And Joe Vosmik was another of the best outfielders I think Cleveland has had. Around 1930 or 1931 he was one of the best-looking hitters I've ever seen. Most underrated player around. I just can't figure things out in his case. Like the Ohio Hall of Fame, he hasn't got into it yet. There are other ballplayers who have been voted into it who can't compare with Joe.

"I think Ken Keltner was a better third baseman than Al Rosen. Kenny was a good fielder and also a good hitter. And he was always in a rough part of the lineup. It seemed like every time Boudreau got a hit and Eddie Robinson followed with another one, then they would knock Keltner down. He was hitting in that sixth spot all the time.

"When Rollie Hemsley was himself he was a nice guy and a good receiver. His enemy was drink, but he handled pitchers real good. It was a shame he had that problem. When he got to Cleveland he got into Alcoholics Anonymous and they straightened him out.

"Joe Gordon was one of the best defensive second basemen. He could do everything around second base. And as a hitter he had power. I don't think he hit .300 too often, but he was a hitter like Yogi Berra. If he hit about .280 he was a tough .280 hitter. When we got him from the Yankees he teamed up with Boudreau around second base and it was quite a combination.

"When Bill Veeck took over the Indians right at the end of the '46 season, he moved the team right away out of League Park and down to the Stadium. And boy we packed 'em in there. I pitched the first game in the Stadium, in 1932, against Lefty Grove. He beat me, 1-0. The crowd was around 82,000 but there were five or six thousand in there as freeloaders. And in the '48 World Series they drew over 86,000 for the fifth game."

Few ballplayers have had a longer association with major league ball than Mel Harder. He is one of a small group of players who have been active in the majors for 20 years or more. And those who match Mel's career of 20 seasons with the same club are even fewer.

Though he had 20 wins only twice, his total of 223 victories puts him in the company of only about 50 other pitchers who have recorded that many wins or more. And he is one of 65 hurlers who have toiled more than 3,000 innings with an ERA of under 4.00. Mel pitched for the American League in four straight All-Star Games (1934-37), winning one and saving two.

Mel Harder says he got a lot out of baseball. And we can add that very surely he gave a great deal back to it.

MELVIN LEROY HARDER
BR   TR   6'1"   195 lbs.
Born on October 15, 1909 in Beemer, Nebraska

YEAR	TEAM	W	L	PCT.	ERA	G	GS	CG	IP	H	BB	SO	ShO
1928	Cleveland AL	0	2	.000	6.61	23	1	0	49	64	32	15	0
1929	" "	1	0	1.000	5.60	11	0	0	17.2	24	5	4	0
1930	" "	11	10	.524	4.21	36	19	7	175.1	205	68	44	0
1931	" "	13	14	.481	4.36	40	24	9	194	229	72	63	0
1932	" "	15	13	.536	3.75	39	32	17	254.2	277	68	90	1
1933	" "	15	17	.469	2.95	43	31	14	253	254	67	81	2
1934	" "	20	12	.625	2.61	44	29	17	255.1	246	81	91	6
1935	" "	22	11	.667	3.29	42	35	17	287.1	313	53	95	4
1936	" "	15	15	.500	5.17	36	30	13	224.2	294	71	84	0
1937	" "	15	12	.556	4.28	38	30	13	233.2	269	86	95	0
1938	" "	17	10	.630	3.83	38	29	15	240	257	62	102	2
1939	" "	15	9	.625	3.50	29	26	12	208	213	64	67	1
1940	" "	12	11	.522	4.06	31	25	5	186.1	200	59	76	0
1941	" "	5	4	.556	5.24	15	10	1	68.2	76	37	21	0
1942	" "	13	14	.481	3.44	29	29	13	198.2	179	82	74	4
1943	" "	8	7	.533	3.06	19	18	6	135.1	126	61	40	1
1944	" "	12	10	.545	3.71	30	27	12	196.1	211	69	64	2
1945	" "	3	7	.300	3.67	11	11	2	76	93	23	16	0
1946	" "	5	4	.556	3.41	13	12	4	92.1	85	31	21	1
1947	" "	6	4	.600	4.50	15	15	4	80	91	27	17	1
	20 yrs.	223	186	.545	3.80	582	433	181	3426.1	3706	1118	1160	25

Pirates' lefthander Larry French made a dramatic big-league debut on **May 7, 1929**, when he pitched a 10-inning, 6-hitter against the New York Giants. After six years with Pittsburgh, French moved on to the Chicago Cubs for seven seasons. He later joined the Brooklyn Dodgers, with whom he had his last and perhaps greatest season, 1942, when he posted a 15-4 record. His career totals of 197 wins put French in the top 100 winningest pitchers of all time, with 40 of those wins being shutouts. French appeared in the 1935 and '38 World Series with the Cubs and in the 1941 Series with the Dodgers.

7

Larry French

The career of Larry French differs from that of most other ballplayers in two significant aspects. When his playing days ended he didn't remain in baseball as a coach, scout, manager, executive or whatever. Instead he went off to two completely different careers, in each of which he enjoyed great success. Also, when he left baseball at age 35 it wasn't because he had outlived his usefulness in the majors. His last season was in some ways his greatest, and he went out at the peak of his form.

The reason for Larry's sudden and final departure from the major league scene was World War II. In January 1943 he accepted a commission in the U.S. Navy and served until the war was won. He remained in the reserve unit and was called back to active duty in 1951 during the Korean War. When he finally retired in 1969 he held the rank of Captain in the U.S. Navy.

And the reason why French didn't return to baseball for the 1946 season was that he had acquired an automobile agency in California. Feeling that it represented his future and required his presence, he declined the opportunity to rejoin the Brooklyn Dodgers. In this he was right, for his car agency business prospered handsomely and helped make his future economically secure.

As far as going out in style is concerned, Larry really did it right. In his last season his won-lost record of 15-4 for Brooklyn gave him the best winning percentage in the league at .789, and his ERA mark of 1.83 was second only to Mort Cooper's 1.78. And he even checked in with a .300 batting average for the season! The most gratifying aspect of it all was that this super performance followed a nightmare year with the Chicago Cubs in 1941 when he suffered through a 5-14 record.

In his 14 seasons in the majors with the Pittsburgh Pirates, Chicago Cubs, and Brooklyn Dodgers, Larry French amassed a total of 197 wins. This is good enough to place him among the top 100 winningest pitchers in major league history.

An interesting and important aspect of Larry's 197 wins is that 40 of them were shutouts. This means that his shutouts-to-wins ratio is better than 20%. A win is more important than a shutout, but the shutout says something about the pitcher's dominance during the win. Another pitching quality of importance is consistency, and here again French rates pretty high with an average of just over 14 wins per season for 14 seasons.

Let's turn the story over now to Larry French himself:

"Well, I was born and raised in California's San Joaquin Valley in a town called Visalia, and like all school kids I played on the high school team. I pitched and was a teammate of Lyn Lary, who played shortstop. Back then they had what was called a Raisin League. It was Sunday ball and they had a bunch of old major leaguers. One of them was Bill Steen, who pitched for the Visalia team. And Dutch Leonard, the first Dutch Leonard, was at Fresno, and Ray Keating was over at Modesto. And so I pitched batting practice to the Visalia ball club a couple of nights a week. Lyn and I were the bat boys for the team. I think I grew up a little faster than the average young kid since I played with the men pretty early in life.

"Then I went on to school. I thought I wanted to go to Oregon State, or Oregon Agricultural College as it was called at that time, in Corvallis. I went up there and my father, who had separated from my mother, had a Chevrolet dealership in southern Oregon. I went to live with him until school opened, and I played summer ball. I pitched a no-hit, no-run game one day against a club from Salem.

"Roy Mack, Connie's son, was the business manager at Portland, and he was there to see another player, a third baseman on the club I was with. When I pitched this no-hitter Roy came down after the game and asked if I'd like to come to Portland for a tryout.

"I asked my father and he said, 'Yeah, you can go but just remember that you've got to go back to school.' I agreed and went to Portland and they signed me to a contract. I played part of the 1926 season with them, from May 15 on. That started me, and so I played '27 and '28 with them, and then they sold me to the Pirates for $55,000 and five ballplayers. That was in the winter of '28, and so in the spring of '29 I went to the Pirates.

"My first contract with Pittsburgh was for $5,750 plus $750 if I stayed with them past the first of May. And Tom Turner, president of the Portland club, also promised me $500 if I stayed beyond May. And of course I collected both of those bonuses. My first contract in five figures was in 1933."

Asked if he remembered his first game with Pittsburgh, Larry replied:

"Wait just a minute and I'll get something to show you. Here it is, a plaque given me by friends which contains the clippings of my first game in the majors and my last game in the majors."

The box score of the game between the Pirates and the Giants in New York on May 7, 1929 shows that Larry French made quite a splash in his debut in the majors. He hurled a 6-hit, 10-inning, 3-2 win against the Giants. After allowing solo home runs in each of the first two innings, he settled down and breezed along to the finish. *The New York Times'* report of the game says in part: "Larry French, the tallest twirler to make a name for himself as a Giant queller, is a 21-year-old southpaw from Portland of the Pacific Coast League."

Larry French spent six years with the Pittsburgh Pirates (1929-34), who finished second three times and fifth three times. In that period Larry won 87 games and lost 83. Then he went to the Chicago Cubs for seven seasons and compiled a total of 95 wins against 84 losses before his last year at Brooklyn which became his greatest one at 15-4.

In 1935 Larry teamed with Bill Lee, Lon Warneke, and Charlie Root to pitch the Cubs to the National League pennant. In winning the flag the Cubs had to put on the most dramatic finish in league history, reeling off a string of 21 straight wins at the end of the season. French hurled the first win in the streak and went on to record five victories in the 21-game string.

The World Series of 1935, pitting the Cubs against the Detroit Tigers, was not so kind to Larry. With the Series tied at one game apiece, he entered the third game in the top of the 10th inning with the score knotted at 5-all. The Tigers won it in the 11th on an unearned run which saddled French with the loss.

The Series then moved on to the sixth game, which found French opposing Tommy Bridges. The ninth inning arrived with the score tied, 3-3. Stan Hack led off the ninth for the Cubs with a triple over Gee Walker's head in center. Billy Jurges struck out. French was due to bat next. Larry tells what happened:

"Charlie Grimm let me hit. I backed away from the plate two times looking for a squeeze sign, but I didn't get anything. And of course I didn't hit the ball very hard off Bridges."

Actually, Larry bounced back to the pitcher, and then Augie Galan flied out. The Tigers scored in the bottom of the ninth with two out to win the Series.

In the 1938 Series, in which the Yankees swept the Cubs in four straight games, French appeared in relief three times, giving up one run and one hit (a homer by Bill Dickey) in three and one third innings.

After going from the Cubs to the Brooklyn Dodgers late in the 1941 season, French appeared very briefly as a relief pitcher in two games of the '41 Series which the Yankees won in five games. Two unusual incidents cost the Dodgers whatever chance they had to upset the Yankees. In the third game Brooklyn pitcher Freddie Fitzsimmons and Marius Russo of the Yankees were locked in a scoreless struggle in the seventh inning when Fitz had to be helped off the field after being struck in the knee by a line drive off the bat of Russo. In the eighth the Yankees scored twice off reliever Hugh Casey to win it, 2-1.

The other incident which cost the Dodgers is one of the most famous plays in baseball history. The fourth game of the Series found the Dodgers leading, 4-3, in the ninth inning, with the ill-starred Casey again on the mound in relief. He got the first two batters on ground balls and then struck out Tommy Henrich to apparently end the game. But somehow the ball got past catcher Mickey Owen and the Yankees capitalized on the big break to score four runs and win. Larry French offers this comment on the unhappy event:

"Well, I didn't see the dropped third strike because I had pitched in that game and went out for pinch hitter Jimmy Wasdell. So I was sitting on the rubbing table in our dressing room, and when we heard the yell go up we just thought the game was over. And you know the rest."

Nineteen forty two was Larry's last season in the majors and he did everything he could to get the Dodgers into the World

Series again. In fact the whole team had a great season, winding up with 104 wins, which was only good enough to let them finish in second place, two games behind the St. Louis Cardinals. Larry likes to talk about the Dodger ball club in those '41 and '42 seasons:

"That was a great bunch of ballplayers and they played well together. Pete Reiser and Joe Medwick were tremendous players. And Dolf Camilli and Billy Herman and PeeWee Reese and Dixie Walker. And Whit Wyatt was a wonderful righthander. In 1942 when the chips were down he pitched three or four tremendous games when all of them were crucial.

"But one of the most interesting things about playing in Brooklyn was that there was something exciting going on in the stands every minute, a fight or something. And Leo Durocher was pretty interesting as a manager, too, because he kept the place stirred up."

When pressed, however, to single out the best ball club he played on, French said:

"Well, I think the Chicago Cubs of '35 probably had the best balanced team I played with. An infield of Cavarretta, Herman, Jurges, and Hack, and the best catcher around in Hartnett. And their outfield of Galan, Klein, and Demaree was pretty fine. A well balanced club, and we had some good starting pitchers with Warneke and Lee and Root and myself. So, of all the teams I played on I believe that was the best ball club. And our manager, Charlie Grimm. He was funny and an awfully nice guy and a real good manager too.

"And Wrigley Field is a beautiful ball park. The dressing quarters and all that are sort of antiquated now. I went there to an Old Timers game recently and those facilities aren't like they are in the new parks, but just the same it's a lovely ball park. And now I hear pitchers saying that it's a horrible park to pitch in because so many home runs are hit there. Well, they hit home runs off us too back in my time. But in those days we regarded that as just being part of baseball."

French was one of the relatively few pitchers to use the screwball frequently. "How did you develop that pitch?" I asked.

"Well, in the Coast League in 1927 or 1928 there was a fellow named Hub Pruett. He had quite a record of having struck out Babe Ruth a lot of times when he was in the majors. He was with the Oakland ball club and so I asked him one day how he threw it. And he showed me. He *really* showed me, and so

I threw it a while on the sidelines and all of a sudden it seemed to be pretty good.

"I wasn't as effective against a left-handed batter as I was against a righthander, due to my screwball. I much preferred to pitch to righthanders. My curveball wasn't anything to write home about. I would have a sore arm from throwing the screwball, and there were times when I couldn't get my hand up high enough to comb my hair. But in those days you lived with those things. It wasn't like it is today when they beg off for any reason at all.

"Speaking of that, I was pitching a ball game, I believe it was opening day, against Cincinnati in Cubs Park in '37 or '38 or somewhere along in there, and Ernie Lombardi hit a line drive at me. I saw it as it left the bat and then lost it, and it hit me here on the right hand driving this bone into this other one and breaking these two fingers. I remember the doctor coming out and he put this finger back in and said, 'That's going to be pretty dad-gummed sore for a little bit.'

"So I said, 'All right' and I put on the glove and the first thought I had was that I was all through for a good while. But we were going on a road trip and Andy Lotshaw, our trainer, said, 'I've got the very thing for you, Larry.' So he ended up with a piece of light lead that could be shaped into any form, and folded that around my hand and put some tape on it. And I put the glove on and I pitched about the third or fourth day afterwards."

"Why didn't you go back after World War II to seek three more wins and reach 200?"

"I can tell you a story about that. Actually, when I went into the Navy on January 8, 1943, they ordered me to the Brooklyn Ship Yard, of all places. So, since there was a curtailment on travel, the Dodgers trained in a fieldhouse at West Point, just up the river. And each weekend I'd go up there and work out with them. And when the season opened I was ready to pitch.

"I petitioned the Secretary of the Navy to let me pitch eight ball games, all to be done on my own time and on weekends in Brooklyn, and I would give the Navy Relief Society $8,000 for the eight games. I was confident I could get my three wins in eight tries. And I was turned down. That decision was setting a precedent at the time, but later on they allowed Joe Louis to fight and then the whole thing opened up, too late for me.

"After the war I wanted to go back and get three wins, sure, but I also had been in the car business, both new and used, out in California, and I wanted an agency when I got out of baseball. I so told Branch Rickey when he came out to have lunch with me on the old battleship New York in the harbor on Navy Day in 1945. We agreed on a contract and I said, 'This is fine except that if I get the car agency I won't come back to baseball.' I got the agency and so I just didn't go back to try for my three wins."

Gabby Hartnett had taken over as manager of the Cubs in the middle of the 1938 season, replacing Charlie Grimm. Though they were good friends and often battery mates, Larry ran into a problem with Gabby in 1939. While this was something Larry regretted very much, it was to lead to an unexpected and very fruitful business deal with Mr. P. K. Wrigley, the owner of the Cubs. Here is Larry's account of the whole matter:

"In '38 I elected to pitch to Gus Mancuso one day instead of to Gabby, who was managing the team at that time and was a good friend of mine. A while later I was having breakfast with Mancuso, and I had won four straight games with him behind the plate. Gabby came by and put his arm on my shoulder and said, 'How about working the first game of the doubleheader with me today?' I said, 'Do you mind if I pitch to Gus?' He didn't, of course, when I put it that way. But he was an Irishman and had an ego like the rest of us. And so I didn't pitch for a week, for two weeks, for three weeks.

"Anyway, I didn't pitch for my three turns in a row and then the All-Star break came along. We had a son up in Wisconsin and so we drove there to see him. On the way I remember telling my wife Thelma, 'I'm going to do something I've never done before. I'm going over the boss' head and right up to the front office. So prepare to go home if this doesn't work out, because I'm going to ask them to trade me. I've got to pitch or get out.'

"So, I made an appointment with Mr. Wrigley and went up to see him. I'll never forget that I said to him, 'If somebody came to me with this request, I'd fire him, but here's my position.' He listened to me and then said, 'Well, you know, when I made Gabby the manager I knew I was dropping from the frying pan into the fire, but he is the boss and all I can suggest to you is that each time you get into a game you do better than you can do.' I remember his words so well they are just stencilled in my mind.

"We were playing an exhibition game that day out in Moline, and when we got off the train all hell broke loose. All the newspapermen started jumping after me. Boots Weber, our traveling secretary, told me, 'Larry, don't say a word, don't open your trap. Just walk with me and come on to the hotel.' I asked, 'What's up?' 'Well,' he said, 'the story got out that you were in Mr. Wrigley's office today.' I replied, 'That's correct, I was.' He said, 'I knew that. Did you tell them?' And I said, 'No, I didn't tell them.' So Wrigley leaked it, I guess.

"They had a Chicago paper with a cartoon showing a doghouse and my ears sticking out of it, and Wrigley was in one corner and Hartnett in the other. Anyway, it did blow over and I did get to relieve in a game a couple of days after we came back. I pitched well and then I got back in the starting rotation, and I won a number of games in a row.

"The end of all this is something I always have felt was very important to my career. Wrigley called me in towards the end of the season and said, 'You've had a good year, Larry, and I'd like to sign you to next year's contract.' And he gave me the biggest contract I'd had up to that time. It was for $17,500.

"Then he said, 'I know you're in the car business on the West Coast. And I know you deal in insurance too. Tell me about that.' I told him, 'Well, mine is all casualty and collisions and fire and theft with regard to cars.' Then Wrigley said, 'How would you like to have my insurance, as part of your contract, for all my personal property on the West Coast?' I could only say, 'Mr. Wrigley, that's beyond my best dreams.'

"So I got to handle the insurance on the Arizona Biltmore Hotel and his mansion above the hotel, and everything on Catalina Island, as well as his house in Pasadena, and I had this for a good number of years. So, if you ask me how good were the Wrigleys, I say they were awfully good to me."

Larry French had by far his worst season in 1941, winning only five games and losing 14 for the Cubs, who traded him to Brooklyn almost at the end of the season. And then in 1942 with the Dodgers he had his great year of 15-4.

"How about this enormous turn-around, Larry?"

"Well, I'll tell you exactly how it happened. It was in the winter before the '41 season. I belonged to the Lions Club in Los Angeles, and we sponsored a kids' softball team. So they wanted to play the old men and we played 'em, and I pitched.

Along in the middle of the game a kid hit a high bounding ball to me and I reached up and broke this left thumb.

"I didn't say anything to anybody, just put it in a cast and went about my business until quail season opened. I went over to Catalina and I wasn't shooting too well. I got a little further into the gun so I could shoot better, and I hurt the thumb again. I went to training camp and signed a contract and then all heck broke loose because I hadn't told anyone I had broken a finger. I had just thought it would get better and be all right. Well, it didn't strengthen up all year and when I was 5-14 they dumped me off to Brooklyn."

Larry agreed heartily when it was pointed out that the broken thumb kept him from reaching 200 wins:

"That's a fact. I think of that so many times, much more than not getting back for three more wins after the war."

Asked to identify his best game in the majors, French had little trouble singling it out. It was his last game, on September 22, 1942, in Brooklyn's Ebbets Field. French hurled a 6-0, one-hit, near-perfect game. The lone hit came off the bat of Nick Etten of the Phillies in the second inning, a lazy liner which PeeWee Reese almost knocked down. A moment later Etten was erased in a double play and French breezed on through, facing the absolute minimum of 27 batters. Nothing like saving the best for last! And what a way to go out!

"Larry, who was the best player you saw at each position during your time in the National League?"

"Bill Terry, all around, was the best first baseman in my day. I think Billy Herman was the best second baseman. Of course, Hornsby played second too and was a better hitter, but he couldn't field like Herman and anyway Hornsby was about through when I got there. Pie Traynor was the greatest third baseman, and the best shortstop I played with was PeeWee Reese.

"Outfielders? Well, Paul Waner. And Joe Medwick, who was an awfully good outfielder and the toughest man for me to get out. And Pete Reiser. Gabby Hartnett would be the catcher. Gus Mancuso was a close second because he caught Hubbell for so long.

"Gus and I pitched and caught like hand in glove, and that's the reason I liked to pitch to him. Gabby hardly every caught a lefthander, if you think back to those Cub days. They had almost no lefthanders in those years and Gabby handled me like a righthander when I came along.

"For the left-handed pitcher on this imaginary team it's Carl Hubbell, of course. And the righthander . . . well, for someone who pitched a long time, I like Charlie Root. He might be the best righthander over a stretch of years that I played with."

Besides being involved in three World Series, Larry French had the good fortune of playing on teams that in most years were contending for the National League flag. In his 14 seasons the clubs he pitched for finished first or second nine times. Also, in the eighth All-Star game, played in 1940 in St. Louis, Larry pitched two scoreless innings in a 4-0 National League win which marked the first shutout in this annual competition. In 1939 French reached his peak as a slugger, blasting his one and only home run in 1,057 trips to the plate. The victim of that unlikely blow was Curt Davis of the St. Louis Cardinals.

During the later years of his baseball days Larry French maintained a nice home in Brentwood, an area of Los Angeles. When Larry went off to spring training and then on to the regular season, his wife and son would stay in Brentwood until the school year ended. At that point they would join Larry and rent the house in Brentwood. For some years their summer tenant in Brentwood was Molly Goldberg of radio fame. Since 1959 Larry has made his residence in San Diego, though only recently has he disposed of the Brentwood home.

In San Diego French served as president of the board of directors of the San Diego Navy Federal Credit Union, and he spent time (involving numerous trips) to establish similar credit unions in Korea and Japan. He also continued to have private business interests in California. Larry was more or less an exception among old ballplayers in that he didn't continue in the game in some capacity after his playing days ended. As he said, "When I left baseball I left it for good. I didn't look back."

After a short illness, Larry French died in San Diego on February 9, 1987, at the age of 79.

LAWRENCE HERBERT FRENCH
BR TL   6'1"   195 lbs.
Born November 1, 1907 in Visalia, California
Died February 9, 1987 in San Diego, California

YEAR	TEAM	W	L	PCT.	ERA	G	GS	CG	IP	H	BB	SO	ShO
1929	Pittsburgh NL	7	5	.583	4.90	30	13	6	123	130	62	49	0
1930	" "	17	18	.486	4.36	42	35	21	274.2	325	89	90	3
1931	" "	15	13	.536	3.26	39	33	20	275.2	301	70	73	1
1932	" "	18	16	.529	3.02	47	33	20	274.1	301	62	72	3
1933	" "	18	13	.581	2.72	47	35	21	291.1	290	55	88	5
1934	" "	12	18	.400	3.58	49	35	16	263.2	299	59	103	3
1935	Chicago NL	17	10	.630	2.96	42	30	16	246.1	279	44	90	4
1936	" "	18	9	.667	3.39	43	28	16	252.1	262	54	104	4
1937	" "	16	10	.615	3.98	42	28	11	208	229	65	100	4
1938	" "	10	19	.345	3.80	43	27	10	201.1	210	62	83	3
1939	" "	15	8	.652	3.29	36	21	10	194	205	50	98	2
1940	" "	14	14	.500	3.29	40	33	18	246	240	64	107	3
1941	2 teams	Chicago NL (26G 5-14) Brooklyn NL (6G 0-0)											
	1941 total	5	14	.263	4.51	32	19	6	153.2	177	47	68	1
1942	Brooklyn NL	15	4	.789	1.83	38	14	8	147.2	127	36	62	4
	14 yrs.	197	171	.535	3.44	570	384	199	3152	3375	819	1187	40

WORLD SERIES

YEAR	TEAM	W	L	PCT.	ERA	G	GS	CG	IP	H	BB	SO	ShO
1935	Chicago NL	0	2	.000	3.38	2	1	1	10.2	15	2	8	0
1938	" "	0	0	.000	2.70	3	0	0	3.1	1	1	2	0
1941	Brooklyn NL	0	0	.000	0.00	2	0	0	1	0	0	0	0
	3 yrs.	0	2	.000	3.00	7	1	1	15	16	3	10	0

Travis Jackson, 15 years a shortstop and occasional third baseman, was part of the best-hitting infield in major league history, the 1930 New York Giants. Here Jackson shakes hands with John McGraw (left) as "Mr. McGraw's" last captain. McGraw ended a 30-year career as Giants' manager in June 1932. Jackson then captained for close friend Bill Terry until he went to the minors as a manager in 1936. He was a 1982 inductee at Cooperstown.

8

Travis Jackson

I n March 1982 Travis Jackson was elected to Baseball's Hall of Fame. News of the honor reached Jackson in his home in Waldo, Arkansas, the small town where he had been born 78 years earlier. Since hanging up his spikes in 1936, he had waited 46 years for this highest recognition baseball has to offer.

When I talked with Travis in his comfortable home three months later, he was still excited and looking forward to the August induction ceremonies at the Hall of Fame shrine in Cooperstown, New York. Like all the great old players of the '20s and '30s who still wait to be included among baseball's select few, Jackson had hoped the honor would arrive while he was still alive to enjoy it. He was lucky.

"Travis, how did you get your start in baseball?"

"I began playing right here in Waldo when I was in high school," Travis told me. "Every little town around here had a team back in those days, like Magnolia, Lewisville, Stephens, Stamps. The way we used to do it was somebody would get up there on Main Street and holler, 'Let's play a ball game!' Word would be sent to Magnolia or some other place and they'd show up. Everybody had to move about in horse and buggy until we got the Model T.

"I played two summers up in Marvell, Arkansas, and worked in a drug store with my uncle. They had an excellent bunch of semipro teams in Marvell, Holly Grove, Clarendon, and Marianna, and so I jerked soda there in the daytime, we'd practice late in the day, and on Friday and Saturday we'd have ball games.

"There were some semipro teams in Little Rock and we'd bring them down. That was my last year in high school and we were playing in Pine Bluff one day when a scout from the Little Rock club of the Southern Association came down there and told me that Kid Elberfeld wanted to see me in Little Rock. It seems they had a shortstop, a little fellow named McGinnity, who broke a leg and they needed someone to finish the season. That was in 1921.

"So, I had a little trouble getting up there because my mother was very religious and she didn't want me to sign a contract. In fact, she would have to sign it for me, and she didn't want any part of that Sunday baseball. It turned out that, although she finally signed the contract, I didn't play ball on Sunday in that first year of 1921. But she relented during the year and in 1922 I started playing every day.

"The New York Giants sent an outfielder named Joe Connolly to Little Rock with the understanding that he could stay there and play center field all season if the Giants could have first pick of the Little Rock players at the end of the year.

"It turned out I was the first pick and at the end of the '22 season they told me to report to the Giants, who had bought me. I got into three games with the Giants and in 1923 I was the utility infielder. After that I was a regular until I finished in 1936."

"Do you remember your first game?"

"Yes, I do. I had one time at bat, against Jimmy Ring, an old-time pitcher who was with Philadelphia then. And he was a mean one. And another thing. I came within an eyelash of starting a triple play on the first ball hit to me at shortstop. There were runners on first and second and a line drive was hit to my left. But instead of being able to catch the ball in the air, I had to take it on the pickup and so we got a double play. If I had caught it we would have had an easy triple play. Imagine almost making a triple play on the first ball hit to me in the major league!"

"How was John McGraw to play for?"

"Well, Mr. McGraw had the reputation of being an awfully rough manager, and he was. And he was smart, he was always ahead of you, he was looking ahead to the next half inning or next inning. He liked to have players who could go for the big inning. He never would sacrifice or anything like that for the first four or five innings.

"And a lot of players didn't like him, because he was rough and tough. But the ballplayers, it was a funny thing, they'd play for him. He'd say, 'If you don't get out there and do this or that, I'll send you down to Timbuctoo or some place.' They were fighting for their lives out there all the time. But if you hustled for John McGraw you could play for him. He'd hold meetings pretty often and he'd tell us, 'Now, just because I do something doesn't give you the right to do it. You do what I tell you and you'll get along fine.' "

"Well," I commented, "it seems like his system was successful."

"Oh, he was successful. And I got along well with him. He made me captain of the ball club. And I'll tell you, his word was good. For example, we had an outfielder named Jimmy Welsh. One day a fly ball was hit out there and it went by Jimmy. He didn't quite get to it. And when we came into the dugout McGraw started to get on Jimmy. He said, 'We told you in the meeting to play this fellow so and so.' Jimmy said, 'Mr. McGraw, Jackson moved me.' McGraw asked me if I moved him and I said, 'Yes, sir.' And McGraw said, 'It's okay then.' He gave me the authority out there to do what I felt best."

"What about Bill Terry?"

"Yes, Bill Terry was a good manager. Mr. McGraw's biggest weakness was in handling the pitchers. He just didn't handle pitchers like Terry could. Or like McKecknie."

"You mean he didn't change pitchers at the right time?"

"Yes. And I've seen him call for 15 or 16 straight curveballs."

"Carl Hubbell told me that McGraw practically wouldn't let a pitcher throw fastballs."

"Oh, yes, he would do things like that. But Terry was a good manager at handling pitchers. McGraw quit and turned it over to Terry early in the 1932 season, and the next year we won the pennant."

"Of course, that wasn't your first World Series."

"No, my first was 1923, when I just pinch hit. Against Herb Pennock. Hit a flyball down in the left-field bullpen and they caught it. That was it. We thought we could beat the Yankees going into that Series."

"Well, the Giants did beat them in '21 and '22."

"By the way, that '23 Series was the first one in Yankee

Stadium. That was when Casey Stengel hit an inside-the-park home run to win the first game."

"Yes," I observed. "And then in the third game he hit one into the right-field stands for the only run in a 1-0 Giant victory. So Casey was the hero in both of the Giants' victories in that Series. Now, what about the 1924 Series? That was a hard one to lose."

"Yes, it was. We were all kind of glad that Washington got into the Series on account of Walter Johnson. He'd never been in a World Series before. And then we hit him pretty hard and beat him twice."

"But in the seventh game he came on in the ninth inning and won it in the 12th."

"One thing everybody should remember about that last game is that it was getting dark in the late innings and with Walter Johnson out there, even if he had lost some of his speed, the way he whipped that ball in from the side you couldn't pick it up until it was right on you. Two things happened in that last inning to make the Giants lose that Series. The first was when catcher Hank Gowdy got his feet mixed up in his mask on a little pop fly that would have retired the side, after which Muddy Ruel doubled, and then that little easy grounder down to Freddie Lindstrom that just hopped over his shoulder."

"And how about the '33 Series, when you beat Washington?"

"There are a couple of things I recall about that Series. Both of them occurred in the fourth game, with us leading two games to one. We were tied, 1-1, going into the 11th inning. Monte Weaver was on the mound for them against Carl Hubbell, who had already won the first game of the Series.

"I couldn't move around as well then as I had earlier in my career, but I remember telling Bill Terry, 'I'm leading off this inning and I'm going to get on somehow, by taking one on the hip or whatever. So have a pinch runner ready for me.' Well, I didn't get hit by a pitch, but I bunted and didn't even draw a throw from Ossie Bluege at third, because they were playing me back figuring I couldn't run anyway.

"After I got to first base I turned around thinking, 'Well, here comes my runner.' I won't mention the boy's name now, for you'll see in a minute why I don't want to name him. But no runner was sent out for me. Gus Mancuso was the next batter and he sacrificed.

"I slid into second base and dusted myself off as I thought,

'Now here comes my pinch runner.' But no pinch runner. So Blondie Ryan singled to left field and I scored, though if the throw had been anywhere near the plate I would have been out.

"I got to the bench and said, 'Bill, what in the hell is going on?' And he said, 'Well, I told this boy that he was going to run and he began to shake all over. And I'd rather have an old man like you in there than somebody that was scared to death.'

"So in the bottom of that same inning Washington loaded the bases with only one out. Then they sent up a pinch hitter against Hub, a left-handed hitter named Cliff Bolton, a young catcher they had called up from Nashville. And Hubbell, you know, a left-handed batter could hit him better than one from the right side.

"Now it happened that one of our players had been hurt and we were allowed to select someone to fill in for us during the Series. And we got Charlie Dressen. We talked out on the mound as to what we were going to do. Dressen had played with this fellow down in Nashville, and Terry called him out from the bench. Bill asked him, 'Can you tell us anything about this fellow?' Dressen said, 'Yes, he hits lefthanders pretty good, but he's slow. If he hits the ball on the ground you've got plenty of time to double him up.' And I'll be darned if that wasn't exactly what happened."

"Well, Travis," I commented, "Al Lopez must be right. He's quoted as saying you were the best bunter he ever saw. He says you had a sort of hitch when you swung and when you were going to bunt it was impossible to detect ahead of time because you'd hitch and then drop the ball down the third-base line. Okay, and in 1936 the Giants faced the Yankees again in the Series."

"Yes, the Yankees kind of blistered us in '36, although the Series did go six games with Hubbell winning the first game and Schumacher another. But Freddie Fitzsimmons lost two, one of them a real tough 2-1 loss.

"Freddie was a real hard worker. He had to work so hard to get what he had. If he went a week without working he'd gain 10 pounds. And that was in the heat of summer, too. He had to work like the dickens to keep in shape the year round or he would balloon up there where he couldn't move."

"Travis, tell me about some of your teammates on the Giants through the years."

"Well, I was a utility player in 1923 but I got into 96 games. Old Heinie Groh hurt his knee and I got my opportunity to replace him at third base for about 30 games. You talk about a green beginner, I was it. Anyway, I played that third bag and must have done a pretty good job. And within a week after Heinie got back, Dave Bancroft came down with pneumonia and so I played more than 60 games at shortstop while he was recovering.

"Then Bancroft went over to manage the Boston Braves in 1924 and McGraw told me, 'You're going to be my short-stop.' And, oh boy, was I pleased and excited. But I wish I could find some of those articles the newspaper people wrote about it. That's the only time, they say, that the writers ever got on McGraw. For getting rid of Bancroft and putting a 19-year-old rookie in at shortstop. You see, when that was announced after the 1923 season I was still only 19."

"Well, you didn't let McGraw down. You hit .302 that year, drove in 76 runs, and hit 11 home runs. Was it tough breaking in as a regular?"

"I don't know, the crowds and everything just never did seem to make any difference to me. I was lucky, though, that the fans never did get on me. The older players sort of took me under their wing. They said, 'Now, on these road trips they're going to knock you down. Don't show any anger, don't try to get back at them, don't give them any satisfaction.' Well, about the second or third trip around the league everything became calm, but on that first trip I was sitting on my tail as much as I was standing up. They did that to every newcomer.

"And I got along with everybody up there. I never had any trouble the whole time. And I was never thrown out of a game, even though I argued with the umpires pretty good at times after I was made captain. Once I had old Bill Klem follow me all the way to the dugout. All he wanted was just for me to look back. If I had looked he would have tossed me out of there.

"We had lots of fine players through all my years there. Like old George Kelly, our first baseman for a few years before he went over to Cincinnati. He was quite a guy, old High Pockets, as they called him. And Jo-Jo Moore and Hughie Critz. Jo-Jo led off for us and Hughie hit second. Joe played at around 145 pounds and Hughie was about 140 pounds, but they were real ballplayers. Irish Meusel, whose brother Bob played for the Yankees at the same time, was our main run-producer for years.

But Irish had a bad arm, which he blamed on me. He said it was from having to throw in all those balls I missed.

"And Ross Youngs was a wonderful guy. He was great. He was fast, had a good arm, was a .300 hitter and could steal some bases, and I mean he was a competitor. But the sad thing is that he died in 1927 at age 30. Ross and Frisch didn't get along. Jealous of one another. They were both great ballplayers.

"One day when we were playing in Brooklyn something happened to Frisch, and we didn't have too many players on the bench at the moment. McGraw took Frisch out and said, 'Now who will I put at second base?' Youngs said, 'I'll play it. Let me go out there.'

"So the next inning McGraw put somebody in right field and told Ross to go to second. And he lasted one inning, because a double play ball came up and the runner reached second before Ross could throw the ball and he got whacked. When he came back to the bench he said, 'Put me back in right field.'

"Hank Gowdy was another great fellow. When I got up there he couldn't hit too well or run much, but he was still a good catcher. He sure could handle pitchers. He and I later coached for the Giants at the same time. Hank was a wonderful person. And he was the first man to enlist in World War I.

"And Bill Terry was terrific as a hitter and a leader. And he was fast despite being a big fellow. Let me tell you a story about that. We used to play a number of games against Washington in spring training, and one time both teams were staying in a Tampa hotel. Sitting out on the porch of the hotel, some of their players said Goose Goslin was faster than anybody we had on our club.

"I knew who was the fastest man on either team and so I got two or three of our boys together and said, 'Let's take 'em up on that.' They asked me, 'Well, who's faster than Goslin?' I said, 'Bill Terry.' And they said, 'Oh, no! You're kidding.' You see, Terry played at around 187 to 190 pounds, and he just didn't look that fast.

"Well, we went out around home plate and got Terry and Goslin on the line. That Washington bunch was just sitting back and grinning. So they started off and you know what? Goslin didn't even finish! When Terry went past him he quit.

"Terry was one of the best all-around ballplayers I ever saw. He could field, he could run, there's no doubt about his hitting, and he had such a strong arm he could have stayed up there as a pitcher. He was a case like Babe Ruth, someone who could both hit and pitch in major league style.

"And Mel Ott was a hitter, for sure. But listen, don't over-look his fielding out there. He had a fine arm. I suppose Joe Moore had the stronger arm, but Mel had the quick release and that's hard to beat. Plus, his throws were accurate. You wouldn't believe how he caught batters trying to take two bases on a hit to right."

"Who were the best players at each position in the National League during your years up there?"

"At first base I'd have to go with Bill Terry over anybody else, but I don't want you to think I'm favoring my own team. Along about that time, when Terry was hitting so much, one of the best fielders that's ever been up there on first base was Charlie Grimm.

"At second you've got Frisch and Hornsby, and I wouldn't want to choose between the two. At shortstop I'd have to go along with Glenn Wright. He was an all-around standout. Hit-ting, fielding, strong arm. Gee, he had a strong arm. And at third base, there's no doubt that it belongs to Pie Traynor.

"The outfield is going to be hard, because you have to choose between Paul and Lloyd Waner, Kiki Cuyler, Edd Roush, Mel Ott, Ducky Medwick. I couldn't pick three from that bunch. And catcher? Al Lopez was pretty good. He sure was. But the two who were always coming at you and would beat you pretty often were Gabby Hartnett and Jimmy Wilson.

"Wilson was smart, like Lopez. Lopez had a way of catch-ing foul balls right back against the screen better than anyone I saw. Somehow he would slide into the screen and catch the ball at the same time. Others would get up close and then shy away from the screen. And Al had the quick release on his throws to second.

"The left-handed pitcher would have to be Hubbell. I'm having trouble on the righthander. Although I hit Dazzy Vance pretty well, he was quite a pitcher."

"Was Dazzy better than Dizzy?"

"Well, no, he wasn't. But if Paul Dean hadn't hurt his arm he would have become a better pitcher than Dizzy. Dizzy didn't have too much of a curveball."

"Well, Travis, who was the hardest pitcher for you to hit?"

"Charlie Root of the Cubs. He was a short-arm pitcher. He stood out there on the mound one Sunday afternoon in

Chicago, and the game wasn't at stake or anything like that, and he just stood up there and said, 'Here, hit it.' I took the biggest cut you ever saw and it went straight up in the air. I just could not hit the guy.

"The only time I did hurt him was after I'd moved to third base, I believe it was in '33, and we were down to the last part of the ball game. We got a couple of men on base and I told Terry. 'Bill, you know I don't hit this guy. Maybe you've got somebody to go up there and hit against him.' He said, 'Aw, go on up there.' And I got a base hit that hurt Root. That's the only time I can remember hurting him."

"And who was one of the easiest pitchers for you to hit?"

"Larry French. When you see him, ask him. I'd beat him in every game he pitched against us that was close."

"Then you must have kept him from winning 200 games."

"I guess I did. I know that one afternoon in the Polo Grounds we had a doubleheader with the Cubs. I've forgotten now whether Larry started the game, but I think he went in about the middle as relief pitcher, and the game went 11 innings. And in the last of the 11th I hit a home run up into the right-field stands to win it, because there was one pitch he would always throw me in spite of the dickens and I just laid back waiting for it.

"And we came back out for the second game and another lefthander was pitching for the Cubs. On his first pitch to me I broke my bat but the ball went into that Chinese place down there in the Polo Grounds for a home run. And that's the way the game ended, 1-0. I beat 'em both games that day. But that Larry, I just beat his brains out."

"Is there any unusual incident that you can think of?"

"Well, we were having a team meeting before a game once in St. Louis. Bill Terry was going over the lineup of the Cardinals and then said that Diz was pitching for them that day. About that time our clubhouse door just busted open, and there was Dizzy himself. He said, 'Terry, what the hell you having a meeting for? I'll go over your lineup for them. I'll tell 'em exactly what I'm going to throw and when I'm going to throw it.' He told us and he went out and did it. He was one man that would say he was going to do something on that ball field and really do it."

"How about your best thrills in baseball?"

"Thrills? Lots of them. When I was sold to the New York

Giants, when I first saw the Polo Grounds, and when I was told in 1924 that I would be the regular shortstop. Then, the four World Series I played in. And being on the 1933 Giants team that won the World Series. In 1934 I was on the National League All-Star team.

"Also, Babe Ruth and his Committee of Baseball Writers selected me to their All-America team in 1927 and 1929. In 1937 I was given the National League Award of Merit for the 14 years I played in the League. In 1960 I was voted into the Arkansas Hall of Fame, and now in 1982 I am elected to the Baseball Hall of Fame."

"After 1936, when you finished playing in the majors, what did you do?"

"I managed Jersey City in the International League during the 1937 season and half of '38. In the middle of '38 I went back to the Giants as a coach. I coached there until I came down with tuberculosis. I fought it for five years."

"Obviously, you whipped it. What did you do from then on?"

"In '46 I went with the old Boston Braves and managed their club in Jackson, Mississippi, in the Southeastern League. At the end of that season Mel Ott called me to come back and coach for him with the Giants. I was there in '47 and in '48 Leo Durocher took over, so that was the last time I was with the Giants.

"Then I went back with the Boston Braves and went with them to Milwaukee. I stayed with their organization for 11 years. I managed in their farm system from 1950 through 1960. I was with quite a few of their clubs. They'd call me and tell me to go over here and go over there.

"Once I was with Bluefield, West Virginia, and I had a bunch of kids there and they were good. And then John Quinn called me. That was in early spring and my wife had just met me in Bluefield. John called early one Saturday morning, before we had even gotten up, and said, 'I want you in Hartford, Connecticut, tomorrow afternoon for a doubleheader.' So my wife and I got up and drove all that Saturday and Saturday night and Sunday morning and got into Hartford just as the first game ended and they were starting the second game.

"I managed for the Braves in Owensboro, Kentucky, and was two years in Appleton, Wisconsin. The Wisconsin State League had to fold because they were too close to Milwaukee.

Then I was at Lawton, Oklahoma for four years and Midland, Texas when they had that new Sophomore League. And then the next year which was 1959 I went to the Siberia of baseball, which was Eau Claire, Wisconsin. It was cold there all the time and they had trips to Minot, North Dakota and to Winnipeg. It was over 500 miles to Winnipeg and more than 600 to Minot."

"How did you travel, by bus?"

"Three station wagons. Man, they were long trips. And the next year I had it made in Davenport, Iowa. Short trips, good bus."

"When you made those long trips to Minot and Winnipeg, you must have had a day off."

"No, no! We didn't have any day off. We'd play a ball game and leave Eau Claire right at midnight, and we'd get into Minot the next afternoon at three or four o'clock and play a game that same night. It was rugged!"

"And after 1960, you came back here to Waldo?"

"I came back here. So many times in Eau Claire I said, 'I'm giving this up. I'm not going to put up with all this kind of stuff, all this traveling. When I get home I'm just going to sit there and sit there!' "

"I notice that you played in only 52 games in 1932 and 53 in 1933. What happened?"

"Well, by 1932 I already had one bad knee. And in a game in old Baker Bowl in Philadelphia I slid into second base and split a bone in my left knee. That made both knees bad. I went on the retired list and thought that was it.

"After I got home I went up to a family clubhouse we had on Indian Bay on the White River in southeast Arkansas. I stayed there for a couple of weeks while they treated those knees and then I came back home. A little later I took my mother and the family back to the lake.

"And they sent a messenger out from Holly Grove, which was close to the lake, to find me. This was in the winter now, and Bill Terry wanted to know whether I would have my knees operated on if the Giants would pay for it. I told him, 'That's a silly question, Bill. I can't walk now and I'd do anything to get fixed up.' 'Okay,' he said, 'when you go home you arrange to come on up here and we'll have them operated on.' And I mean they operated on both of them at the same time. Ligaments and things."

"You had to be laid up for quite a while, right?"

"Oh, I was laid up for the rest of the '32 season and through the winter, but I did go to spring training in 1933. And the games I played that year were in the latter part of the season and most of them at third base. Then in '34 I came back strong. I made the All-Star team."

"In '35 you had a good season, too."

"Yeah, but '36 beat me. If it hadn't been for '36 I would have ended up with a career batting average of .301, I believe it was."

"Your overall memories are pleasant and favorable?"

"Oh, very much so. Good gracious alive, we had some wonderful times. But people tend to overlook what a family has to go through. I'd go to spring training and then I'd go up to New York, and my wife would have to stay here until school was out. Then she'd get in a car with those two children and drive from here to New York in three days. And that was before they had these super highways. She'd leave here in the morning and drive into Nashville by night time, with those two children in the back seat fighting most of the time. And every time she'd come to a filling station they'd want to stop."

"What do you think of the move the Giants made from New York to San Francisco."

"That hurt a lot of ballplayers. What I mean is, for the old-timers who had played in the Polo Grounds it seemed like all the things they had played for were concentrated right in that ball park, and then they even tore that down.

"We're left out of the Old Timers games the Giants have in San Francisco. They seem to feel that we weren't the Giants, that the Giants are only the ones who have played in San Francisco. I must say that the Dodgers have not forgotten their old ballplayers, not like the Giants have."

"Travis, there must be one game or two that will always stand out in your memory."

"Well, yes, there are two. Once in Cincinnati I drove in eight runs in one game. Another time in Pittsburgh I drove in seven runs with two home runs, a triple, and a double."

Travis Jackson, not surprisingly, was nicknamed Stonewall, after the great Confederate general and in tribute to Travis' stalwart defense. In time the Stonewall was often shortened to Stony. Travis contributed his part to the best-hitting infield in major league history, that of the 1930 New York Giants. The combination of Bill Terry at first base (.401), Hughie Critz at second (.265), Travis at short (.339), and Fred Lindstrom at third (.379) produced an average between them of .349.

There is further evidence that the Giants of the 1920s must have had about the best infield in baseball. No fewer than seven of their infielders from that decade are now in the Hall of Fame—George Kelly and Bill Terry at first base, Frankie Frisch and Rogers Hornsby at second, Fred Lindstrom at third, and Jackson and Dave Bancroft at short.

As a matter of added interest it may be noted that the first seven batters in the Giant lineup during the 1924 World Series are now all in the Hall of Fame: Lindstrom, Frisch, Ross Youngs, Kelly, Terry, Hack Wilson, and Jackson.

Today at 83 Travis Jackson lives with his wife of more than 50 years, Mary, in Waldo, a town of 1,585 population some 50 miles east of Texarkana. In this quiet town where he was born and raised and which he has always called home, Jackson is probably the most prominent citizen and he basks in the warm friendship of his fellow townsmen. He keeps close track of baseball happenings and personalities, and understandably enjoys entering into a conversation which causes him to relive in memory many moments and deeds of his bright career which led him to the sport's highest honor, the Hall of Fame.

TRAVIS CALVIN JACKSON
BR   TR   5'10½"   160 lbs.
Born on November 2, 1903 in Waldo, Arkansas
Hall of Fame, 1982

YEAR	TEAM	G	AB	R	H	RBI	2B	3B	HR	BB	SO	SB	AVG.
1922	New York NL	3	8	1	0	0	0	0	0	0	2	0	.000
1923	" " "	96	327	45	90	37	12	7	4	22	40	3	.275
1924	" " "	151	596	81	180	76	26	8	11	21	56	6	.302
1925	" " "	112	411	51	117	59	15	2	9	24	43	8	.285
1926	" " "	111	385	64	126	51	24	8	8	20	26	2	.327
1927	" " "	127	469	67	149	98	29	4	14	32	30	8	.318
1928	" " "	150	537	73	145	77	35	6	14	56	46	8	.270
1929	" " "	149	551	92	162	94	21	12	21	64	56	10	.294
1930	" " "	116	431	70	146	82	27	8	13	32	25	6	.339
1931	" " "	145	555	65	172	71	26	10	5	36	23	13	.310
1932	" " "	52	195	23	50	38	17	1	4	13	16	1	.256
1933	" " "	53	122	11	30	12	5	0	0	8	11	2	.246
1934	" " "	137	523	75	140	101	26	7	16	37	71	1	.268
1935	" " "	128	511	74	154	80	20	12	9	29	64	3	.301
1936	" " "	126	465	41	107	53	8	1	7	18	56	0	.230
	15 yrs.	1656	6086	833	1768	929	291	86	135	412	565	71	.291

WORLD SERIES

YEAR	TEAM	G	AB	R	H	RBI	2B	3B	HR	BB	SO	SB	AVG.
1923	New York NL	1	1	0	0	0	0	0	0	0	0	0	.000
1924	" " "	7	27	3	2	1	0	0	0	1	4	1	.074
1933	" " "	5	18	3	4	2	1	0	0	1	3	0	.222
1936	" " "	6	21	1	4	1	0	0	0	1	3	0	.190
	4 yrs.	19	67	7	10	4	1	0	0	3	10	1	.164

Joe Moore's entire 12-year career was spent with the New York Giants as an outfielder. Known as "Jo-Jo," "The Gause Ghost," and "The Thin Man," Moore had a 23-game hitting streak in 1934, ending that season with a .331 average. His career average with the Giants was .298 and he played in three World Series and appeared in numerous All-Star games. (Photo credit: NBL)

9

Joe Moore

J oe Moore was born in Gause, Texas, on Christmas Day in
1908. He would later go to the major leagues and have a
distinguished 12-year career with the New York Giants. Then
he would return to Gause, some 85 miles northeast of Austin
with a population of about 500. He lives there today with his
wife of more than 50 years.

Joe Moore today is a well-tanned, relaxed man in his late
70s. He has put on 20 or more pounds since he played for the
Giants at a weight of about 155. Joe is a friendly, down-to-earth
Texan with a warm personality and a positive outlook on life.
He has only good memories of his career in baseball.

"How did it all start, Joe?"

"I was playing semipro ball in Crystal City, south of San
Antonio. One of the owners of the San Antonio ball club was
a coffee salesman in the Crystal City area and he made all the
ball games every week. He talked with me about someday playing with San Antonio and naturally I was mightily interested.
It wasn't like it is today. I wasn't interested in making a million
dollars. I was just interested in playing.

"So, I finished high school and he gave me my first contract with San Antonio. But some of us were later sent out to
Coleman in the reorganized West Texas League. It was a young
league until the East Texas League folded, after which we got
an influx of players from over there. That made quite a change
in the league. I played out there for two years. That was in '28
and '29.

"Around the middle of the second season I was sold to the

105

Waco club of the Texas League on a trial basis. So I went over to Waco and they had a bunch of old fellows there. Naturally, I was scared to death being with all those old professionals. And an old Italian fellow named Joe Martina was pitching for Waco on the day they put me into a game. I went out there and I dropped a ball. That sent me back to Coleman.

"During the winter of 1930 the West Texas League folded. I tried to make contact here and there and wrote to a lot of clubs but never did hear from any of them until I got a reply right back from San Antonio, which had owned me before. I went to see them and they offered me a contract for $250 a month. Big money!

"During the 1930 season I was having a terrific year, leading the Texas League in hitting with about a .380 average. We started playing night ball at that time, and in one of our first night games a left-handed pitcher in Shreveport hit me on the arm and broke it. The Giants had already sent a scout who was on his way down to look at me. San Antonio was naturally in a hurry to get me back in the lineup, and I got back in too quick. I couldn't swing the bat and I finally wound up hitting .330 or something like that.

"But the Giants had bought me and called me up at the end of the season. I played in about three or four games with them, the first one in the Polo Grounds against Chicago. That was when Hack Wilson had his big year for the Cubs. They put me in center field, which was a spacious place in that park, and I was playing old Hack so deep I could hardly see him. I believe he hit a home run that day. My first base hit was against a Philadelphia pitcher named Ray Benge, who later coached baseball down here at Sam Houston State."

"How did you get the nickname of Jo-Jo?"

"I don't know how I got that. Actually, I don't. I had two or three nicknames but none of them stuck too firmly. They called me 'The Thin Man' and 'The Gause Ghost' and then 'Jo-Jo.' "

"When you went to the Giants, Joe, they were still under the leadership of one of the premier names in baseball during the first third of this century. What was John McGraw like?"

"I never played much for Mr. McGraw. Actually, he sent me over to Jersey City the last year he was manager, in '32. I had had a good spring with him, too. Of course, you know, Mr. McGraw, he was the boss. And another thing about him.

Mr. McGraw had his ball club pretty well picked before the season opened. He knew who was going to be playing unless something very adverse happened. You just didn't hardly break into his lineup unless you did something outstanding.

"I'll say one thing for him, though. He took up for me one time after I rejoined them in 1931. We were playing in St. Louis and they had the bases loaded. Somebody hit a ball out toward me in left field, and I charged the ball and booted it. The pitcher began to eat me out back in the dugout for charging the ball. 'You didn't have any play,' he said. McGraw stepped in right then and said, 'Man, with the bases loaded you've got a play somewhere.' There was one thing about McGraw, he could eat you out but nobody else could get away with it. And he was for his ballplayers. Of course, he had softened up some when I got there."

"Early in the '32 season John McGraw resigned as manager and Bill Terry took over. How was he?"

"Bill Terry was the best manager in baseball. I'll tell you, when he was a playing manager he was great. It may not have been a mistake, but I think it hurt his managerial career when he took over as general manager too. He had too many irons in the fire when he had to sign all the players and a lot of other things. It took away from him as a manager and he lost contact with the players.

"And I think the loss of contact with the players is something that's happening in baseball now. Not only with the players, but also among the players. In our time we would play each game over in discussions among ourselves. And they tell me now that when the ball game's over they don't see each other until the next day.

"Our ball club was a family back in those days. We all lived in the same neighborhood, up on Manhattan Island, with several families living in the same building. It was a cooperative-owned building, and we'd sub-lease. We all lived up there and we had good family relationships, the kids all played together, etc. And we had some mighty fine ballplayers on our club in those years.

"I don't think anybody was in the same class with Carl Hubbell when it came to pitching. There were people who had more stuff than he had, but if I had to choose one pitcher for the big game I'd take him. He could lead you up to a certain pitch better than anybody. He was the easiest guy to play behind too, for if he said he was going to pitch a batter a certain way, then he'd pitch him that way.

"Mel Ott and I were good friends. Mel was the best little man ever. And he hit a lot more home runs than even Bill Terry. And Freddie Lindstrom, he was one of the youngest guys ever to play in the World Series, in 1924. In the last Old Timers game I played in out in Los Angeles, he was there too. I think it was about 1971. Fred was the youngest older man you'll ever see.

"Fat Freddie Fitzsimmons was the hardest loser I ever saw. When we got beat by the Yankees in the World Series in 1936, Freddie booted a ball and he was the best fielding pitcher in baseball. They beat us, 2-1. And Freddie booted the ball that let 'em tie the score on us.

"We still might have won that game but for a tough break. You talk about fortune falling for or against you, it does happen that way. Bump Hadley was pitching for them and they had Lazzeri at second and Crosetti at short. You know, you play differently when the score is tied or you're ahead or behind. Well, we had runners on first and second with two out and I was batting. Bump Hadley pitched to me when both Lazzeri and Crosetti were out of position. And so help me if I didn't hit a line drive as square over second base as you could hit one. And Lazzeri, because he was playing out of position and over by second base, was able to catch it and retire the side.

"Our shortstop, Travis Jackson, had the best throwing arm in baseball, I guess, at that time. And I didn't see how anyone could have a better arm now. Travis could hit too. I remember one game in Pittsburgh, when Larry French was pitching against us and we had a rain delay for about two hours. They were ahead but we hadn't played five innings yet, so they did everything in the world to dry that field out. They burned gasoline on it and they scraped and everything. Larry had two strikes on Jackson when the rain delay came along, and when they finally got started again Jackson hit the first ball Larry threw him up in the right-field seats with two men on and beat him.

"French was what I called true in his pitching and I could hit the true guys. I hit Larry real good. Even though he was a lefty and I batted left-handed, it didn't make any difference to me. The only chance I ever had to hit three home runs in a game was against lefty Bill Walker when he was with St. Louis. I had already hit two off him, but he wound up beating us, 3-2. Man, you can remember things like that.

"And we had old Hal Schumacher too. He was out of St. Lawrence College and he had been with San Antonio, which of course is where I started too. Hal was a good pitcher, a hard worker, and he was at his best when the weather was a little cool.

"We had Lefty O'Doul for a couple of years in '33 and '34, at the end of his career. Now, he was a hitter. He wasn't too serious except when he was at bat. I'll tell you one thing, Lefty helped me a lot. When I first went to the Giants I was a slap hitter. Lefty told me, 'You ought to learn how to pull that ball.' And he showed me things and helped me and I learned to pull the ball real good. I don't think it helped my average any but it probably helped some on extra base hits. Lefty had a bad arm and couldn't hardly throw a ball across the infield. He'd rub himself with some kind of liniment he had which I called his 'stay-in-the-league' liniment. Boy, that was the hottest stuff! You put that on and it'd burn you to a crisp. Lefty always said, 'I gotta have it. I can't stay in the league without it.'

"And Dick Bartell was one of our good ballplayers. I don't want to make a statement critical of anybody, but I'll say that Dick had to learn to play after he came to the Giants. He'd played on a losing ball club at Philadelphia and I think it had an effect on him. He wasn't long in learning, for he had ability. Dick was a fighting little guy, I'll guarantee you. He was rowdy and he'd do anything to win. He and Van Lingle Mungo got into it all the time. Brooklyn fans hated Dick. When we'd walk out on the field in the Ebbets ball park, the fans would shower Dick with all kinds of fruit and stuff.

"Cliff Melton was a good pitcher but he just lacked that one pitch. He was a fastball pitcher and you got to have something else to go with it. And he never did develop a good changeup or curve. If he could have, he would have been real good for he won 20 games his first season with us.

"We had Zeke Bonura, a colorful guy, with us one year. Old Zeke could hit that ball, and he led the league in fielding every year because he couldn't get to the balls hit near him. On any ball hit to his right, he'd say, 'Come on, Whitey.' Burgess Whitehead was our second baseman. We called him Whitey and he covered lots of ground. So if a ball was hit anywhere between first and second, Zeke would yell, 'Come on, Whitey.' "

"Joe, you got into a World Series pretty fast, in your second year as a regular."

"Yes, that was in '33 and all the games were close except one when Crowder was pitching for Washington. We had a big inning and I got two hits in one inning off the same pitcher. The last two games went into extra innings, with Hubbell winning one and Dolf Luque the other. Now if you want to talk about an old relief pitcher, there's one, old Adolfo. He'd say to me, 'Me throw for him fastball, him looking for curve.' "

"And then you lost to the Yankees in the World Series in both '36 and '37."

"You know, DiMaggio went to the Yankees in 1936 and that turned them around. That's the only time I ever saw one man absolutely turn a team around. He did it. There's no doubt about him being a great ballplayer. And Gehrig hit that ball hard wherever he hit it. He played in the shadow of Ruth for a long time.

"You know, Christy Walsh took Gehrig and Ruth and kind of handled their money for a while. I was talking to Christy in New York the summer that Gehrig died, and he told me, 'You just can't imagine that a man with the physique that Lou had could look the way he does now.' He told me Lou weighed only 86 pounds by the time he died, and Gehrig weighed well over 200 pounds when he was playing. The last time I saw Gehrig was when they had the special day for him over in Yankee Stadium. We all went over there. He was crippled as he walked out to home plate that day."

"How good a leftfielder were you, Joe?"

"They said I was pretty good. And I was selected seven or eight times on the National League All-Star team. But Joe Medwick was the better hitter and he'd always get the starting assignment. Bill Dickey once told me, 'You know, I've caught behind lots of guys but I've never had anybody hit the ball right out of my mitt the way you do.' He was telling me I hit the ball later than anybody else he'd caught behind. My best year was 1934 and if I had been a lucky hitter I would have led the league that season. I hit .331 and I was hitting the ball sharply. I'll tell you one thing, the type of hitter I was and both the Waners too, if we'd had the hard surface infield a lot of ball parks have now, we'd have hit 15 or 20 points higher. The ball really goes through the infield now.

"An old fellow who scouts for Cleveland now and who played with me through the lower and upper minors came to my door here one Saturday. When I went to the door he said,

'You don't know me, do you?' And I said, 'I sure do.' Even if I hadn't seen him in 20 or 25 years. We got to talking and he said, 'Man, if I'd been playing in the infield now, these guys would knock me right out into the outfield. It's really amazing the way that ball goes through the infield.' "

"Who was the toughest pitcher for you to hit?"

"The toughest pitcher I hit against, I believe, was Cy Blanton over at Pittsburgh. I didn't get many hits off him but nearly every time I did I hurt him. It was one of those things. They had another lefthander in Pittsburgh named Ralph Birkofer that I'd rather hit against more than anybody else. Man, I could tee off on him and hit him like I owned him. And I hit old Red Lucas pretty good. I'll tell you who I hit pretty good that had good stuff was Paul Dean. But Cincinnati had a righthander named Benny Frey, a little fellow who didn't have too much of a fastball, but we'd go in there and he'd just pitch the greatest game against us. He could get our big bats out."

"What was your favorite park to hit in?"

"Forbes Field in Pittsburgh."

"And what parks did you dislike?"

"Well, the park that most of us disliked was Wrigley in Chicago, but I hit pretty well there. It used to have that little center-field bleacher that gave the batter a white background to hit against, and it was hard to pick up the ball. Also, the Cubs had guys who could pitch out of that background—Charlie Root, Guy Bush, Lon Warneke, and Pat Malone."

"How was Horace Stoneham to work for?"

"Horace was good, but he was too easy. He was a soft touch. I think he liked me and his daddy did too. In the mid-30s, after I'd had some real good seasons, I was holding out and I thought I was going to get to talk to Horace in Pensacola where we were training. But it worked out that I never did get to talk to him and so I didn't get too much of a raise. Horace had a bunch of leeches who followed him around. And they kept him broke all the time."

"What did you think about the move of the Giants to San Francisco?"

"I think that's the worst move they ever made. They were a real popular ball club in New York."

"Of course, you'll have to admit there were some problems in New York, Joe. The Polo Grounds was an old park and the parking problem around it was growing worse. But I think

Stoneham let Walter O'Malley talk him into making the move."

"There's the guy that got the gravy. And there had to be two teams making the move west. So O'Malley got the gravy and Stoneham got fooled. O'Malley got the best franchise in baseball."

"What was your best game in the major leagues?"

"Well, I can't remember the exact year but there was a game in Cincinnati that several sportswriters told me afterwards was the greatest exhibition of playing left field they ever saw. I had about eight putouts, diving catches and everything. It was in old Crosley Field, which had a short left field and an incline leading up to the wall. It was a hard field to play and took some figuring to play it good. Our club was strong on knowing what we had to do, and the best part was that we could carry it out. And I'll tell you another thing. I never once lost a flyball in the sun. I can't get over the way players do that all the time now."

"Maybe it's because they play too much night ball," I suggested.

"Well, that might be. Let me tell you another thing. The way I see it, today the pitcher suffers more than anybody else, because he has to throw a new ball practically all the time. If it just hits the ground the umpire is probably going to throw it out. Some of those old pitchers, if they got a little rough spot on that ball they could really make it do something.

"Even so almost none of the hitters today hit as much as .300. I can't understand it. I sure don't know why these people can't hit that smooth ball."

"Who were the best players at each position in the National League during your playing days?"

"Well, I think Bill Terry was the best first baseman. And Charlie Grimm was another one. Charlie had old big meat hands and he'd catch balls barehanded lots of times. And Jim Bottomley was a mighty good first baseman too.

"At second base you'd have to go a long ways to beat Frankie Frisch. When he was an old man he was still a real good second baseman. He wasn't as good a hitter as Hornsby but I'll tell you one thing, Frisch could get a hit when it would hurt you most.

"There were a lot of good shortstops in that time. Billy Jurges was a good one, Bartell was good, Arky Vaughan was another one and a good hitter too, and Slats Marion was a good shortstop. And two others who had been great shortstops were about at the end of the line when I got up there. I mean Travis Jackson and Glenn Wright.

"Pie Traynor was the best third baseman. But I'll tell you one thing about it. That first baseman had better get back over to the bag fast when a ball was hit towards Pie. He just couldn't hold the ball. When he got hold of it he had to let it go for first base.

"As for outfielders one of the best I saw while I was playing was Terry Moore, though not as much in hitting as some others. But he was just like having another infielder out there. Joe Medwick wasn't a bad outfielder and he was sure a great hitter. And both Paul and Lloyd Waner were real good in the field and real good at the plate. Little Waner could really go get that ball, just like Paul.

"Catcher? Al Lopez was as good a receiver as ever lived. But I couldn't really take him over Gabby Hartnett overall, because Gabby's hitting was so good. As for the left-handed pitcher it would have to be Carl Hubbell. Among the right-handers Lon Warneke was a good one and he was good for a long time. Dizzy Dean was a good pitcher until he hurt his arm. That started when he broke a toe in the All-Star Game in 1937.

"Speaking of that, this ball I've got right here is the one President Roosevelt threw out to start that game. He threw it out and I got it. The President autographed it, but it almost took an act of Congress to get it to him for him to sign. The Secret Service wouldn't let you come near. I tried sending it up to him by the batboy and then I tried to go myself. So Calvin Griffith finally got that ball autographed for me."

"So, after your last season with the Giants in '41, what did you do?"

"I played in the American Association, with Indianapolis. Frank McKinney was the owner and Gabby Hartnett was the manager. McKinney talked to me after the first year about replacing Gabby as manager. I was interested but I was a good friend of Gabby's and I just couldn't do it. I think a friendship is the greatest thing a person can have, and just a little misunderstanding can destroy it lots of times."

"Did the players' pension plan go into effect before you left the majors?"

"No, it went in just a little later. I didn't get in on it. I wish I had, for it's a good one. And the money from All-Star Games went to that fund in the years I was playing. They could have given everybody a small pension, I think."

Besides playing on three pennant-winning teams and being on the National League All-Star squad a half dozen times or more, Joe Moore has lots of other pleasant memories. In 1934 he had a 23-game hitting streak en route to a .331 season average. The longest streak ever by a Giant player was set by Charles Hickman in 1900 when he hit safely in 27 straight games.

Joe also recalls a couple of games in which he went five-for-five. One was against Red Lucas and the last hit was the icing on the cake when it landed in the stands for a home run. On another occasion, in Baker Bowl in Philadelphia in 1933, Moore had five hits and on his last at bat missed a sixth one when outfielder Chick Fullis hauled in a line drive which had all the earmarks of a sixth hit.

The most unusual play Joe Moore ever had a hand in occurred in a game against the Cincinnati Reds. It was in the Polo Grounds and the Reds had the bases loaded with none out when Ernie Lombardi hit a low line drive to left-center. Hank Leiber was in center field for the Giants and Joe was in his usual spot in left. Both raced for the ball. Leiber dove but couldn't quite make the catch. Seeing Joe right on top of him, however, he showed great presence of mind by slapping the ball at Joe, who caught it, whirled, and threw to the infield. With the Red runners all on the go, it proved no problem to complete a most unusual triple play.

All ballplayers are participants or witnesses in lots of amusing incidents. One Joe remembers happened when the Giants were playing Frankie Frisch's St. Louis Cardinals in New York. In a rain-delayed game in the era before lighted fields, the Cards were leading and darkness was settling in fast. Frisch demanded that the game be called on account of darkness, but to no avail. As the next inning began Frisch took his place in the third base coaching box waving a flashlight around in protest, and the umpire promptly thumbed him out of the game.

I asked Joe about his overall memories of baseball.

"My memories are good. Baseball was good to me because we played in a time, at the start of my career, when times were bad. I mean, you couldn't hardly get ahold of a dollar. People can't believe that unless they lived in that era. In New York

I saw street corner after street corner where they had soup kitchens, and the people waiting would be four abreast and the lines would run for several blocks."

"After you finished your playing years, what did you do? Did you come back here?"

"We came back here. We've owned this land since I started buying it in 1935. We do some farming, but not much. We've had cattle mostly. We've had a good life and we've enjoyed it. We still enjoy one another. We get cross now and then but everybody gets cross, don't they?"

JOE GREGG MOORE
BL   TR   5'11"   155 lbs.
Born on December 25, 1908 in Gause, Texas

YEAR	TEAM	G	AB	R	H	RBI	2B	3B	HR	BB	SO	SB	AVG.
1930	New York NL	3	5	1	1	0	0	0	0	0	1	0	.200
1931	" " "	4	8	0	2	3	1	0	0	0	1	1	.250
1932	" " "	86	361	53	110	27	15	2	2	20	18	4	.305
1933	" " "	132	524	56	153	42	16	5	0	21	27	4	.292
1934	" " "	139	580	106	192	61	37	4	15	31	23	5	.331
1935	" " "	155	681	108	201	71	28	9	15	53	24	5	.295
1936	" " "	152	649	110	205	63	29	9	7	37	27	2	.316
1937	" " "	142	580	89	180	57	37	10	6	46	37	7	.310
1938	" " "	125	506	76	153	56	23	6	11	22	27	2	.302
1939	" " "	138	562	80	151	47	23	2	10	45	17	5	.269
1940	" " "	138	543	83	150	46	33	4	6	43	30	7	.276
1941	" " "	121	428	47	117	40	16	2	7	30	15	4	.273
	12 yrs.	1335	5427	809	1615	513	258	53	79	348	247	46	.298

WORLD SERIES

YEAR	TEAM	G	AB	R	H	RBI	2B	3B	HR	BB	SO	SB	AVG.
1933	New York NL	5	22	1	5	1	1	0	0	1	3	0	.227
1936	" " "	6	28	4	6	1	2	0	1	1	4	0	.214
1937	" " "	5	23	1	9	1	1	0	0	0	1	0	.391
	3 yrs.	16	73	6	20	3	4	0	1	2	8	0	.274

Masterful on the mound and mean with the bat, George Uhle was both a dominating American League pitcher in the 1920s and the best-hitting pitcher in major league history. His 17-year career was spent primarily with Cleveland and Detroit, with brief stays with both the Yankees and Giants in New York. Uhle compiled 200 lifetime wins, including seasons of 26 wins (1923) and 27 (1926).

10

George Uhle

At his best few American League pitchers were so dominating in the 1920s as George Uhle. But periodic arm trouble prevented his being at his best all the time. Even so, laboring mainly for the Cleveland Indians and Detroit Tigers between 1919 and 1936, Uhle compiled a career record of an even 200 wins against 166 losses. There is every reason to believe he would have threatened the 300-win mark had his arm been sound all the time.

Twice Uhle led the American League in wins (26 in 1923, 27 in 1926) and in those same seasons he topped the league in innings pitched. Of the 368 times George started a game he threw 232 complete games, for a completion rate of 63%. In 1926 he went the route in 32 of 36 starts.

It must be noted, however, that George Uhle was not only a very able pitcher. He also was the best hitting pitcher in major league history. Even Babe Ruth, in his early years as a premier pitcher, never equalled Uhle's marks as a batsman. George finished with a career batting average of .288, which is the highest for any pitcher who went to the plate 1,000 or more times.

If all pitchers hit like Uhle the designated hitter idea would never have been dreamed up. One year he had a total of 52 base hits, a record which has been tied only by his old teammate Wes Ferrell when he was with the Red Sox in 1935. George's value as a batter is reflected in the fact that he was sent up to the plate as a pinch hitter on 169 occasions, on 44 of which he delivered with a hit for an average of .260. One year he even led the league in pinch hits.

117

Another interesting aspect of George's career is that he never played a day in the minor leagues until his major league career was finished. Born on September 18, 1898, baseball lured him to the Cleveland sandlots before he reached his 15th birthday. By the time he was 16 he was involved in industrial ball in Cleveland, and at age 21 he was good enough to hang up a 10-5 record with the Indians.

I found George and Helen, his wife of more than 50 years, in their home in Bay Village, just outside of Cleveland, on a pleasant July afternoon in 1982. Until bronchial trouble sidelined him a few months earlier, he had been a salesman for Arrow Aluminum Casting Company for more than 30 years. But it was his baseball career I wanted him to talk about, and George was more than willing.

"When I was 16," he told me, "I was pitching for the Dubsky Furniture team and we were playing for the Class D championship in Cleveland. We went down to one of the final games before we lost, 2-0. Our shortstop threw away both runs on bad throws to first base. That was when the final game in Class AA or whatever they called it between Omaha and some other team drew 100,000 people down in Cleveland's Brookside Park.

"We had played our game right around the corner from the stadium on what they called Brookside #2, right next to where the zoo is today, and we went back over to the stadium to watch that game. We sat under some trees way up on the side of the hill. Like I said, they had over 100,000 people there and they drew that kind of crowd for the championship game regularly for three or four years.

"Anyway, sitting up there on the hillside, I wasn't wearing any sweater or sweat shirt or anything like that and, as it happened, the only one who had a sweater was the shortstop. This was right after I had pitched that nine-inning game. He offered me his sweater, but I was so mad at him I wouldn't take it.

"The next morning I woke up and couldn't bend my arm. I thought I'd never be able to play ball again. And as it turned out, the following year our team moved up into Class C, and doggone it I still wasn't able to pitch. There was something wrong with my elbow. A very fortunate thing happened for me then. In the middle of the season there was a carnival at Storer Avenue and 65th Street. Some of us happened to go there and they had a stand where you throw balls at bottles. So I took the balls and threw one or two or maybe all three, and suddenly something popped in my elbow. After that I was all right.

"And so I went back to pitching again. Thereafter the only trouble was that, early in my career, I had trouble with my elbow from time to time. I'd go down to Bonesetter Reese in Youngstown and he'd pop something in my elbow and fix it each time. I was his very first athlete customer.

"The next year I joined Jimmy O'Donnell's Bailey Company semipro team. We traveled around the state and played in such places as Massillon, Canton, Toledo, and Cincinnati. Then the following year some fellows who had been playing in pro ball came back here, and the Standard Parts team was organized and entered the Class AA league. I got a job with the company and they paid me $15 or $20 a ball game for pitching. It was a high class organization. We got paid both for playing and for our job, as well as getting a cut of the gate receipts to divide among us. We had a pretty experienced team for semipro ball.

"Glenn Liebhardt, Heinie Berger, and another lefthander whose name I don't recall had all been in the big leagues for a short while. And we had two of the famous Delahantys, Jim and Frank, both of whom had played in the majors and were brothers of the great Ed Delahanty. Our manager and rightfielder was Del Young, who had played for the Cincinnati Reds.

"Well, anyway, Glenn Liebhardt went to the Cleveland ball club and recommended me to Mr. Barnard, who was the president then. That was in the fall of 1918. They called me over to talk with them and I signed a contract. Since they paid so little even in the majors at that time, I made them put it in the contract that they couldn't send me down to the minors, because I could make just as much money around here holding a job and playing semipro ball.

"So I went to spring training with Cleveland in 1919, and it turned out they wanted to find out real quick what I had, because they pitched me in the second game of the season in St. Louis. I started and won, 4-2, though I think I was relieved in the eighth inning. And the Browns had a pretty good team in those years, with George Sisler, Baby Doll Jacobsen, Ken Williams, and others. Then we came back home and I'll be dog-goned if they didn't start me again as soon as St. Louis came in. And the game turned out exactly the same as the other one. I won, 4-2.

"The following series was against the Chicago White Sox. I'll never forget it because I went great for about five innings, and all of a sudden they started belting me around and really hitting the ball. Eddie Collins was just crossing home plate when Les Nunamaker, our catcher, was bawling the dickens out of me. 'Keep that curveball out away from them,' he yelled at me. Eddie Collins turned around and said to Les, 'Did you ever stop to think it might be your fault?'

"It didn't dawn on me then just what he meant, but before the year was out it finally sank in that I was tipping off my pitches myself. I was throwing my curve overhand and my fastball kind of sidearm. And neither our catcher nor anyone else on our club noticed it. But the Chicago club picked it up right away. Fortunately, the other clubs didn't that first season, for I went on to win 10 and lose 5.

"In 1920 when we won the pennant, I was used more in relief and they only started me now and then. Towards the end of the season I was warming up to start a game when Urban Shocker of the Browns, who was a fine pitcher and was from Cleveland, walked by on his way to the dugout. I said to him, 'Shock, ain't I coming more overhand with my curve than with my fastball?' And Shocker replied, 'Yes, and everybody in the league knows it.' And after that I started coming overhand on my fastball just enough to keep the batters guessing, and from then on I didn't have any more trouble about that.

"Tris Speaker was about to start me in the last game of the World Series against Brooklyn, because I was going good and had relieved twice in Brooklyn without letting them hit a ball out of the infield. But Speaker finally told me, 'Gee, if I start you and you should happen to lose, everybody will say that we were trying to extend the Series to take in more money.'

"In those days that was a common feeling on the part of the public if a Series went down to the last game. And it would have been suspected even more in that Series, since both parks had less than 30,000 capacity. In Cleveland we seated 22,000 but with ropes all around the outfield they could cram in 29,000. And with those ropes out there, you could spit from second base into the outfield crowd!"

"George, after Ray Chapman was killed in 1920, how important was Joe Sewell in winning the pennant?"

"He was very, very important to us and he sure was a fine hitter. Joe couldn't run like Chappie, who was very fast and was great at pushing bunts between the pitcher and the first baseman. And Chappie covered a lot of ground, but he wasn't quite as good a hitter as Joe."

"Was there any feeling that Carl Mays threw at Chapman with that pitch, or did it just get away from him?"

"I don't know. Ballplayers who played with and against Mays before my time said that he used to challenge hitters and tell 'em he was going to knock 'em down. That's all I know. I wasn't there to see it; I had twisted my knee in Detroit and I was here at home under the doctor's care. In my mind I don't think Mays meant to hit him like that. They tell me that Chappie never moved his head or anything. It might have been in Chappie's head to push the ball, and then he just stood there frozen when it was a ball he couldn't push for a bunt. Otherwise I think he would have ducked."

"Do you think Chapman might not have been hurt badly if he had been wearing a modern-day batting helmet?"

"Well, I don't know. When you get hit that square it's hard to say whether it would have protected him or not. Because they say he never moved or anything and didn't give with the ball."

"What do you think was the best game you ever pitched?"

"Oh, I had a lot of tough ones, both wins and losses. But two games stand out in memory that Eddie Rommell and I pitched against one another within three or four weeks. I think it was in 1926. In Philadelphia he beat me, 2-0. I think we got two hits and they got four, and the game lasted an hour and 15 minutes. Here in Cleveland we hooked up again on a Sunday and both teams had to catch a train to go back east. We started maybe 5 or 10 minutes ahead of the usual time of 3 o'clock, so that we could catch the train. Anyway, it wound up that I beat him, 2-0, and they got only one hit, a line drive that landed in front of our rightfielder in the first inning. Neither of us walked a man and we didn't get over about four hits. We were in the clubhouse before 4 o'clock, which means the game lasted just over an hour."

"What would you call your biggest thrill in baseball?"

"Well, one of my biggest thrills was against the St. Louis Browns, early in my career. In the ninth inning Win Ballou got me out on a curve that I hit off the end of my bat down to the third baseman. The game went to the 11th and as I went to bat I hoped he would throw me that curveball again. And when he did I hit it away up in the wooden bleachers here in Cleveland, a good 400 feet away."

"Tell me more about your hitting."

"Another real kick I got was when I had five hits off Ted Lyons in a 21-inning game I pitched against him when I was with Detroit. In the 21st inning I led off with a base hit and they put a runner in for me. He scored and so I got credit for the win. I don't know how I happened to pitch that long, except that every time Bucky Harris started to take me out I'd tell him I was coming to bat in the next inning and wanted to stay in."

That game was played in Chicago's Comiskey Park on May 24, 1929. There have been only 15 longer games in modern major league history. The official account of the game shows that Uhle had four hits instead of the five he remembers.

In today's terms perhaps the most amazing aspect of this 21-inning game is that it was completed in only 3 hours and 31 minutes. Plenty of nine-inning games nowadays run longer than that.

"George, I see that you hit .361 in 1926 and were over .300 in more than half of your 17 seasons. And you got a lot of pinch hits."

"Yeah, I remember one pinch hit in particular. It was against my old teammate Wes Ferrell. He was then with the Red Sox and I was with Detroit. He was ahead of us, 1-0, when I went up to pinch hit in the ninth with two men on. I got a hit to drive in both of them and win the game, 2-1."

"How about Tris Speaker?"

"Tris was the greatest centerfielder that I know of. It was really marvelous the way he could slide along on one knee as he caught a low liner. And it was something the way he played the count on the batter, as well as who was pitching, so that he could catch a drive against the scoreboard or one right back of the infield. He would move and position himself according to all the factors involved. He moved a few steps one way or another on every ball pitched."

"What about Steve O'Neill as a catcher?"

"Steve was a great catcher and a wonderful target. There were lots of fine catchers, like Luke Sewell and others, but Steve was the only one who, if he wanted a low outside pitch with a runner on third, would come to the mound and say, 'Don't be afraid to get it in the dirt; I'll block it.' And they had such small catcher's mitts in those days."

"And how was Stan Coveleski?"

"Oh, Covey was the greatest spitball pitcher I ever saw. And in my day there were quite a few spitball pitchers. Covey, just like a good pitcher who can let up on you with a good change of pace, could throw a slow spitter with a 2-0 count and get it over the plate, and then when he got the second strike he would break it off real good."

"Was he better than Red Faber?"

"I definitely think so. Faber was a good one but he didn't have Covey's knack of throwing a slow spitter."

"George, who were the toughest hitters for you to get out?"

"Well, it's funny, but the toughest hitter for me was Bob Fothergill, who really was a pretty good hitter. He seemed to guess me right all the time. And Bibb Falk was a left-handed hitter who seemed to guess me right."

"How did you do against Babe Ruth?"

"Well, at the end of the '21 season when we were fighting the Yankees for the pennant, he beat me in New York with a little pop fly home run that was barely fair and barely cleared the fence. The Polo Grounds had the shortest right-field fence in the country in those days. And that was the only home run Babe Ruth hit off me until 1933, my last year with Detroit. Then he hit a real tape measure drive that went out of the park and across the street. I fed him curveballs and change of pace nearly all the time.

"Let me tell you there never was any ballplayer better than Babe Ruth. Babe could throw, he never threw to the wrong base, he could run the bases good, and how he could hit! I remember one time we had a player who tried to score from second on a ground ball hit through the infield, and he was thrown out at the plate. Speaker really chewed him out, saying there was no excuse for being thrown out on a ground ball hit through the infield.

"About two weeks later we were playing the Yankees and Speaker tried to score from second on a ground ball that was hit over first base in old League Park. The ball was hit down the line and Babe Ruth picked it up and threw Speaker out by several yards. Speaker wasn't even close enough to slide. Ruth threw a line drive into home plate and the catcher was just waiting for Speaker, who never said a word after that about not scoring on a ground ball through the infield."

"What did you think of Ty Cobb?"

"Cobb's greatness was in hitting and running. He couldn't play the outfield with Speaker, and he couldn't throw too well. He threw like a lot of outfielders today—rainbows. But he was a corker on the bases! He knew how to slide and as you were tagging him he knew how to kick the ball out of your hands."

"When you went to Detroit in 1929, were you traded or sold?"

"I was traded for Ken Holloway, a pitcher, and Jackie Tavener, a shortstop. Cleveland thought I was through. My arm was absolutely dead and I couldn't hardly raise it. And Emil Yde, a pitcher who had been with Pittsburgh before coming to Cleveland and who lived on the West Coast, told me about a doctor named Spencer out there. I talked with Detroit about this and went out two weeks before the Tigers would start spring training on the coast. Doc Spencer found that my trouble was all due to adhesions. He stretched my arm for a couple of weeks and he had me just about crying on the table in the first three or four sessions.

"My arm was wonderful when he got through. When the season started I won nine straight, and one of them was that 21-inning ball game. After that game was in the papers Dr. Spencer sent a wire to our manager Bucky Harris and gave him hell. The doc said it was a crime, as bad as my arm had been, to let me pitch more than a doubleheader in one game.

"Well, I was overworked while winning those nine straight. I lost the 10th one, and I know I couldn't even raise my arm when Bucky came out to see me in the last inning. I had a different soreness, under my shoulder blade, and it was the sharpest pain I ever had. And the next game I tried to start I pitched one inning against New York, but the pain was still there and I couldn't hardly throw. But after a while we got the pain out of there by stretching the arm.

"The next spring we drove over to where Mark Koenig lived in San Jose, with the car windows down since we didn't have air conditioning. And in a day or two I got that same pain under my shoulder blade. I jumped right on the train and went down to see Doc Spencer and he stretched it out for me. He told me I had caught a good cold back there which had affected a nerve."

"Now, George, comment on a few of the Tigers you played with in Detroit."

"Well, Charlie Gehringer was a great second baseman and a fine hitter. Harry Heilmann was a wonderful hitter. He could slug that ball. Tommy Bridges had a marvelous overhand curveball, though I don't think it broke any more than mine did when I was in my prime. And Whit Wyatt was a young fellow who could throw real hard, but he had no breaking ball. Later he came up with enough of a slider or something like that to become a big winner in Brooklyn. And Waite Hoyt came there when he was on the downgrade. He didn't like playing for the Tigers because they weren't scoring enough runs. He wanted out of there as soon as he arrived. Earl Whitehill was a good pitcher with a fine curveball. He was a fighter who would battle you every minute of the way."

"Was either Goose Goslin or Heinie Manush in the outfield for Detroit in your years there?"

"No. They both played for St. Louis and Washington in my Detroit years. I remember pitching against Goose one time and he hit a home run off me. I think I had thrown a hundred different changeups and slow curves and things like that, and then I threw him one fastball and I'm darned if he didn't park it. So I said to myself, 'Well, that son-of-a-gun will never see another fastball from me.'"

"Do you remember your 200th win in 1934?"

"No, I don't. I never had any idea. If I'd known it I would have grabbed the ball, for one thing."

"Now, in '36 you came back for a while with the Indians. How was that?"

"Steve O'Neill was the manager then and he needed some help out in the bullpen. My arm felt pretty good in pitching batting practice, so I told Steve that if he wanted to put me on the active list I could come in once in a while and face a batter or two. So he did, but he used me mostly as a pinch hitter. I had good success in that role."

"You sure did. Eight hits in 21 trips to the plate. After that season, what did you do? Did you stay on as a coach?"

"I stayed on as a coach the next year, then Steve was let out and he went off to manage Buffalo, so I went with him as a coach there. And just before the playoffs I went on the active list, and in the playoffs I saved two games for him. I pitched to one or two men with the bases full in the ninth inning and saved both games."

"After that, did you stay connected with baseball in one way or another?"

"I was a coach with the Chicago Cubs in 1940. My job was to work with the pitchers. Gabby Hartnett and I got along real good and I was going to be with him again the following year. But I guess Gabby made some remarks around a fire station that there wouldn't be many of the same Cub players around the next season. The players got wind of it and wrote to Wrigley saying they didn't want to play for Hartnett any more.

"And even though Wrigley had told Hartnett he was the manager for next year, and Gabby had told all us coaches that we would be back with him, he was gone. By the time I got home after the season the Cubs had signed Jimmie Wilson, the old catcher, as their new manager. So the ballplayers really got Gabby fired for popping off in some fire station or something like that.

"Then in '41 and '42 I went with Brooklyn, working with their young pitchers and scouting. Leo Durocher was the manager and Charlie Dressen was one of the coaches."

"Who were the best players you ever saw at each position?"

"Well, I didn't see him too long, but George Sisler was the best first baseman, and a great hitter too. Of course, Gehrig was a terrific hitter, too. But when I pitched against him he never got a home run off me until that last year I was in Detroit. Then he just slapped a fast curveball over the left-field fence, just poking at it. As for the second baseman, I'll have to say that Bill Wambsganss was awfully good in the field and great on turning the double play. But he couldn't hit with Tony Lazzeri or Charlie Gehringer."

"How about shortstop and third base?"

"Well, Joe Sewell was the best hitter. And that fellow who became president of the American League, Joe Cronin, was a marvelous shortstop and a fine hitter. Lou Boudreau was another one, but he was after my playing days. Larry Gardner was a very good third baseman and a corking good hitter with men on base. Jimmy Dykes was another one. Ken Keltner was a great one, but after my time."

"Three outfielders?"

"Well, you have to take Babe Ruth in right field. And you

have to take Speaker in center, that's for sure. Charlie Jamieson would be hard to beat in left. He had an accurate arm too, but not quite as strong as Ruth and Speaker. He could go and get that ball."

"And the catcher?"

"I would say Steve O'Neill and Luke Sewell."

"Right-handed pitcher?"

"It's hard to get away from Walter Johnson. He may have been along toward the end of his string when I broke in, but he still had it. I remember one game in about 1921 when Charlie Jamieson led off the first inning with a triple, and then he struck out Bill Wamby, Speaker, and Elmer Smith on nine fastballs that they couldn't even follow. On nine straight pitches! That was a great game. Someone for Washington led off with a triple too in the first inning, but like Johnson had done, Coveleski got out of it without the run scoring. We finally got a run and that's the way it ended, 1-0."

"And the best lefthander in your day?"

"It's a question of whether you're picking pitchers or throwers. If it's throwers, it would be Lefty Grove. For pitchers, it's Herb Pennock."

"Did you pitch any night games, George?"

"Only after I was out of the majors, with Buffalo. And I don't like it myself. The pitchers have such a big edge at times when it's not dark and it's not light. The lights are on but they don't do any good at that time. I think that's why you pick up the paper so many times and read that somebody had a no-hitter until the sixth or seventh inning."

"What are your feelings about the designated hitter?"

"I don't like it at all."

"I guess you naturally wouldn't like it, as a good hitting pitcher."

"Oh, it's not just for that reason. I remember a game I pitched against Lefty Grove in Philadelphia one time when the temperature was 102. I was determined to pitch my best and stay in there long enough to make them use a pinch hitter for Grove if we could just get one run ahead. It was scoreless until the seventh, when I bunted a runner over to third and we scored him. Then they put in a pinch hitter for Grove and we got to the relief pitcher for four or five more runs and won the game. Under the designated hitter rule Grove would have stayed in there all the way and we might not have won."

"Were most of the players in your day in the game for the money or because they loved to play baseball?"

"Well, they had to love the game, for sure, because they weren't going to make big money. After I'd been up there four years they told me that to make as much as $7,500 you had to be a big star. Of course, back in those days $50 a week was good money, too."

"George, besides your fastball and your curve and your changeup, what other pitches did you have?"

"Well, I think I was the first one to throw the slider. At least, I happened to come up with it while I was in Detroit. And I gave it its name because it just slides across. It's just a fastball you turn loose in a different way. When I first started throwing it the batters thought I was putting some kind of stuff on the ball to make it act that way."

"Can you think of any other game where you had a big day?"

"Yes, I can. But it was my hitting more than my pitching that made it a day to remember. Once in 1921 I drove in six runs in one game. It was against the Tigers in Cleveland and four of those RBIs came on a grand slam homer off the old Dutch Leonard."

George Uhle's whole career is one that stands high on the rolls of major league stars. Seventeen seasons in the big time, a 200-game winner, two years with 26 and 27 victories, the best hitting pitcher in the history of the majors. It seems enough to make anyone believe that George should be enshrined in the Hall of Fame.

After a long illness George Uhle died of emphysema on February 19, 1985.

GEORGE ERNEST UHLE

BR   TR   6'   190 lbs.

Born on September 18, 1898 in Cleveland, Ohio
Died on February 19, 1985 in Lakewood, Ohio

YEAR	TEAM	W	L	PCT.	ERA	G	GS	CG	IP	H	BB	SO	ShO
1919	Cleveland AL	10	5	.667	2.91	26	12	7	127	129	43	50	1
1920	" "	4	5	.444	5.21	27	6	2	84.2	98	29	27	0
1921	" "	16	13	.552	4.01	41	28	13	238	288	62	63	2
1922	" "	22	16	.579	4.07	50	40	23	287.1	328	89	82	5
1923	" "	26	16	.619	3.77	54	44	29	357.2	378	102	109	1
1924	" "	9	15	.375	4.77	28	25	15	196.1	238	75	57	0
1925	" "	13	11	.542	4.10	29	26	17	210.2	218	78	68	1
1926	" "	27	11	.711	2.83	39	36	32	318.1	300	118	159	3
1927	" "	8	9	.471	4.34	25	22	10	153.1	187	59	69	1
1928	" "	12	17	.414	4.07	31	28	18	214.1	252	48	74	2
1929	Detroit AL	15	11	.577	4.08	32	30	23	249	283	58	100	1
1930	" "	12	12	.500	3.65	33	29	18	239	239	75	117	1
1931	" "	11	12	.478	3.50	22	18	15	193	190	49	63	1
1932	" "	6	6	.500	4.48	33	15	6	146.2	152	42	51	1
1933	3 teams	Detroit AL (1G 0-0)			New York NL (6G 1-1)			New York AL (12G 6-1)					
	Total	7	2	.778	5.85	19	7	4	75.1	81	26	31	0
1934	New York AL	2	4	.333	9.92	10	2	0	16.1	30	7	10	0
1936	Cleveland AL	0	1	.000	8.53	7	0	0	12.2	26	5	5	0
	17 yrs.	200	166	.546	3.99	513	368	232	3119.2	3417	965	1135	20

WORLD SERIES

1920	Cleveland AL	0	0	—	0.00	1	0	0	3	1	0	3	0

James Luther (Luke) Sewell, younger brother of Joe, was also a University of Alabama alumnus who lasted long as an outstanding catcher and could hit well enough. Sewell, a 20-year man and the only manager ever to win a pennant for the moribund St. Louis Browns, spent most of his career with Cleveland. Here, he wears the "W" of the Washington Senators, a club he helped to a surprise pennant the year he joined them, 1933.

11

Luke Sewell

I t's not an uncommon thing in baseball history for two
brothers to play in the majors at the same time. There are
dozens of such combinations, including many well-known
pairs—Mort and Walker Cooper, Bob and Irish Meusel, Wes and
Rick Ferrell, Gaylord and Jim Perry, Paul and Lloyd Waner. And
a few cases of multiple brothers come to mind, such as the
Boyers (Ken, Clete, and Cloyd), the Alous (Felipe, Matty, and
Jesus), and the Delahanty clan around the turn of the century
(Ed, Jim, Frank, Tom, and Joe).

Among the cases of multiple brothers to reach the majors
are the Sewells of Titus, Alabama. Nearly every baseball fan
knows that Luke and Joe Sewell are brothers, but few probably
are aware that a third brother also made the majors. Barely.
Tommy Sewell made a single appearance as a pinch hitter for
the Chicago White Sox. But this shortest of all possible careers
is more than compensated for by his famous brothers. Joe played
for 14 seasons, was on two World Series winners, and is in the
Hall of Fame. Luke was around for 20 seasons and was a manager for 10 more, plus playing in one Series and managing in
another.

An interesting aspect of Luke's career is that he couldn't
make his high school team, didn't play in college until his
junior year, and never spent a day in the minors before join-
ing the Cleveland Indians in 1921. Yet he came on to be recognized as one of the very finest receivers during the 20 years he
performed in the American League. Here's the way he tells
about it:

"I didn't play too much there in Titus where I was born. I was too small. I was the bat boy and the water boy. Sometimes when the catcher wouldn't show up they'd let me catch. But they wouldn't let me play any place else. And I never could make the high school team. Didn't play at the university until my junior year. After I graduated at Alabama I got my first contract directly with the Cleveland ball club. I went to Cleveland on May 23, 1921.

"I remember that my first time at bat was against Carl Mays. It was the year after he had hit Ray Chapman. And they were yelling at him from the bench, 'Don't throw at him.' Mays had one front tooth knocked out, and as he looked down at Wally Schang, the catcher, he shook his head and I thought, 'That's the meanest-looking man I ever saw.' "

"Did Mays' submarine delivery make it more difficult to see the ball?"

"Not particularly." Luke replied. "I could always pick up an underhand or sidearm pitch better than I could an overhand one. Back in those days they had advertising signs out on the wall in center field and the pitchers would throw out of those signs, making it a little hard to see. Connie Mack had a scoreboard out there that his lefthanders would pitch out of. There were all kinds of tricks in those days. They've made the game safer now—batting helmets and such."

"Didn't you play at all in the minors, Luke?"

"I played about three weeks at Columbus in 1921. Steve O'Neill broke a hand, and the Indians had an old Giant catcher, Art Wilson, down at Columbus. So they brought him up and sent me to Columbus. But they put Art in a couple of games and found he wasn't the answer, so they sent me back to Cleveland.

"In 1924 Cleveland traded O'Neill to Boston and then Glenn Myatt and myself sort of split the catching for a couple of years before I became the regular in 1926. My brother Joe and I were together at Cleveland from 1921 until he was traded to the Yankees in 1931.

"You know, I had a hand in getting Wes Ferrell going in the majors. In 1929 Cleveland was ready to send him out to Terre Haute. But they needed a pitcher for a game one time, I guess it was in May. They came around to me and asked, 'Who should we start?' I said. 'Pitch that kid Ferrell.' 'Oh,' they said, 'he can't pitch.' I said, 'Try him.' And Wes went on to win 20 or more games in each of his first four seasons, the only time it's ever been done."

"Tell me about some of your teammates."

"I thought Tris Speaker was a better ballplayer than a manager. Back in those days the rookies didn't count for much. I went to four training camps under Speaker before I got to take batting practice in spring training. They just wouldn't let us in that batting cage. Four or five of us young players would go out after practice sessions and pitch to each other. We'd get the balls by going out at 8 in the morning and sneaking some balls out and hiding them. I got to catch a lot of batting practice but I didn't get any hitting. Of course it was different for Joe when he went up there because they had to let him step right in as a regular.

"Riggs Stephenson? Well, when he was young he had a broken arm or something and it never got fixed right. His arm didn't really flex and he couldn't throw well, so he had to sort of heave the ball. He was an infielder then, and at second base he just couldn't make the snap throw to first. They tried him in the outfield and he fell down one day. The Indians shouldn't have let him go because he really could hit.

"Stan Coveleski was a great spitball pitcher. We'd hold meetings before games and when he was asked how he would pitch to a certain batter, he'd say, 'I'll fire my spitter at him.' He was the first spitball pitcher I ever caught, and I think he hit me on the toes as much as he did on the mitt. He'd laugh like everything. A great fellow.

"If George Uhle's arm had been good and strong all the time, he would have ranked very high among all pitchers. He was about as good a 'one-game' pitcher as I ever saw. In other words, if you had one game you really needed to win and he was in good shape, I'd trust it to him more than anybody. And George was a real good hitter and knocked a lot of his own runs in.

"Sam Langford was quite a fellow. We used to play a lot of poker. We got a game going one time and Sam got into debt to me for about $20. It was on the train coming back from St. Louis just at the end of the season. I said to him, 'Sam, don't forget the $20 you owe me.' He said, 'I'll pay you right now.' He went back and opened his suitcase and took out a World War I German Luger pistol. He asked if I would take it for the debt and I said yes. And I have it upstairs right now. A lot of boys in those days couldn't pay up, and if you didn't get it by the end of the season you'd never see it.

"Earl Averill was a good hitter! When he first came up we were playing Detroit in League Park and Earl Whitehill was pitching against us, a real good lefthander. The first pitch he ever threw to Averill was a big sidearm curveball and Averill hit it over the right-field wall. Whitehill stood there wide-eyed as if to say, 'Who was that fellow?' Averill had tremendous power for a little fellow. Great arms and shoulders. You know how we got him, don't you?

"Billy Evans was general manager of the Indians, and in 1928 Averill, Roy Johnson, and Smead Jolley were playing the outfield for San Francisco in the Pacific Coast League. All three were hitting above .350. The highest price tag was on Roy Johnson. Smead was a little clumsy, but I think he was leading the others in hitting. So Averill was the cheapest and Evans bought him because he was the cheapest. And he got the best of the three. Evans told me this story himself. He said, 'I would have bought Johnson for the same price, or Jolley, but that was all we could spend and so we took Averill.

"Roger Peckinpaugh as a manager? Average. He didn't keep good records on the players, which you have to do when you're the manager. And he was too much of a 'book' manager. I think he was afraid that the press would get on his back. A manager has to be a riverboat gambler now and then. It was too easy to figure what Peck was going to do. I thought some years we should have finished higher than we did."

"Luke," I asked, "when you went from Cleveland to Washington in 1933, were you traded?"

"Yes, I was traded for Roy Spencer, a catcher. I had had a little argument with Mr. Bradley, our owner, over a salary agreement I made with Evans which Bradley wouldn't honor, so the result was that he traded me to Washington."

"Well, it had the advantage that you got into the World Series right away there in Washington."

"Yeah, we got in, with a bunch of old ballplayers. But nearly all of them had a good year in 1933. We had Joe Kuhel at first, Buddy Myer at second, Joe Cronin at short (and also the manager), Ossie Bluege at third, and Goose Goslin, Fred Schulte, and Heinie Manush in the outfield, with a pitching staff made up mostly of Alvin Crowder, Earl Whitehill, Lefty Stewart, Jack Russell, and Monte Weaver.

"In the Series our power hitters couldn't do anything against Carl Hubbell, who won two games for the Giants. Brother, he had a good screwball. They had a real good club and it was more consistent than ours.

"And Clark Griffith, you could write a book on Griff alone. He sure didn't like to spend money, but he was supporting four or five families during the Depression and you had to appreciate that. Normally, you know, when a club clinches the pennant they pop champagne and all that sort of thing. Well, when we clinched the pennant in '33 old Billy Smith, a long-time friend of Griff's and his concessions boss, came into the clubhouse with a concession boy loaded with a couple of cases of orange pop which they made down there under the stands. That was our celebration. But Griff couldn't afford anything else. And he would argue with you about a nickel.

"That was about the time that air conditioning was coming in on the trains. They had a kind of locker under each end of the car and they'd put six 300-pound blocks of ice in them and blow a fan over them to bring cool air into the car. I'm telling you, it was hot riding those cars without any air conditioning, especially on long trips. So we were after Griff to get us some air conditioned cars. But he said, 'No, it's bad for the pitchers' arms.' We had a trip in the middle of the summer, with the temperature over 100, from Washington to St. Louis, about 22 hours. And we went to Griff and said 'If you'll let us have air conditioned cars, we'll pay for the ice.' And right away Griff said, 'Why don't we try it?' "

"Well, after a couple of years in Washington you went over to the White Sox."

"That's right. In 1934 I got a broken finger in spring training and the doctors never got it set right. The only injury I came out of baseball with. It's broken in the joint and I can't bend it. Griff thought that with this broken finger I'd never play again."

"But you had a fine season with the Sox, hitting .285 in 118 games."

"I'll tell you a good one about that. Al Simmons was with the Sox then and I outhit him that season. Simmons said, 'The league is upside down when you're outhitting me.' We had some good names on that Sox team—Simmons, Mule Haas, Luke Appling, Jimmy Dykes, Zeke Bonura, Ted Lyons, Sad Sam Jones.

"After four years in Chicago and before the 1939 season Larry MacPhail of the Brooklyn Dodgers called me at home one night and said, 'I've just bought your contract from the White Sox.' I asked him, 'What are you taking me for? I'm through.' 'Oh,' he said, 'I have plans for you.' He wanted me to meet him in Detroit for a talk. Durocher was going to be in his first year of managing the Dodgers. And Durocher and I had been at odds for a few years. So I met MacPhail in Detroit and told him, 'Larry, I won't finish spring training with you.' But MacPhail said he had two things he wanted me to do for him.

"He told me he had got Red Evans, a pitcher, from the Boston Braves. Evans was a bottle man, a drinker. He wanted me to room with Evans, and then he wanted me to teach Babe Phelps to catch. Phelps could hit but he didn't know which hand to catch the ball with. So, I went to Hot Springs for pre-training. I roomed with Evans and talked with him a lot about how he could make the team and everything if he would give up drinking. He told me he was all through with that stuff. Well, I left for the spring training site in Clearwater, Florida, and the night I left Evans didn't come in all night. So that experiment went by the boards.

"Well, I got to spring training and tried working on Phelps. The trouble with lots of catchers, especially nowadays, is that they get down and give the sign and then try to catch the ball with their mitt going down. And the ball drops down and they pick it up and take a hop, skip, and jump, by which time the runner has taken four steps on them. That's why a lot of the base stealing is going on. They aren't stealing so much on the pitchers. All the pitcher has to do is stop 'em. Just don't give 'em the running start. Then if the catcher will catch the ball with the mitt coming up he's got a chance to throw the runner out.

"I was trying to get Babe to stop knocking all the balls down and to catch them with the mitt coming up. When he tried it the balls were hitting him on the throwing hand, and he would jump out of there yelling and shaking his hand. I told him, 'Babe, try putting your right hand behind you and just catch the ball in your mitt.' Well, the batter fouled one and it hit the batting cage and caromed back, and you know where it hit him? Right on that hand! I got to laughing and Durocher got mad because I was laughing at Babe. 'What you trying to do? Make a joke out of this spring training?' he demanded. Well, I stayed with them until they released me back in Brooklyn, and then I came over with the Indians again.

"One reason I came back to Cleveland was that their catchers were Rollie Hemsley and Frankie Pytlak. As long as they could keep Hemsley sober, he was tremendous. But he could catch just so long and then he couldn't resist going on a binge. They would put Pytlak in and he was a good little catcher, though not as good as Hemsley.

"When Rollie would sober up and return to catching, Pytlak would take off and go home to Buffalo. Then they would have to send an old third baseman who was scouting for them over to Buffalo to bring Frankie back. Well, they got me as a player/coach. When Frankie would go home, I'd catch a few games after they put me on the active list. When Frankie returned they would take me off the active list and I'd be a coach. After we had done that about four or five times, a rule was put in saying that you could only move a person back and forth between coach and player one time in a season."

"So, you went over to manage the St. Louis Browns in 1941 and in '44 earned the distinction of being the only person ever to manage the Browns to a pennant."

"That's right. In 1940 I was offered the manager's job in Cleveland three different times. They were having a lot of player/manager problems under Oscar Vitt. Mr. Bradley and the Board of Directors came to me three times, the last one in New York when they said, 'You've got to take it.' I told them, 'I don't have to take it. And what's going to happen to Oscar?' They said, 'We're going to put him in a sanatorium.' I said, 'Oh, no! You couldn't think of a thing like that.'

"Then I asked, 'If we could stay in this pennant race until the last week of the season, would you be satisfied?' Bradley said, 'Oh, definitely.' I told him that we would be there, and we were, right up to the last day. We lost it when a Detroit rookie named Giebell beat Bob Feller, 2-0.

"I was thinking of giving up baseball at that time, but Bradley himself called and said, 'Don Barnes wants to talk to you about managing the Browns.' I told him, 'Mr. Bradley, I'm satisfied right where I am.' He replied, 'No, you owe it to yourself to go over and talk to him.' So I went over, and after talking with them for a while they were willing to give me everything I asked for, so I couldn't turn them down. But you never saw such a misfit outfit in your life as the Browns were then."

"Well, by 1944 you had shaped them up a good bit. And you gave the Cardinals a pretty good run for their money in the World Series."

"We actually had a chance of winning that Series, if we had won the second game. We misplayed a bunted ball which kept us from winning, 2-1, in nine innings and then they scored in the 11th to win, 3-2.

"The last play of the final game of the regular season in 1944 gave me my biggest thrill in baseball. We were leading the Yankees, 5-2, with two out in the ninth inning and Oscar Grimes popped a little fly outside of first base. George McQuinn went over and camped under it and caught it. That clinched the pennant for the Browns and it was the greatest thrill I ever had.

"Don Barnes, a vivacious little fellow who owned the club, was in his box seat right there and he was so excited I thought he was going to have a heart attack. He said, 'Luke, come over here.' And tears were running down his face. I never saw a man so emotional over anything."

The lineups of this pennant-clinching game did not feature a single future Hall of Famer. World War II had decimated—indeed, much worse than that in most cases—the rosters of all major league teams, so that the seasons of 1944 and 1945 in particular were not showcases of baseball at its greatest. Nevertheless, the St. Louis Cardinals were able to field what appeared to be the strongest lineup in the majors in 1944 and coasted to their third straight National League title with 105 wins against only 49 losses. They were heavily favored to whip the Browns.

The heady atmosphere of the World Series seemed at first to spur the underdog Browns to greater heights. Denny Galehouse outdueled the much-heralded Mort Cooper in the opener, 2-1, on George McQuinn's two-run homer. As Luke Sewell says, the second game may have determined the outcome of the Series. At the end of nine innings it was tied, 2-2, both Cardinal runs being unearned, and in the 11th they scored the winning tally to snatch a game which the Browns might easily have won. Since Jack Kramer pitched the Browns to a 6-2 triumph in game three, it is more than likely that the Browns could have picked up the pay-off fourth win in one or another of the remaining four chances.

Sewell managed the Browns until near the end of the 1946

season and then became manager of the Cincinnati Reds in the final days of 1949.

"Well," Luke says, "I went to Cincinnati as a coach. Warren Giles had made Bucky Walters his manager. Bucky had been a fine pitcher and a great favorite down there. Giles at heart didn't think he would make a good manager, but he gave him the job and then got me to come down and help Bucky. And poor Bucky had the worst ball club I ever ran into, even worse than the Browns. It liked to have killed Bucky. He got ulcers and couldn't eat and couldn't sleep, and he would walk the streets at night until 2, 3, or 4 in the morning. It was a pity. Giles asked me to take over at the very end of the season and then I stayed through '50 and '51 and until August of '52. But we had a terrible club."

"What did you do after 1952."

"Well, Branch Rickey called me about Jack Kent Cooke, who owned the Toronto minor league team and was trying to get a major league franchise. Cooke told the city council up there, 'If you build a ball park I'll get a franchise.' The council said, 'You get a franchise and then we'll build the ball park.' That's the way it stood.

"Rickey said to me, 'They don't have anyone up there who has been around the major leagues at all. Why don't you go up there? I'll talk to Cooke and maybe they'll get a franchise and something good will come out of it.' Cooke called me and I met him in Atlanta, and we made a deal for me to manage his Toronto club.

"Cooke was like Steinbrenner. He'd go into the clubhouse and lecture his players. Those poor kids, some of them didn't know the way home. He'd give them pep talks and everything. I made a deal with him that he was to stay out of the clubhouse and I'd handle the players. And he stayed out. We won the pennant that year and we won the next year and we made Cooke a lot of money. And I finally arranged it so that he could get a franchise.

"The Athletics were still in Philadelphia then, and I ran into Roy Mack in Rochester. I asked him what they were doing with the franchise and he said, 'We're trying to sell it.' Roy had 20% of the club and Earle had 20%. They were Connie's sons by his first wife. With his second wife he had Connie, Jr. and a daughter. They and the second wife had the remaining 60%.

"The Macks owed the concessionaire, Jacobs Brothers of Buffalo, over a million dollars and an insurance company another million or more. But they owned the ball park and Bob Carpenter of the Phillies would buy the park. And the Jacobs Brothers said they would take theirs out in concessions. The sale of the ball park would pay off the insurance company. It would cost Cooke $600,000 to buy out the other 60% interest in the club. It was a great deal!

"So I got back with Cooke and went over everything with him. He sent a cost accountant to Philadelphia to go over the books. There was so much red in the books that he said not to touch it with a 10-foot pole. But I said to Jack, 'You take the ball club and I'll go and manage it for you next year. You keep the team in Philadelphia for a year and if you can't get it transferred to Toronto, you can sell it and make yourself some money. I didn't have any money at the time or I'd have bought the club myself.

"Cooke considered it for a while but finally told me he couldn't take the deal for the Athletics because he was going to put everything he had into an offer for a newspaper, the *Globe-Mail*. So the whole deal fell through. And to top it off, a few months later I got a call from Cooke, who told me, 'I lost out on the paper bid.' It seems the paper was appraised at 9 million, he bid 9.5 million, and a fellow out of Toronto bid 10.5.

"Then Gabe Paul got me to go out to Seattle on the same kind of deal. The people out there, hoping to be bankrolled by Mr. Sick of Sick Brewery, were looking for a major league franchise. Paul told me to go to Seattle and see what I could do to help them. They offered me a contract for more money than I had ever made in baseball in my life. I went out and stayed there for some months. Then Mr. Sick got emphysema and couldn't breathe and finally told me one day, 'I'm not going to put a cent into baseball.' So I quit and came home."

"After that, what did you do?"

"I had been connected with a small rubber company off and on for about 15 years. The offices were here in Akron but the factories were down south—in Muscle Shoals, Alabama and one over in Georgia. We got into the rubber and vinyl flooring business and had a tremendous development starting in about 1948. Later I went into a bronze business and stayed with that until 1972."

"Can you identify the best players you saw while you were a player?"

"George Sisler at first base, Gehringer at second, Bluege at third—he was the best and that's including Brooks Robinson and all of them.

"At shortstop, Boudreau had one or two really good years. But the best defensive shortstop I ever saw was a Cuban named Rodriguez. Everybody classified him as a third baseman and he couldn't play third base, but he was a whiz at shortstop. Joe Cronin was just an average fielder.

"In the outfield, I'd name Cobb, Ruth, and Speaker."

"Best right-handed hitter?"

"I think the best right-handed hitter I saw in this league was Harry Heilmann. Overall, Hornsby would be best."

"And the best catcher?"

"Before I answer that, let me tell you a true story. We used to train out in Pasadena, and one time I went to a Boy Scout meeting where they were trying to raise money for some project. After my little talk I said, 'I'll give $5 to the boy who asks the most interesting question. You keep half and give the other half to your fund.' One little fellow sitting down in front raised his hand and asked, 'Who is the best catcher in the league, and why are you?' Without a word I handed him the $5. Now, I think I could outcatch Dickey and Cochrane, and outthrow them too, but I sure couldn't hit with them. And Ray Schalk was a mighty good defensive catcher. It would be hard for me to rate the best catcher I ever saw.

"As top pitchers, Grove was the best all-around pitcher I saw. I saw Walter Johnson when he was on his way down. I could hit Walter but I couldn't hit Grove."

"Luke, you played many years when baseball was strictly a day game, and you also were around when it became mostly a night game. Any comments on the difference?"

"Night ball gives a decided advantage to the pitcher. And to the owners. I remember how Clark Griffith would say, when night ball was just coming in, 'Baseball is made to be played in the daylight.' The first night game in the American League was played in Philadelphia, and everybody was there to see it. The fans were just hanging from the rafters. Griff was there and I said to him, 'Griff, what do you think of this?' And he said, 'This would be the very thing for us now.' "

"Luke, can you give me an interesting anecdote from your experience?"

"Well, we had a pitcher in St. Louis named Bob Muncrief, and one day we were playing the Red Sox. Joe Cronin was through playing but would sometimes put himself in to pinch hit. He would get up to the plate and crouch way down like he was looking for a curveball, but he really wanted the pitcher to throw a high fastball. We were a run or so ahead and Cronin came up to pinch hit with a couple of men on base.

"I went out to the mound and said, 'Now listen, Bob, he's going to crouch over but you just keep throwing that ball right at his knees. Don't throw that fastball up here, and make him hit a curveball.' Well, the first ball he threw was a fastball about letter high and Cronin just raised up and drilled the ball into the galvanized tin out on our scoreboard. I started for the mound on the run but just about the time I got to the foul line Muncrief said, 'Skip, you were right. Next time I'll know better.' "

Sewell then showed me his first contract in the major leagues, and as I was studying it he asked, "See what the pay was?"

"I see it but I can't believe it. $350 a month—and in the majors!"

"I was still in college at the time," he told me, "and we could play in the summer with teams in the small towns. I had played in a little town named Madison, Georgia, east of Atlanta. There I got $125 a week and expenses. And they let us stay in a little hotel on the square and every night they sent up an ice-cold watermelon. Then I signed in the major leagues for $350 a month and had to pay my own expenses. My, how things have changed!"

During his long and successful career in the majors, Luke Sewell was the central figure in two of the most bizarre double plays in the history of baseball. One of them occurred in 1933 when the Washington Senators were in New York playing the Yankees. Luke tells about it this way:

"We were locked in a tight pennant race with them at the time. It was the last of the ninth and as I recall we were two runs ahead. Our pitcher was Monte Weaver, who had pitched the entire game and looked exhausted. Lou Gehrig was the first batter and he walked. Then Dixie Walker singled but Gehrig had to stop at second. The next batter, Tony Lazzeri, hit a screaming line drive to right-center. Gehrig apparently thought it was going to be caught and tagged up at second, while Walker ran almost all the way to second. Goose Goslin was playing right and made a great attempt to catch the ball but just missed. Gehrig started running with Walker right on his heels, and the Yankee third base coach, Art Fletcher, sent them both on to the plate. The ball caromed off the wall right into Goslin's hands and he relayed the ball to Cronin, who had gone into the outfield. Cronin made a perfect throw to me just in time to tag Gehrig sliding home on the outside, and he spun me around in time to tag Dixie sliding on the inside.

"Lazzeri had an easy double which should have tied the score, but he stood there at second amazed with the happenings which left them with two outs and no runs. I went to the mound and Weaver seemed to be in somewhat of a daze. I told him all he had to do was get one more out and we would win. He took a deep breath and proceeded to strike the next batter out. That seemed to be the turning point in our race with the Yankees and we went on to finish six or seven games in front of them."

That was one of the very rare instances when a catcher has tagged out two runners at the plate on the same play. Carlton Fisk did it in 1985, also against the Yankees. But the other double play we're talking about is even harder to believe because Luke didn't tag out the runners at the plate but rather at second base! This one took place in 1927.

There was a runner on second with nobody out. The batter hit a grounder to the shortstop, who threw to third and trapped the runner coming from second. Sewell went out to help in the rundown. Luke got the ball and chased the runner down just as he was about to slide back into second. The batter at that moment was trying to advance to second, so Sewell turned around and tagged him too as he slid in. It's highly doubtful that any other catcher in baseball ever made an unassisted double play at second base.

Luke Sewell also was the catcher in three no-hit games, thrown by Wes Ferrell of the Indians in 1931, Vern Kennedy of the White Sox in 1935, and Bill Dietrich (also of the Chisox) in 1937.

Luke Sewell died at the age of 86 on May 14, 1987, in Akron, Ohio. He had been living in Akron in the home he had purchased there in 1938 and had been active and in good health until late in 1986.

JAMES LUTHER SEWELL

BR TR   5'9" 160 lbs.

Born in Titus, Alabama on January 5, 1901

Died May 14, 1987 in Akron, Ohio

YEAR	TEAM	G	AB	R	H	RBI	2B	3B	HR	BB	SO	SB	AVG.
1921	Cleveland AL	3	6	0	0	1	0	0	0	0	3	0	.000
1922	" "	41	87	14	23	10	5	0	0	5	8	1	.264
1923	" "	10	10	2	2	1	0	1	0	1	0	0	.200
1924	" "	63	165	27	48	17	9	1	0	22	13	1	.291
1925	" "	74	220	30	51	18	10	2	0	33	18	6	.232
1926	" "	126	433	41	103	46	16	4	0	36	27	9	.238
1927	" "	128	470	52	138	53	27	6	0	20	23	4	.294
1928	" "	122	411	52	111	52	16	9	3	26	27	3	.270
1929	" "	124	406	41	96	39	17	3	1	29	26	6	.236
1930	" "	76	292	40	75	43	21	2	1	14	9	5	.257
1931	" "	108	375	45	103	53	30	4	1	36	17	1	.275
1932	" "	87	300	36	76	52	20	2	2	38	24	4	.253
1933	Washington AL	141	474	65	125	61	30	4	2	48	24	7	.264
1934	" "	72	207	21	49	21	7	3	2	22	10	0	.237
1935	Chicago AL	118	421	52	120	67	19	3	2	32	18	3	.285
1936	" "	128	451	59	113	73	20	5	5	54	16	11	.251
1937	" "	122	412	51	111	61	21	6	1	46	18	4	.269
1938	" "	65	211	23	45	27	4	1	0	20	20	0	.213
1939	Cleveland AL	16	20	1	3	1	1	0	0	3	1	0	.150
1942	St. Louis AL	6	12	1	1	0	0	0	0	1	5	0	.083
	20 yrs.	1630	5383	653	1393	696	273	56	20	486	307	65	.259

WORLD SERIES

YEAR	TEAM	G	AB	R	H	RBI	2B	3B	HR	BB	SO	SB	AVG.
1933	Washington AL	5	17	1	3	1	0	0	0	2	0	1	.176

LUKE SEWELL AS MANAGER

YEAR	TEAM	G	W	L	PCT.	FINISH
1941	St. Louis AL	113	55	55	.500	6
1942	" " "	151	82	69	.543	3
1943	" " "	153	72	80	.474	6
1944	" " "	154	89	65	.578	1
1945	" " "	154	81	70	.536	3
1946	" " "	126	53	71	.427	7
1949	Cincinnati NL	3	1	2	.333	7
1950	" "	153	66	87	.431	6
1951	" "	155	68	86	.442	6
1952	" "	98	39	59	.398	7
	10 yrs.	1260	606	644	.485	

WORLD SERIES

YEAR	TEAM	G	W	L	PCT.
1944	St. Louis AL	6	2	4	.333

12

Babe Herman

E ver since the late '20s the legend has circulated here and there in baseball that Babe Herman once tripled into a triple play. Not so.

The colorful slugger of the old Brooklyn Dodgers did, however, double into a double play, a feat which though rare is not unique in major league history. But he emphatically denies the triple play bit. "It's crazy to say I hit into a triple play, because there was already one out." Moreover, he couldn't have tripled into anything, for he was called out at third.

The truth is that the bases were loaded one day when Babe hit a drive off the right-field wall. The runner on third of course scored easily. Dazzy Vance, running from second, rounded third and should have reached home in a walk, but after advancing some 30 feet he changed his mind and returned to third.

Chick Fewster, the runner from first, probably would have scored too and Herman would have been safe at third. Yet all of a sudden the three of them were having a reunion at third. Confusion galore.

Vance was clearly entitled to occupy third, and Babe was called out for passing Fewster on the basepath. In all the commotion Chick no doubt could have wandered safely back to second, where he was entitled to be. Instead, he made a break for it and was tagged out, ending the bizarre inning.

Thus did Babe Herman double into a double play. But as he points out in injured pride, "Everybody overlooks the fact that the run I knocked in on that play was the winning run."

Among baseball's more colorful players Babe Herman

145

Floyd Caves (Babe) Herman spent the greater part of his 13-year career with the Brooklyn Dodgers. Breaking in as a first baseman, he was then permanently stationed in right field. Pictured here with Babe Ruth, Herman himself stood out among the game's best hitters, with a lifetime average of .324, tied for 33rd place with Joe Medwick on the lifetime batting leaders list. Herman's best years were 1929 and 1930, when he hit .381 and .393, respectively.

would rank in the upper echelon. And if you're talking about natural hitting talent, he has to be one of the first mentioned.

Babe was a big leaguer for 13 seasons, mostly with the Brooklyn Dodgers. In his prime it was generally agreed that he hit the ball harder than anyone else in the league. His career batting average of .324 leaves him tied with Ducky Medwick and one point behind Joe DiMaggio and Jimmy Foxx.

Herman's two best years were 1929 and 1930. In '29 he had 21 homers, 113 RBIs, and batted .381, second only to Lefty O'Doul's .398. And then in '30 he upped his statistics to 241 hits, 35 home runs, 130 RBIs, and an average of .393. Even then he didn't lead the league in hitting because that season Bill Terry posted a mark of .401.

Babe amassed other slugging honors during his sojourn in the majors. Twice in one season he hit for the circuit, and he is the only player to perform the feat three times in a career. Once he clubbed three homers in a game and missed the fourth by a scant two feet. He led his team in RBIs in seven of his first eight seasons in the big leagues.

These days Rodney Dangerfield is always complaining that he "don't get no respect." This was somewhat true of Babe, in his earlier years especially, largely because in his time the Dodgers, under the genial leadership of the rotund Wilbert Robinson, were commonly referred to as the "Daffiness Boys." There's no denying that the Dodgers of that time were known on occasion to lose flyballs in the sun, throw to the wrong base, and even suffer nearly inexplicable mishaps on the basepaths. Things of that sort plague almost every ball club on occasion.

Yet the sportswriters of the day (and one suspects particularly those partial to the Giants and the Yankees) magnified the foibles of the Dodgers and soon created the impression that these daffy doings occurred routinely in every game. And the faithful Flatbush fans encouraged this belief through the affectionate name they coined for their heroes—"Dem bums."

Since Babe was the standout on the ball club (even more than Dazzy Vance) and was an outgoing, uninhibited sort, the media types settled on him as the symbol of the lovable, bumbling Dodgers, who in tribute to Robby were also known in those years as the Robins. Herman's 190 pounds distributed over his 6' 4" frame and his long arms gave him a gangling yet imposing appearance. More than that, his exceptionally colorful personality made him from the beginning the people's choice in Brooklyn.

Babe Herman reached the majors as a first baseman. His height made him a fine target for the other infielders and, despite an occasional case of tangled feet, he played the bag so well that following his first year in 1926 he was named to Babe Ruth's All-America team which was chosen by a panel of sportswriters from around the majors.

But in 1928 Babe was stationed in right field, so as to get Del Bissonette's bat into play at first base, and this became his permanent position thereafter. He thinks now it was a mistake to let them move him away from first base. It pretty surely was a mistake in his first year or two in the outer gardens, for he was unfamiliar there and experienced difficulty in adjusting to playing the sun field. Max Carey solved that problem after he came over from Pittsburgh to the Dodgers. Max observed that Babe was letting the ball go through the sun on the way up and again on the way down, thus giving himself two chances to lose it.

Before that got straightened out, however, Babe had done a lot of wavering under flyballs and actually let one hit him in the chest after he lost it in the sun. In fact, a late-inning replacement for Babe let one bounce off his head one day, and Herman got the blame because nobody had noticed the replacement enter the game. So the writers had a ball penning highly exaggerated accounts of how it was always a 50-50 bet as to whether Babe would catch a flyball in the glove or on the head.

Yet there is evidence from numerous ballplayers of that era to show that Babe Herman, after his first few years, became a really good rightfielder. He had fine speed and a throwing arm that matched just about anyone in the league. Moreover, he became quite adept at playing the angles off the walls in all the National League parks. Nevertheless, the myth has endured that Babe was just a bumbling clown in his outfield play.

"I was born in Buffalo, New York, in 1903," says Babe. "In 1904 my father went to California to look everything over and in 1905 he brought us all out here. I was the fourth of five children. My father was a carpenter, a brick mason, and later a contractor. In those days I was a paper boy. After grammar school I went to Glendale High and played on the first football team they ever had. When they held the first practice only 10 fellows showed up. So we had to go out and draft a fellow who was a fat kid. He said. 'I can't play football.' And we told him, 'You're gonna.' We put him at guard and he turned out to be real good before the season was over. We had several players who went on to be stars in college.

"I wanted to go to Berkeley to play football for Cal. I had been offered eight or 10 scholarships at other places. But just at that time I met someone around Rafferty's Sporting Goods store who offered me a contract to play baseball for Edmonton in the Western Canada League for $175 a month. I signed the contract and went home and my father said, 'Bah! They don't pay you for playing. You stay around here and learn the contracting business and you'll be worth something some day.'

"So that's the way I got into baseball. Heinie Manush and I were both signed to go up to Edmonton, and we were both sold to Detroit in 1921. Before the next season started Heinie was optioned out to Omaha, and I got to go to Augusta, Georgia, for spring training with the Tigers. Ty Cobb was then player/ manager. That's where I am supposed to have pinch hit for Ty Cobb and hit a home run with the bases loaded. Like nearly all such stories, it's exaggerated.

"There were two men on when Ty said to me, 'Dutch (he always called me Dutch), get ready to go up and hit for me.' It was cold and I was all bundled up on the bench. By the time I got uncovered the batter had walked, which loaded the bases. And I hit a ball through the box for a single.

"Ty decided I should be a first baseman. In the outfield he already had himself and Veach and Heilmann, plus Fothergill, Heinie Manush, and Johnny Mohardt. So he sent me out to Omaha. Everybody knocks Ty but he treated me great.

"Out at Omaha I was hitting .468 and still the older fellows said they ought to be getting more money than me. Anyway, after various doings I wound up leading the league with .416 and Heinie was second with .398. I had led the league in Canada and he was second there too. We roomed together for two years and Heinie used to stand in front of the mirror and say, 'Boy, can I hit!'

"When Mr. Navin traded me from Detroit to the Red Sox in 1923, the Boston manager, Frank Chance, asked me if I wanted to sit on the bench as a pinch hitter. I said no, so he sent me down to Atlanta. The next year I went to spring training with the Red Sox again. Lee Fohl was the new manager and

I got sent out to San Antonio. I didn't like the Texas League, but I played 50 ball games without an error and hit about .350.

"Nevertheless, I asked them to get me out of there. Kid Elberfeld, the manager of Little Rock and an ornery little bugger, asked me if I'd play for him. I said sure and so I got assigned there.

"In 1925 my son Bob was born and I asked the Boston club to let me come out to the West Coast. So they sold me to Seattle. Spencer Abbott, a scout for the Dodgers, saw me one day while he was scouting somebody on the Portland club. I hit a couple out of the park that day and he went back and told his boss about it, and the Brooklyn club bought me.

"I always had to laugh at Garry Hermann of the Reds. He saw me play in Frisco when I had a good day, and he went back east and said, 'There are two guys out in the Coast League that I'd like to buy. One is a second baseman/pitcher named Red Lucas and I can't think of the other guy's name.' Of course, I was the other guy and the name was the same as his own. When he finally woke up to who it was, he contacted the Seattle club and was told they had already sold me to the Dodgers.

"So that was my start in the big leagues. And the funny thing is, they sent me a contract for less than I was making in the Coast League. When I got the Brooklyn contract I tore it up in disgust, something I knew later I shouldn't have done, but a young kid doesn't think of those things.

"So they didn't hear from me and I didn't hear from them, until finally I got a wire offering me a thousand dollars a month. After we were up in Brooklyn, Robby said to me one day, 'Hey, I hear you play the outfield.' I said, 'Well, I don't know if I can play it to suit you.' Anyway, I played right field against right-handers and first base against lefthanders, replacing Jack Fournier. Later on in the season I took over first regularly.

"I was leading the league at .356 pretty late in the season when I came into home plate a little hard one day trying to take the catcher out on a close play. But he had time to get set real firm, and when I hit him my momentum brought me right up to a sitting position and I banged into his shin guards and broke a rib. But you know, I didn't take any time off. The next day they taped me and I went on playing for the rest of the year, winding up with a .319 average.

"In 1927, my second year at Brooklyn, I had some troubles and ended up hitting .272. After the season it turned out I had several crowned abscessed teeth which had been my problem. And then by the next year the Dodgers had brought up Del Bissonette to play first."

"How was Robby as a manager?"

"Well, Robby was a wonderful fellow. I think he sometimes got a little tired at the end of the season. And once in a while he'd be talking to somebody about Dover Hall and the third base coach would be hollering at him trying to get a sign. But one thing about him was he knew how to handle pitchers, and he had good luck with Luque and John Quinn and other old guys who were supposed to be through. He had been a catcher, you know. No, I don't think there was anything against Robby."

"In your day did rookies ever get to take batting practice during spring training?"

"Let me tell you my experience. Ty Cobb said to me one day when we were training in Augusta, 'Dutch, you're going to play today, and you'll hit in the lineup after me.' So I was shagging flies in the outfield until Ty came to the plate in batting practice. Then I dropped my glove, trotted in, picked up a bat, and got ready to hit. Bobby Veach said to me, 'Hey, where are you going?' I told him, 'I'm playing today, so I'm going to hit.' 'You're sure as hell not going to hit,' he replied. I said, 'You're sure as hell not going to stop me.'

"So Ty stepped out of the batter's box and asked what the argument was. I reminded him he told me I was playing and was to bat after him, so I was going to get my hitting practice after him. Ty said, 'No, Dutch, get down to first base and I'll hit you some.' That's the way it was then. Later, when I was scouting, I'd see a manager say to a veteran, 'Get out of there. I want to see this kid hit.' You see, any time a kid came in there and wanted your job in the old days, there was trouble."

"How about Dazzy Vance?"

"Dazzy was the Koufax of his day. He had the best curve and the best fastball of anybody in baseball. I mean anybody that threw both pitches. And he threw a knuckleball that nobody could catch. That's the way he was as a pitcher, and if he had had Grimes' disposition I don't think any team would ever have beaten him. He was too easy going and he wouldn't throw at you.

"The first game I hit against him after I was traded to Cincinnati I got four hits. He threw me a fastball high and inside and I hit it right through the box. When I got to first base he said, 'I'll stick one right in your ear next time.' The next time up he threw one the same place and I got another base hit. Then he threw me a knuckleball and I hit it up into the stands. And the fourth time he threw me a curveball. I'll never forget how I started swinging away up here and just kept coming down and finally hit the ball past the third baseman. Old Daz had a fit. He was a nice fellow. I played a lot of golf with him and personally you couldn't say anything against him."

"Burleigh Grimes wasn't quite that way, was he?"

"In his own mind Burleigh never lost a game. There was always something that went wrong. He was a good hard-nosed pitcher. He had a good spitball. One of the best I ever saw with the spitter was Red Faber. While I was with the Cubs Red pitched against us in the City Series. His spitter acted like it broke twice. Grimes got so he could break the spitter in or out by turning his wrist, making it a little more like a screwball."

"In 1930 the Dodgers came in fourth but only six games out of first. Did you make a challenge for the pennant that year?"

"We led the league for a while and should have won the pennant. Two things probably kept us from doing it. Robby made a mistake in holding Vance back to pitch against certain teams and then rain prevented him from doing it, so for 18 days Dazzy did us no good.

"And then Johnny Frederick got hurt. He was the most underrated ballplayer of the whole bunch. Without those bad breaks we would have won the pennant. It was easier playing right field next to Johnny than with anyone I ever played next to—Douthit, Crabtree, Hafey, Cuyler, Merv Jacobsen, Jigger Statz. I always knew where Johnny was and whether he could get the ball.

"And we all knew how to run into the wall, this way, so we could catch the ball and not get hurt. But they don't know how to do that nowadays. There are a lot of things they don't do in the outfield now that we used to. When we caught a ball we had to get rid of it in one step. We didn't go three steps— that's 18 feet more for the runner. How many runners you gonna throw out by 18 feet?"

"Was Max Carey a good base runner?"

"I think Max was the greatest base runner I ever saw. He didn't steal bases unless it meant something. He wasn't like they do today. And I've seen him advance a base on a ball that was almost an infield fly. If he was on third and the shortstop went back for a short fly with his back to the infield, Carey would always make it to home safe. I never ran much on the bases because Robby never gave me the steal sign. Finally Robby told Max to take me under his wing. So he did and in mid-season I was leading the league in stolen bases before I pulled a muscle. Then Robby said, 'What do you want to run for, anyway? We want you in there hitting.' But I was fourth in stolen bases in '29 and second in '30.''

"In 1929 and 1930, when you hit .381 and .393, did you have your sights on .400?''

"I was over .400 nearly all year. I just got so darned tired I didn't run out a couple of swinging bunts. I only needed a few more hits to stay up there. Robby used to say he'd give me a week off after July 4 to get rested up. But he never let me take a day off. I've had my leg swollen up two inches with a charley horse and when it was just about down again Robby would say, 'You can hit one. Go on up and hit.' And then if I hit one on the ground and tried to run it out, the leg would get all puffed up again.''

"Who are some of the best ballplayers you played with or against?''

"I'll tell you about Lefty O'Doul. I knew him awfully well and he was as fine a fellow as you'd ever want to meet. He was brought up in a tough group in San Francisco, but he was a high class guy and a great competitor. He started out as a pitcher but hurt his arm and then became an outfielder with Salt Lake City of the Pacific Coast League. That year of 1925 O'Doul and Paul Waner and Charlie Root and I all came up out of the Coast League. Lefty was an average fielder with a weak arm, but he ran real well and could he hit!

"And Ernie Lombardi, a great catcher who could really hit. And he could throw, too. A funny thing, one day. Red Lucas was a good control pitcher, but once he threw a sidearm ball that went two or three feet outside the plate. Schnozz just reached out, grabbed the ball barehanded, and picked a runner off first base. And Lucas had a fit. 'Gee whiz,' he said, 'here you are catching me barehanded.'

"I got Van Mungo his first start in the majors. In a double-header with the Giants, Luque had beaten them, 1-0, in the first game and Ray Phelps was scheduled for the second game but something went wrong. Robby was looking around for someone to pitch and I said to him, 'Robby, it's already getting hard to see out there. You ought to put that big Mungo kid out there and tell him to throw hard and keep the ball low.' Robby did and Mungo and Hubbell went 0-0 for seven innings before the game was called for darkness.

"Van was one of the real characters of baseball. He mumbled, you know, and was hard to understand, but he could throw that pea. I'll tell you, I'd rather hit against Nolan Ryan than face Mungo the way he could throw then. And he didn't care if he stuck the ball in your ear. Mungo and Dazzy were both faster than Dizzy.

"Speaking of Diz, did you know he jumped the club for two weeks in '34 and still won 30 games? I had a field day in a doubleheader against Diz and Paul on the day they tore their uniforms up, against the Cubs. They both jumped the club, but Paul came back in time for his next start. Diz stayed away for about two weeks. With that much rest I don't think he lost another game after he came back.

"Something most people don't know about Dizzy Dean is that he had the best motion on a change of pace that I ever saw. One day he came in with nobody out and three men on and struck out the next three batters, two of them Paul Waner and Arky Vaughan. With a three and two count he would throw you that motion and come in with that change of pace. A great competitor. He was an outstanding fellow, too. I never heard Diz knock anybody. Paul didn't like that Dizzy and Daffy stuff, but he was a high class guy, too.

"I played a lot with and against Fresco Thompson and I liked him, even if he did start a lot of jokes about me. I remember one day in spring training in Clearwater when we played the Phillies. There was only one dressing room and a bunch of their guys came in and asked if they could dress with us. Thompson shared my locker. When we came back in after hitting practice I yelled jokingly, 'Get that .240 hitter out of my locker. It might rub off.' And Thompson said, 'Well, what about me? Sharing with a .240 fielder? That might rub off too.' He had an answer for everything.

"Del Bissonette was a real nice fellow. 100% true blue. He was what you like to call a friend. He was the kind of guy that, regardless of whether it's going to hurt him or not, the truth was the truth. I was glad for him that I did go to the outfield, though I think it was a mistake for my own career.

"And I liked Dave Bancroft. I knew him when he was managing the Boston Braves and then he was with us in Brooklyn in '28 and '29. He was a Dapper Dan and liked to go around with the upper class. When my boy Bob was a kid he was nuts about Banny and would often go over to have dinner with the Bancrofts.

"Al Lopez was my roommate his first year up and we've always been friends. They don't come any better than Al. I think he's the best receiver I ever saw. I thought Dickey was the best hitting catcher, Mickey Cochrane the best leader, and probably Hartnett the best all around.

"Sloppy Thurston was another buddy of mine. I used to hunt with him a lot. One time when we went over to play in Havana I asked to get us a suite and I'd pay the difference. Glenn Wright and Thurston roomed together, and Lopez and I. And from that time on, nothing was ever said about it, but every hotel we went to we had that same setup, with a bath between the two rooms. That went on for several years.

"Another one I liked was old Eppa Rixey. I even took out insurance from him. I've got two policies yet that he wrote. I had pretty good luck hitting against him, and he was quite a pitcher. One time I hit a drive out of the park off him. I broke the bat doing it and a big sliver came out of the bat right where the trade mark is. Eppa said, 'Gee whiz, he even hits 'em out of the park on me with a broken bat!' "

"Babe, when you went from the Dodgers to Cincinnati before the 1932 season, was it in a trade?"

"Yeah. Ernie Lombardi, Wally Gilbert, and myself for Tony Cuccinello, Joe Stripp, and Clyde Sukeforth. I think it was one of the worst deals Brooklyn made, for Lombardi was quite a guy and won the MVP twice. The whole deal came about as the result of a salary squabble I had with the Dodgers.

"After I agreed to terms they reneged. I bowed my neck and wouldn't sign and they got stubborn and wouldn't give me the contract we had agreed on. One night Dan Howley, the Cincinnati manager, called and said, 'You're a big Red now.' I said, 'I've been called worse than that, Dan.' He went on to tell me, 'I just made a deal for you.'

"Dan Howley treated me better than anyone I ever played ball for. And I think the world of him. Dan gave me my nickname when he was my coach back in '22. He said to me, 'Hey, kid, what do they call you?'' I replied, 'Well, my nickname's

Lefty.' He said, 'No, that's not it for you.' Then I told him, 'Well, there was a fan with a foghorn voice up in Edmonton who used to call me Tiny Herman. Sometimes, he would yell, 'Come on, baby.' 'That's it,' said Dan. 'From now on you're my Babe.'

"It's funny, but when I went back down to the minors, I beat Dan's Toronto team opening day in Jersey City with a home run with two out in the ninth. I hit it clear out of the park and that had never been done before. Three men on, too. Then we went up to Toronto to open his season there, and again I had about three hits, winning the game with a three-run homer in the ninth.

"Dan had invited me out to dinner at his house that night and had told me where his car was parked. So I was sitting in his car when he came along, and he said, 'Get out of my car. Gee, you beat me on opening day in your park and now again in my park.' I went on out to his house with him and we had a wonderful dinner. But, you know, his wife never spoke to me. Boy, was she mad!

"Before spring training in '33 Dan Howley called me and said, 'Babe, we've got to trade you. The club needs the money and you're the only guy we can get any money out of. Do you want to go to the Giants or the Cubs?' I told him, 'Gee, Dan, I'd rather be in New York. But the Cubs won last year and I think they'll win again. And I'd like to get in one World Series. Let's make it Chicago.' So he traded me to the Cubs and got five ballplayers and $75,000 in cash. The players were Bob Smith, Johnny Moore, Lance Richbourg, Rollie Hemsley, and some minor leaguer."

"When you first got to the majors with the Dodgers in 1926 what was your contract for?"

"It was for $6,500. That was a good salary. I heard Tommy Thevenow only got $3,500 that year, and he was a star in the World Series."

"Do you remember your first hit?"

"Yes. It wasn't too long after opening day and we were playing the Braves up in Boston. Robby had to go somewhere but he left word to use me if the situation presented itself. And he had said, 'Tell that big guy not to take a strike but to hit the first ball that's in there.' So we're behind in the last inning and I go up as a pinch hitter.

"On the first pitch the umpire called 'Strike one!' I looked back at him and asked, 'That ball in there?' He said yes. I told him I thought it was a little outside. Just then he said, 'Strike two!' I said to myself, 'Gee, I'm on my way to L.A.' I took the next pitch also and then was afraid it was better than the other two. But the umpire said, 'Ball one!' The following pitch I slashed down the left-field foul line and drove in a couple of runs. We went on to score three more and win."

"It must have been a thrill. Any special hitting feats you remember?"

"Well, one time in 1933 in Wrigley Field I hit three home runs in a game, and I just missed a fourth one by a couple of feet. And there were a couple of times when I had nine straight hits. Once on the 10th try I hit one out of the ball park and Cuyler jumped up and it hit his glove and he fell over the fence. He came up with the ball in his glove and they called me out.

"A long time later on a fishing trip to Florida a fellow from Brooklyn told me, 'I was 14 years old when that happened, and I was sitting right out there where I could see it. Cuyler didn't catch that ball. When he fell the ball dropped free and he reached over a few feet to pick it up and then stood up with it in his glove.' I got three straight hits after that, so I really should have had 13 hits in a row, which would be the record."

"Who was the toughest pitcher for you to hit?"

"Well, I had days against all of them, and some of them had their days against me. The hardest was probably Wild Bill Hallahan. He had a curveball bigger than Koufax's and just as quick breaking. And he was wild."

"Can you recall any funny incident right now?"

"One day when I was with the Cubs, Bill Klem was umpiring behind the plate. We had three men on against one of the Dean brothers, and Chuck Klein hit a ball about nine miles high up over by the stands. The wind was blowing out, and hard. The Cardinals' catcher went over towards the stands but the ball kept coming out and he began backing up and up, until finally the ball landed in fair territory. Lon Warneke was on third and when he saw the ball drop he ran for home.

"Frankie Frisch was managing the Cardinals and he came charging out of the dugout claiming the infield fly rule should have been called. Klem said no, because the catcher was never in position to make the catch. The argument went on hot and heavy until suddenly Frisch slumped to the ground right in front of home plate. And Klem bellowed, 'Dead or alive, Frisch, you're still out of the ball game.'"

"After leaving the Detroit Tigers in the 1937 season, what did you do?"

"The Detroit club asked me to go to Toledo and try to help Fred Haney win the pennant there. I went over and we won our last 10 ball games. But we only gained half a game and lost the pennant by half a game. The Columbus Red Birds had Mort Cooper, Max Macon, Nelson Potter, and Bill McGee for starters and Nate Andrews for relief pitcher. They also had Enos Slaughter and Johnny Rizzo in the outfield, so they had eight or nine guys that went on to the big leagues. And they were the ones that beat us out.

"And then in 1945 Brooklyn asked me to come back for a while. I had the ranch and I quit playing at the end of the Coast League season in September. And they wanted me to come back and pinch hit for them. So I took the family and went because we hadn't been back to Brooklyn for about eight years and I wanted to see it again.

"But I don't think it was a smart move. It meant that I had to wait five more years, until 1950, before the baseball writers could consider my name again in the voting for the Hall of Fame. My last full season was '36 and by '50 a lot of writers who knew me best were no longer around, and I think that hurt my chances."

After leaving the Tigers in 1937 to go and help Toledo put on a gallant finish that just missed capturing the American Association pennant, Babe Herman passed a number of years in the high minors, mostly in the Pacific Coast League. Wherever he played he was the plague of pitchers.

In 1943, playing for Hollywood at the age of 40, Babe hit .354 and as a pinch hitter one day slammed three home runs in a doubleheader. If you wonder how he could be a pinch hitter three times in a doubleheader, the answer is that in one game his team batted around in one inning. Babe came up twice in that inning and in both instances whacked the ball into the outfield seats.

After that, Herman turned to coaching and scouting, which he did for 22 years (1946-67) for the Pirates, Yankees, Phillies, Mets, and Giants. He scouted and signed such future stars as Vern Law, Pat Corrales, and Paul Blair. On his recommendation Max West and George Metkovich were drafted by big league teams.

When Hollywood decided to make the movie *Pride of the*

Yankees, based on the career of Lou Gehrig and featuring Gary Cooper and Teresa Wright, it was Babe Herman who was chosen as Cooper's stand-in to do all of the batting scenes.

Through it all and right up to the present Babe's home has remained in Glendale. He and his wife Ann, now married for well over 50 years, both continue to be not only active but energetic. They participate in affairs of the community, in which they are widely known and respected. Babe also knew how to invest his earnings wisely and has prospered through the years. He has been a turkey and chicken rancher and has property and holdings of consequence in Glendale.

Babe has played a lot of golf through the years, and his natural talent has shown itself in that sport as well. As an example, on his 66th birthday he toured a tough course in 67 strokes. For a hobby he has developed into an expert in raising orchids and has served as president of the Orchid Society of Southern California.

Through it all, Babe says, he has practiced and preached what his own father used to tell him: "Your word is your bond and don't ever break it."

FLOYD CAVES HERMAN
BL TL   6'4" 190 lbs.
Born in Buffalo, New York on June 26, 1903

YEAR	TEAM	G	AB	R	H	RBI	2B	3B	HR	BB	SO	SB	AVG.
1926	Brooklyn NL	137	496	64	158	81	35	11	11	44	53	8	.319
1927	" "	130	412	65	112	73	26	9	14	39	41	4	.272
1928	" "	134	486	64	165	91	37	6	12	38	36	1	.340
1929	" "	146	569	105	217	113	42	13	21	55	45	21	.381
1930	" "	153	614	143	241	130	48	11	35	66	56	18	.393
1931	" "	151	610	93	191	97	43	16	18	50	65	17	.313
1932	Cincinnati NL	148	577	87	188	87	38	19	16	60	45	7	.326
1933	Chicago NL	137	508	77	147	93	36	12	16	50	57	6	.289
1934	" "	125	467	65	142	84	34	5	14	35	71	1	.304
1935	2 teams Pittsburgh NL (26G — .235) Cincinnati NL (92G — .335)												
	Total	118	430	52	136	65	31	6	10	38	35	5	.316
1936	Cincinnati NL	119	380	59	106	71	25	2	13	39	36	4	.279
1937	Detroit AL	17	20	2	6	3	3	0	0	1	6	2	.300
1945	Brooklyn NL	37	34	6	9	9	1	0	1	5	7	0	.265
	13 yrs.	1552	5603	882	1818	997	399	110	181	520	553	94	.324

Knuckleballer Dutch Leonard never had the good fortune to perform in a World Series, but compiled a lifetime record of 191 wins and was one of the few players to perform effectively past the age of 40. Pictured here in a Cub uniform, near the end of his career, Leonard broke into the majors with Brooklyn, becoming the second "Dutch" Leonard to perform in the majors. After four years with Brooklyn, Leonard went to the Washington Senators, where he spent the majority of his pitching career.

13

Dutch Leonard

Some nicknames seem almost automatic. Like "Dusty" for anyone named Rhodes. Or "Lefty" for a good many left-handed pitchers—Grove, Gomez, and Carlton. In other cases a player is slapped with the nickname given earlier to someone with the same family name. That's what happened to Emil Leonard when he got into baseball.

Before World War I a pitcher was brought up by the Boston Red Sox named Hubert Leonard. He proved to be a good one over 11 seasons, compiling in 1914 an 18-5 mark with an eye-popping ERA of 1.01. He seemed to be fond of that latter figure, for in helping the Red Sox capture the World Series in 1915 and again in 1916 he pitched one complete win in each and his ERA both times was a neat 1.00. But he was rarely known as Hubert because early on he picked up the name of Dutch.

Less than a decade after the first Dutch Leonard hung up his spikes, the Brooklyn Dodgers unveiled his successor. With the exploits of the earlier Leonard still fresh in mind, sports-writers, players, and fans alike quickly tagged Emil Leonard with the same monicker of Dutch. And, while he never got to perform in the World Series, Emil ably lived up to the name and fame of Hubert. In some ways he surpassed him—20 seasons as compared to 11, 191 wins against 138.

Our Dutch Leonard is another player who came out of a small town to achieve stardom and then later returned to live in his hometown. In Dutch's case it was Auburn, Illinois (1980 population: 3,616), located some 75 miles north of St. Louis just off Interstate 55. I found him there on a pleasant summer afternoon.

As we talked and he warmed to the subject of his baseball days, it became evident that I was face to face with a person of sincere human warmth, devoid of pretentions. Always a family man, he typified the solid values of rural mid-America. I asked him how he got started playing ball. His story was not sensational, but compelling.

"I was born and raised here in Auburn. This is home. I began playing semipro ball here. I went down into the coal mine with my dad, and boy I didn't like that. He said, 'Well, you see, I've tried to feed and clothe you kids all these years, and it's hard work.' I know he worked hard.

"When I got out of high school I left home and went to Chicago and got a job digging ditches for the Public Service Company of Illinois. They were going to have a baseball team, and I asked if I could come out and pitch batting practice. After I did this a couple of times they said, 'How about you pitching for the team?' That suited me fine.

"We played for the sempiro championship of Chicago and I beat old Hippo Vaughn, who had been a star with the Cubs, 1-0. After the game a guy named Jerry Stannard who caught me said, 'My brother is playing in the Southern League, and if you want to play pro ball I feel sure he can get you a job.' I said, 'I'll take a shot at it.' And that's how I started in pro ball, in Mobile, Alabama. That was in 1930.

"The next year I got an infected hand and came home. The following season I started over here in Decatur, in the Three I League. After a month I had four wins and three losses when the league blew up. It was the Depression, you know.

"Frank Dessault, who was with me in Decatur, lived in York, Pennsylvania and he wrote to say if I'd come there he thought he could sell me to a Triple A club or even a major league team. I said to myself, 'I'm going to give baseball one more shot.' So in 1933 I went to York and won 14 ball games, and in the middle of the year I went up to Brooklyn. I stayed with them until the middle of '36 and then went down to Atlanta. In 1938 I went to Washington in the American League and stayed with them nine years."

"How did you develop the knuckleball?"

"Before I ever left home I got hurt playing basketball. Our high school only had a baseball team one year while I was there, and I couldn't make the team because I couldn't raise my arm very high. When I went to Chicago and started pitching batting practice I could throw hard but not like before, when I was really fast. So I started experimenting with the knuckleball because I heard somebody talking about that kind of pitch.

" I threw mine with the end of my fingers, since it didn't feel comfortable putting my knuckles on it. Of course, that's the way Hoyt Wilhelm threw his knuckler too. He said he'd read about how I threw mine and imitated it.

"The big thing was that when I went to Atlanta from Brooklyn, Paul Richards was down there. He caught me and he'd put his glove down like this and say, 'Now I want the ball down here, down here!' I got to the point with him where I could throw eight strikes out of 10 pitches and keep them below the waist. Then I went right back to the majors and stayed 16 years. Paul Richards really helped me a lot. Later, when he was managing Baltimore, he worked with Wilhelm too."

I asked Dutch about his first game in the majors.

"Well, I got into a game as a reliever. Before the game we were talking over the opponents' hitters. Casey Stengel was our manager and he said, 'If Frankie Frisch comes up hitting left-handed, try to pitch him outside and high to make him hit a flyball to left field.' When Frisch came to bat that flashed through my mind. I threw it high and outside and he hit an easy flyball to left field. It turned out just right.

"Then in my first start I got beat in Pittsburgh, 1-0. That first season I think I was two and three. The next year I won 14. In 1935 my dad died and I had a rough time and had to come home. Then in '36 they sent me to Atlanta."

"When you went to Washington in 1938, who was your manager?"

"Bucky Harris. I thought he was a great manager. He wasn't loud or anything, and he was smart. Even if you made a couple of bonehead plays he didn't raise his voice. He would just say a few words and you felt like crawling under the table. And the next day that was all over with.

"Bucky left me in the ball game one time when our pitching staff was pretty well wrecked. They got three unearned runs off me in the first inning and another in the second. Bucky came out to me and said, 'Dutch, if you can go on for most of the game today it'll give our staff a break.' Well, it wound up I got beat, 9-0, but I pitched the whole ball game.

"Like I say, you don't fool the fans. I gave it everything

I had and they didn't boo me one bit. In the dressing room after the game Bucky said to the team, 'I'll say one darn thing. He never did quit out there.' That made me feel good. Then I went out and won eight straight games. I had been having a hard time getting started because of my control, but that work was just what I needed."

"Dutch, I seem to remember that Washington had four starters who were knuckleballers in 1944."

"That's right. We had Mickey Haefner, Johnny Niggeling, Roger Wolff, and myself. But that was the year we finished last. The very next year we came in second, only a game and a half behind the Detroit Tigers. That was the only time we ever came close. That year it happened that we finished the season a week ahead of Detroit and had to sit around and sweat it out to see who got the pennant. The reason we finished our season early was that Griffith had rented the stadium out to the football team and we had to get our home games over with a week early. Our manager that year was Ossie Bluege, a nice guy and a real good manager."

"I guess your best season ever was in 1939, when you were 20 and 8."

"That's right. I think we only won 65 ball games. And my next best was in 1945 when I went 17 and 7. But that led to my biggest disappointment in baseball. Even though I had such a good year I came up with a sore arm toward the end and Griffith blamed me for our not winning the pennant, saying I should have won two or three more. He wanted to cut my salary by $500 and told me I would have to pay my own expenses in spring training in '46.

"Then we got together and he told me everybody was taking a cut because some fellows were coming back from the service, like Cecil Travis and Buddy Lewis. I told him, 'Well, if that's the way it is, I'll do my part and play for what I got last year.' That's what he wanted in the first place.

"So I was real happy the first month of the season and had four wins and one loss. Then one morning I picked up the paper and read a headline saying everybody on the club got a raise but one. Of course, I knew who that one was. And then the bottom dropped out for me.

"To make a long story short, I wound up the season winning 10 and losing 10. A couple of weeks before the season ended I asked Bluege, 'Does the old man figure on me in his plans for next year?' Bluege said he did. Then I told Ossie what had happened and he said, 'Why in hell didn't you tell me this months ago?' Anyway, I told him, 'I can still pitch up here. I can help you if you give me a chance to.'

"Joe Cambria was a scout for us and a long-time close friend of Griff's, and he didn't think I could get myself back in shape. You see, I had let myself go and had got up to 225 pounds and really wasn't in shape then. So they believed Joe and sold me to the Phillies. As soon as the deal was made I told my wife, 'I'm going to show that gray-haired old guy that I can still pitch up here.' And I went on a diet right then and there.

"I started working out here in Auburn, running and running and running. I went to spring training and I never had a glass of beer or highball or even a Coke. All I drank was black coffee. I worked out with the sweat suit on. I ate broiled fish till it came out of my ears, and no dessert. Grapefruit and stuff like that. And I took off those 25 pounds but still kept my strength.

"So I came back and won 17 games for Philadelphia in '47, and I was real close to the top in earned run average. But the next year I lost 17, even though I had a 2.51 ERA with a sixth place ball club. I was happy in Philadelphia, but I didn't think I got a good deal in Washington at the end."

"Can you recall one or two of the best games you pitched?"

"One of the best was the game that decided the American League pennant in 1944. The St. Louis Browns and the Detroit Tigers were tied on the last day of the season. I pitched in Detroit against Dizzy Trout. As I recall, I allowed only one hit going into the ninth inning and I won the ball game and helped the Browns take the pennant. They had a big party the next night in St. Louis and they called me and my wife to come down for it. We went and had a great time. A furniture company which sponsored the radio broadcasts of the games in St. Louis gave my wife two beautiful table lamps. We enjoyed it all very much.

"There's a story about that game. Before the game someone called on the phone and offered me a lot of money not to have a good day. I said I wasn't interested and then I told our coach, Clyde Milan, and he went to Bluege and told him what happened. I had talked it over with George Case, our rightfielder, and he told me, 'Dutch, if someone happened to overhear that phone call, you could be thrown out of baseball for life.' After

Ossie heard about it, he came over to me and said, 'You're still my pitcher.' I liked that and started warming up.

"I never thought about it again during the game, because once I started warming up I never did see anybody or hear anybody. I couldn't tell you whether there were 10,000 or 50,000 people in the stands, for I never heard them. You know, some players have been run right out of baseball by listening to the fans and not being able to take it.

"Also, I pitched against the Yankees in New York when they had 'Lou Gehrig Day,' and I won that one too. Pitching that game was a thrill for me, but the ceremonies were the saddest thing I ever saw. Over 60,000 people were in the stands and there wasn't a person in the place who didn't have tears in his eyes.

"Lou had been such a big strong fellow, and he had so much trouble walking to the mike, but he didn't want any help. Babe Ruth was there too. When Gehrig took the mike he said, 'I'm the luckiest guy in the world. I've got a wonderful wife and a wonderful mother.' And then it wasn't too long after that when he died. It was a sad thing."

"What was your biggest thrill in baseball?"

"Well, I had a few of them and one comes to mind right now. When I went to the American League I didn't have any money, and my wife and I didn't have any kids then. In those days, if you paid $250 a month for an apartment and got sent to the minors right after the first of the month, you didn't get any refund like you can nowadays. So we stayed at a boarding house some other ballplayers told us about.

"Right after we got there I had to pitch one night against Bob Feller, and I beat him, 1-0, in 13 innings. I didn't walk a single man and gave up six hits. That was probably my biggest thrill. And then I had another one right after the game when they called me into the office and said, 'Get yourself an apartment. You're going to be with this ball club.' And I stayed with them for nine years."

"Dutch, isn't the knuckleball a somewhat uncertain pitch? That is, it won't always behave the same, will it?"

"No, the wind has a lot to do with it. But I got to the point where I knew about what it was going to do according to my point of release. I had a pretty good fastball, but I threw that sinker all the time. In the American League sometimes I would only throw 12 to 14 knuckleballs in the whole game. But they were looking for my knuckleball and that made my fastball better. Joe DiMaggio thought I was one of the fastest guys in the league.

"When the catchers used to warm me up, they'd put on shin guards, mask, breast protector, and everything. 'Cause that knuckler sometimes was unpredictable. But Rick Ferrell was a great knuckleball catcher. He had relaxed hands and he let the ball come to him. Rick would take most of the padding out of his glove and then use a little sponge in it. So it was flexible like a first baseman's mitt. And he didn't drop many balls, so he could throw guys out.

"I had two or three moves to first base to keep the runners close and give Rick a chance to throw 'em out. I never had problems with Jackie Robinson or anybody stealing on me. But these pitchers with the high leg kick now, gee whiz, the runner's halfway down to second before they release the ball. Steve Carlton has a good move to first and picks off some runners. But some of these righthanders, I don't know. And a lot of pitchers today are all off balance when they release the ball and aren't in any position to field a ball hit back toward them."

"Who were the toughest batters for you to get out?"

"Well, guys like Ted Williams, Joe DiMaggio, Stan Musial —all great hitters. You can almost expect them to get two or even three hits off you on lots of days. Some days they won't get any, of course. When they're hitting around .350 as they usually did, it means they are getting base hits off everybody in the league. You just try to keep them from beating you in the ball game.

"There was a little guy named Don Heffner, you remember him, he was an infielder. Man, I think he got 12 hits in a row off of me. Finally it came to the point I said to him once, with nobody on base, 'Don, here it is. You do whatever you want.' And I just took the ball and threw it soft like that for a strike. He was a little guy, you know, and he reared back and hit the ball as hard as he could. It was an easy out. He didn't say anything.

"Next time he came up, the same thing. I said, 'Here it is.' I was just lobbing it in and he had to furnish his own power. Well, he was determined he was going to hit the ball out of the park, but he couldn't. This happened three times, and when he came to bat for the fourth time he was calling me every name he could think of. And so after that I never had any trouble with him.

"But you couldn't do that with guys like Musial, DiMaggio, and Williams. I'll tell you, DiMaggio was the greatest all-around ballplayer I ever saw or played against. And I'm not taking a thing away from Willie Mays or Mickey Mantle or any of those guys. Ted Williams was the greatest hitter I ever saw, and to me Musial was almost on a par with him. I think Stan would swing at a few more bad balls than Ted would.

"With those big guys, you don't want to let 'em beat you. In the last three innings, if I have a four-run lead, I'll lay it in there and make 'em hit it. I won't walk 'em. But in the ninth with a one-run lead, they're going to hit my pitch or else I'll walk 'em and take my chances with the next guy. That's the way I pitched all those years.

"And I loved to pitch against the best—Feller, Ted Lyons, Charlie Root, Gomez. It always brought out the best in me. What a battler Ted Lyons was. He and I fought each other in at least three great games. And all of them lasted only about an hour and 23 minutes each for nine-inning games.

"In one of them we were playing in Washington and I'm the leadoff batter in the last of the ninth with the score 0-0. I think to myself that I've got to get on base somehow. So I laid down a bunt along the third-base line. It stayed fair and I beat it out. Holy cow! Lyons raised the devil and was still talking at me when he pitched to the next batter, who also bunted. And Lyons threw the ball into right field, leaving us on second and third. He walked the next guy purposely and then the following batter hit a long fly to left-center. I tagged up and took off for the plate and scored.

"I didn't stop after crossing the plate, for in the old Washington ball park the little stairs going down to the clubhouse were right near home plate. I heard somebody running right behind me, and it was Lyons. He said, 'You big so-and-so!' I ran right on into the clubhouse and he ran to the door and stopped, just looking in. He couldn't believe what had happened.

"And the next day he came out and we just grinned at each other. He said to me, 'Boy, that really got me. I thought you were going to go for the downs, and then you beat out that little old bunt.' Of course, I didn't care what he called me then. Ted was a really great competitor.

"Talking about fast games, I pitched in one nine-inning

game that was over in 61 minutes. I don't know how these pitchers now can stand out there on the mound so danged long before throwing the ball. Boy, when that batter got up there we were ready to throw. And the batters take even more time than the pitchers. I think the umpires are partly at fault. They could make everybody speed it up."

"How about some of your teammates in Brooklyn?"

"First of all there was Al Lopez, the catcher. Besides being a great catcher, he was a great guy, and he's in the Hall of Fame. Sam Leslie played first base at that time, Jersey Joe Stripp was at third, Tony Cuccinello at second, and Lonny Frey was the shortstop. In the outfield we had Hack Wilson, Johnny Frederick, and Danny Taylor. Watty Clark was a left-handed pitcher, and Van Lingle Mungo could throw as hard as anybody for about six innings. And old Tom Zachary and Ray Benge and Fred Frankhouse were on the pitching staff. Ray Berres was another catcher, and he could pick guys off first base."

"Who were some of the outstanding players with Washington in your time there?"

"Well, Wes Ferrell was with Washington during most of my first season there and he was something, both as a pitcher and as a personality. One time he was pitching against Detroit and we got an early lead of 11-1. Then it started raining in the fourth inning and we had a 20-minute delay. When Wes went back to the mound he walked one and threw a wild pitch and allowed a hit or two before he got the first out. By the time he got the second they had about five runs. On the bench Bucky said, 'Well, he's bound to get this next guy.' And before Bucky could get a reliever in there they had tied the score.

"Ferrell came in and sat on the bench. Nobody said a word, because Wes had a temper, mostly at himself. He had a brand new glove and he took it and tore it right in half. Then he pulled all the stuffing out of the glove and put it all in a little pile and said, 'Wes Ferrell, you dumb so-and-so.' And he went like this and hit himself in the chin. When he did that his head snapped back and hit the back of the dugout with a big pop. And he was out cold. Nobody moved. They didn't dare to. We finally lost that game.

"After the game, in the clubhouse he went over to the little trunk where the players left their watches and valuables during the game. He reached in to get his watch and as he was putting it on it fell to the concrete floor. He just looked down at it and then ground it to pieces with his heel as he said, 'You didn't keep good time anyway.' In those days I didn't even own a watch and it nearly killed me to see him ruin one like that. Wes would get mad at himself, not at anybody else. That's the way he was when he played golf. I've seen him throw bag and everything in the bay down there at Clearwater.

"We had some other good players in Washington too. Zeke Bonura and then Mickey Vernon at first, Buddy Myer at second, Cecil Travis at short, Buddy Lewis on third, and George Case, Sammy West, and Al Simmons in the outfield, with Rick Ferrell doing most of the catching.

"Other pitchers besides Wes and myself were Ken Chase, Sid Hudson, and Joe Haynes. Later we had Early Wynn and Bobo Newsom and those other knuckleballers we mentioned earlier. But those Yankees had too much power, and Boston and Cleveland too. I enjoyed my nine years in Washington. Of course, I was at my peak then.

"Then I had two good years with the Phillies before I was traded to the Cubs for Eddie Waitkus. And the following year the Phillies won the pennant. Of course, I'd never been in a World Series, so I was sorry to have missed it by one year.

"Two years ago they had an Old Timers game in Chicago between the Cubs and Detroit, who played each other in the '45 Series. I went up there and I saw guys from the Detroit team I hadn't seen in 15 years or more. I was messing around and having a lot of fun and finally Charlie Grimm came up and said, 'You're my starting pitcher.' I said, 'What? I've never been on a pennant winner in my life. These other guys have played in World Series.' He repeated, 'You're my starting pitcher.' Darned if I didn't start the game, and we won. I got a big thrill out of that.

"In '49, my first season with the Cubs, Frankie Frisch took over as manager from Charlie Grimm before the end of the year. They were both characters. Sometimes Frisch would be reading a book or something on the bench and then get mad at the umpire and throw the book out on the field. And Charlie was funny just to look at, the way he'd move his hands and everything. He was just meant to be funny. And I think he's a hell of a nice guy."

"Your '49 Cubs team had some good names on the roster but didn't do too much."

"Yeah, Phil Cavarretta, Emil Verban, Andy Pafko, Hank

Sauer, Mickey Owen. I saw Mickey over at Springfield last year when the Cardinals had an Old Timers game there. Rube Walker and Bob Scheffing were the other catchers. Frank Baumholtz was in center field. Roy Smalley was at shortstop. I thought he was going to be real good, but he was one who had rabbit ears and let the fans get to him.

"Among the pitchers we had Johnny Schmitz and Bob Rush. Now Rush was a guy that had the tools. But he was a guy who thought he had to have that high kick. Brooklyn stole four bases off him in one game, and then he came to me and wanted to know what he should do. He was afraid he couldn't get much on the ball if he didn't use his kick. I told him he would get plenty on the ball and the main thing was to get rid of the ball faster. So he won his next two games trying it that way and then he went right back to his old style."

"What about the knuckleball pitchers in the majors today?"

"Well, the Niekro brothers and Charlie Hough are about the only ones I think of at this moment. In '74 I think it was I got to talk to the Niekros. Eddie Matthews was then manager of Atlanta and both Phil and Joe were on his pitching staff. It was spring training and I was down there in Florida.

"When I showed up at the ball park Eddie said, 'Just the guy I want to see.' I said, 'I'm glad to see you too. But what's up?' He said, 'I'd like to have you talk to Phil Niekro and his brother Joe.' I told him, 'Why, I'd be happy to if they want to.' We went into the clubhouse where he introduced me to them. He got three new balls and gave one to each of us and then said, 'You three guys sit down here and discuss the knuckler.'

"We sat there for over an hour and talked about the grip and how you have to move your fingers sometimes a little bit, back or up. Now Phil was afraid to throw the fastball. I told him, 'Your knuckleball makes your fastball better. You've got to throw it, and it'll make your knuckleball more effective.' The next day he shut the Cardinals out and he's been going fine ever since."

"Who were the best players you saw at each position in the majors?"

"At first base I didn't see Gehrig too much, but he was a great one. And Hank Greenberg made himself into a great one. At second I saw Gehringer some and he was great. And Joe Gordon too. Phil Rizzuto and Pee Wee Reese were the best shortstops, though Marty Marion and Joe Cronin were mighty good too. At third, Ken Keltner and Red Rolfe. The outfield would be Musial and Williams and DiMaggio. There were a lot of fine catchers—Bill Dickey, Roy Campanella, Al Lopez, Gabby Hartnett. Lefty Grove and Lefty Gomez for the left-handed pitchers, and Bob Feller for the righthander."

"When you left the majors, what did you do, Dutch?"

"I came back here and started working for the State of Illinois. I was with the Recreation Department and I conducted baseball schools and clinics for kids from 7 to 17 from one end of the state to the other. I conducted about four a week from April to October for 50 to 250 kids. And I'd pitch batting practice for every one of those kids. We started at 9 o'clock in the morning and I'd run straight through. I didn't want two workouts a day. I'd get wringing wet sometimes but boy it felt good.

"The thing was, we'd play game conditions. We'd have a team in the field and I'd pitch. Every kid would get to play his favorite position and get to hit. I had more fun doing that for 18 years. I retired from that not too many years ago. I'd be away from home one or two nights at the most. That would be when I went to Chicago or north of Chicago. If I was working 50 to 60 miles from here, I'd come back home every night, and that was great.

"I used to talk to the kids a lot about staying in condition, getting proper rest, how they could learn baseball by watching games on TV, and about not giving their parents trouble. The parents ate it up, of course. A lot of them told me later that it really helped change the attitude of their kids. I enjoyed it all and met lots of nice people. In fact, I got such a kick out of it that I didn't try to get a coaching job in the majors."

"When you were in the majors, I suppose all the traveling and being away from home so much must have been one of the worst features."

"For me it was. I was a family man. When I went to spring training, especially in the last few years of my career, man, if it wasn't for that telephone I don't know what I would have done. I'd call home two or three times a week and for 15 minutes or so it just seemed like we were together.

"I missed my family, my wife and kids. When I got married I got married for good. On the road when girls would call the room wanting to know if they could come up and see me, I'd say, 'Well, just a minute. I'll ask my wife if it's okay.' End of call. My family was my whole life. And that's the way I feel about it now."

Dutch Leonard was one of the relatively few ballplayers able to perform productively in the major leagues well past the age of 40. In 1953, his final season, he appeared in 45 games as a relief pitcher for the Chicago Cubs at a time when he was already past his 44th birthday. When I talked with him in midsummer of 1982, he seemed trim and strong, though he told me he had had a bit of heart trouble.

Just nine months after we had our pleasant conversation, Dutch Leonard died of congestive heart failure on April 17, 1983 at the age of 74. All who knew him realized that the world had lost a splendid human being who in his younger years had contributed meaningfully to the annals of baseball.

EMIL JOHN LEONARD
BR   TR   6'   175 lbs.
Born in Auburn, Illinois on March 25, 1909
Died April 17, 1983 in Springfield, Illinois

YEAR	TEAM	W	L	PCT.	ERA	G	GS	CG	IP	H	BB	SO	ShO
1933	Brooklyn NL	2	3	.400	2.93	10	3	2	40	42	10	6	0
1934	" "	14	11	.560	3.28	44	20	11	183.2	210	34	58	2
1935	" "	2	9	.182	3.92	43	11	4	137.2	152	29	41	0
1936	" "	0	0	—	3.66	16	0	0	32	34	5	8	0
1938	Washington AL	12	15	.444	3.43	33	31	15	223	221	53	68	3
1939	" "	20	8	.714	3.54	34	34	21	269.1	273	59	88	2
1940	" "	14	19	.424	3.49	35	35	23	289	328	78	124	2
1941	" "	18	13	.581	3.45	34	33	19	256	271	54	91	4
1942	" "	2	2	.500	4.11	6	5	1	35	28	5	15	1
1943	" "	11	13	.458	3.28	31	30	15	219.2	218	46	51	2
1944	" "	14	14	.500	3.06	32	31	17	229.1	222	37	62	3
1945	" "	17	7	.708	2.13	31	29	12	216	208	35	96	4
1946	" "	10	10	.500	3.56	26	23	7	161.2	182	36	62	2
1947	Philadelphia NL	17	12	.586	2.68	32	29	19	235	224	57	103	3
1948	" "	12	17	.414	2.51	34	31	16	225.2	226	54	92	1
1949	Chicago NL	7	16	.304	4.15	33	28	10	180	198	43	83	1
1950	" "	5	1	.833	3.77	35	1	0	74	70	27	28	0
1951	" "	10	6	.625	2.64	41	1	0	81.2	69	28	30	0
1952	" "	2	2	.500	2.16	45	0	0	66.2	56	24	37	0
1953	" "	2	3	.400	4.60	45	0	0	62.2	72	24	27	0
	20 yrs.	191	181	.513	3.25	640	375	192	3218.1	3304	738	1170	30

Terry Moore, masterful centerfielder and captain of the St. Louis Cardinals' 1942 and '46 world champions. Moore, who joined the Gas House Gang in 1935, missed three war seasons. The swift ball hawk once (1939) hit two home runs inside the park in a game at Pittsburgh.
(Photo credit: NBL)

14

Terry Moore

Of the several thousand ballplayers who have made an appearance in the big leagues, the Moore clan is well represented. Remember Joe Moore of the New York Giants? And Wilcy Moore, who had a tremendous rookie season with the Yankees in 1927 as both starter and reliever? And Johnny and Ray and Gene and Barry and Jim and Eddie Moore? To say nothing of Roy and Whitey and Earl and Jim and Dee Moore. And of course there's Donnie, now with the Angels, and Charlie, who gave Milwaukee a strong performance in the '82 World Series.

Terry Moore was a fine centerfielder for the St. Louis Cardinals between 1935 and 1948, with time out for World War II. Like the Sewell brothers and Riggs Stephenson, Terry was born in Alabama, though more than 10 years later. And unlike those three, Terry left Alabama at age 10 and subsequently lost the soft southern accent.

Though he is himself now well past 70, Terry Moore looks and acts a great deal younger. His weight is not too different from what it was in his playing days, and it doesn't take much imagination to see him racing to deep left-center to snare a long drive and squelch a would-be rally. Terry and his wife Pat have been married for 30 years and now live comfortably in their home in Collinsville, a few miles from St. Louis on the Illinois side of the Mississippi River.

"I started playing baseball in the St. Louis municipal league," Terry told me, "and then I was in a semipro league over in Illinois. In 1934 the Cardinals sent me a contract and

175

I joined their Columbus Red Birds club, which was Class AA at that time. We won the pennant and the Little World Series that year. That same year the Cardinals won the real World Series against Detroit.

"I joined the Cardinals in spring training in 1935 and I was lucky enough to stay. And that's how my career began. That was kind of a rough club, you know, the Gas House Gang. Everybody was loyal to each other on that club and when a rookie tried to come in they didn't even look at you.

"A funny thing, they wouldn't let us take batting practice. All the rookies would get out there early in the morning, and we'd pitch to each other and shag the balls. After the rest of the club had their workout during the day we'd stay until almost dark getting in more work. That's the way it was. I said to myself, 'Boy, I'll never be on this club.' But what happens, you know, is if somebody is hurt and you get in there, then if you've got what it takes you've got it made."

"Well," I commented, "you got into 119 games in your first year, and you hit for a .287 average."

"Yeah," Terry replied, "but I broke my leg towards the end and missed the last two weeks of the season. I broke it trying to steal second. I was going down the line as hard as I could and watching the ball to see which side of the bag it was coming in on. All of a sudden I looked down and I was there before I knew it. I hit the bag hard and twisted my ankle and broke a bone. We were on top of the league at that time, but then the Cubs won 21 straight to beat us out for the pennant."

"Do you remember your first game in the majors?"

"Sure, my first game was on a cold day in Chicago, opening day. Lon Warneke was pitching for them and I didn't get any hits. And a long ball to left-center, that I should have caught, I barely missed. I think it cost us the game and Frisch really got on me about it. In fact, I didn't get any hits in that first series, but then we went over to Pittsburgh and I got my first hit, a double. After that I went ahead and started getting settled. But like I said, as a rookie and especially playing with that rough group, you could get into a lot of trouble."

"Would Paul Dean have become as fine a pitcher as Dizzy if he hadn't had arm trouble?"

"Oh, no. Paul never had the good curveball and also he didn't have a change-up. You see, Diz could get every pitch over any time he wanted to. Heck, he was liable to have you 3 and

0 and throw you a change and get it over. Or he'd get you 3 and 2 and throw you a good curveball. Paul was more of a fastball pitcher, and his fastball moved and was just about as good as Dizzy's. But he had only what we call a nickel curve.

"I'll tell you what happened to Paul, and in a way to Diz too. You know, they were always holdouts, and then they'd try to get in shape at the last minute. They would say they were ready, but that's how they ran into trouble, especially Paul. The trouble for Diz started in the '37 All-Star Game when Averill hit him on the big toe with a line drive. And you know, you could never believe Diz. He joined us in Philadelphia after that All-Star Game and he told Frankie, 'I got a sore toe.' He kidded so much that Frisch didn't believe him. So he started pitching and then he began favoring that toe, and that's how he hurt his arm.

"I think the '42 Cardinal club was the best I was with. If the war hadn't come along I feel we could have won maybe six or seven pennants in a row. I left for the service, and Enos Slaughter too, as well as Jimmy Brown, Johnny Beazley, and Ernie White. Beazley hurt his arm in the service, that's what happened to him.

"You see, that's when the big league clubs were playing service teams with big leaguers on them. In spring training in '46 Beazley told me, 'I wasn't really in shape in the service and I'd get out there and they'd start hitting me, and then I'd try to bear down, and along the way something just gave.' He would have been a great pitcher. He was 21-6 in his first year in '42.

"Like I say, but for the war I think the Cardinals would have won the pennant for at least six more years. We had so many great young players then, and we came up with a lot of others in the next few years. Beazley's arm wouldn't have been hurt, nor Ernie White's either. He was in the Battle of the Bulge, pinned down in freezing water, and was never the same after that. And we had several others who saw combat duty in the war—Harry Walker, Murray Dickson, Howard Krist.

"I myself was in the Air Force, a Supply Sergeant with the 6th Air Force Headquarters Squadron in Panama. I had my regular duty as Supply Sergeant and then during the baseball season they put me in special service for the team. They play baseball down there during the winter, for two months. I spent more than three years in the service."

"After the great year in '42, the Cards went on to take the

pennant again in '43, '44, and '46, and the only year they lost the World Series was in '43," I remarked.

"Well, the '42 team was the best I played on. Stan Musial, Johnny Beazley, Whitey Kurowski were all rookies, and Mort Cooper was in his second year. They were all young boys, and I was the captain and the oldest of the regulars. I could see early in the year what a terrific club it was becoming, and we were red hot coming down the stretch. On the last day of the season we played a doubleheader and had to win one of them to beat Brooklyn, which we did. The Dodgers won 104 games that year, but we won 106.

"Of course, the Yankees had a great club that year, too. They had people like Dickey, DiMaggio, Keller, Rizzuto, Gordon, Crosetti, and Henrich, plus Ruffing, Chandler, Bonham, and Borowy on their pitching staff. Ruffing beat Mort Cooper in the first game but then we won four straight, with Beazley getting two of the wins. They couldn't believe it.

"Connie Mack saw the Series and said, 'I have to take my hat off to the Cardinals. They played the game the way it ought to be played. They took advantage of everything and didn't give anything. I think that's the greatest club I've ever seen.' That '42 World Series was my biggest thrill in baseball.

"After the war when I came back for spring training in 1946 I banged up my left knee, and I was in and out of the lineup all season. So I played in that '46 Series with shots of cortisone to kind of deaden it. I played all seven games. Then after that I had it operated on. But I wasn't the same player when I came back from the service. Maybe I could have been if it hadn't been for the knee. If I had been younger, like Slaughter and Musial, maybe I could have come back the same. And those years I was in the service should have been my best ones.

"In 1946 that fellow Jorge Pasquel down in Mexico was luring big league players to go and play in the Mexican League for more money. He got Freddy Martin, Lou Klein, and Max Lanier from our team, and he tried to get Musial, Slaughter, and myself. He offered me almost as much as he did them, but I said, 'No way. I'm about through and I'm not leaving here.' And I said to Musial, 'You've got a great career in front of you. You and Slaughter would be crazy to go. You'll make more money in time up here. Forget it. It looks good now but you've got years to play.'

"And they did make better money after the war, when TV

came in. Mr. Breadon called me in after he heard about the whole thing and talked with me about it. Then he went down to Mexico and talked with Pasquel, and after that they never did try to get any more of our players. Breadon gave me $1,000 because I had discouraged Slaughter and Musial from going. Before that, every time we went into New York to play, the Pasquel agents would get hold of us. Remember, they got Sal Maglie, Vern Stephens, and Mickey Owen, among others."

"Tell me about Pepper Martin."

"Well, I'll tell you about him. He was an exciting ball-player. We don't have many of that kind today. Pete Rose would be about the only one who would compare to Pepper in that regard. Pepper was a good base stealer. But I'd like to see him run the bases today like he did then, and every time he ran he'd dig up about six inches of dirt when he took off. I wish I could see him run on this Astroturf where you don't lose any footing at all.

"Pepper was the kind of fellow that sportswriters would love to have around these days. Now Pepper and Diz, they were two characters. You never knew what they were going to do. On the field Pepper was always bearing down. He wasn't the greatest fielder, you know, but he had a great arm. Off the field he was really a character.

"In 1936 we were in Philadelphia when the Democratic Convention was going on in the Bellevue-Stratford. We didn't start games then until about 3:30 in the afternoon, so we all sat around in the morning with a lot of time to kill. So one morning Pepper and Rip Collins and Heinie Schuble and Dizzy Dean went to some hardware store and bought white coveralls and painters' caps and tools and things. The rest of us didn't know anything about it.

"At about noontime we saw them go through the lobby, dressed in those things and carrying their equipment. First they went into a little room off the lobby where there was a group of women meeting. They didn't have air conditioning yet in those days, and so there were oscillating fans on the walls.

"They told the manager, who didn't recognize them, that they were air conditioning people sent to find out if air ducts could be installed. To do this they would have to take the fan down from the wall in the room where the ladies were meeting. They took it down and put it right in the middle of the table, and then they left, saying they would be back soon.

"The next stop was the kitchen, where they posed as government inspectors. They started looking at pots and pans and threw a lot of them on the floor, saying they didn't meet the standards. The chef came running out of the kitchen towards the front desk. So they left and went downstairs where there was a barber shop.

"They told the head barber they were sent to find out where they could put ducts for air conditioning. They told him, 'We're going to have to move that chair over there.' A guy was stretched out in the chair getting a shave, but the four of them got down and lifted the chair with him in it and put it over in the corner. Then they left, saying as they did, 'Well, we'll be right back.'

"Then they went upstairs to where the convention was going on, with someone talking into a microphone. They dropped a ladder on the stage and did a lot of moving back and forth. All this time the speaker was trying to go on with his talk. Finally, someone recognized them and then the whole hotel was in an uproar.

"Other times Pepper would get some sneezing powder, roll it up in a paper, and then walk through the lobby, letting most of it escape as he did so. Then he'd go up to the mezzanine and watch everybody sneezing like crazy down below.

"Another thing he would do is to get some of those small bombs that jokesters attach to a spark plug in a car to make an explosive noise. In the evening when some fancy affair would be scheduled at the hotel, big cars would pull up in front with a chauffeur who would get out and escort the lady up the steps to the entrance. Some of us would stop the chauffeur on his way back and start asking him for directions to different places. That's when Pepper would put one of his bombs on the guy's car. When Pepper would come walking past us a few minutes later, we would thank the chauffeur and let him go on back to the car. He would get in, start up the motor, and right away there would be this big noise with lots of smoke. And the chauffeur would leap out and dash off looking for the police while we went on our way.

"I remember one time when we were in Boston and it was hot. But I mean hot! By then we were playing night ball, just a few games a year. So Pepper and Diz got some Indian blankets and went out by third base and built a fire, and they sat there by the fire smoking these big old pipes. Nobody had more fun than Pepper and Diz.

"Pepper and Rip Collins and Jack Rothrock had a game they played, flipping the ball back and forth with lots of acrobatics. They would always put that show on, and people came out early to watch them. While the other team was taking batting practice, they would be in front of our dugout putting on this pepper game. The people would be screaming, and heck, I watched it every day myself. The fans really enjoyed Pepper. I never did hear anybody boo him as long as I played with him.

"Towards the end of his career they moved Pepper to third base. But he hated to play third. Once we were in Boston while Casey Stengel was the manager and Buddy Hassett was the first baseman. Before the game Pepper walked over in front of the Boston dugout and said, 'If any of you guys bunt toward me today, I'm going to throw the ball right at you.'

"Sure enough, when Hassett came to bat he bunted down toward Pepper, who came in and did just like he said he would. He threw it right at Buddy, who was sort of watching as he ran to first base. Hassett got out of the way of it and Pepper's throw caromed on into right field. A run or two scored on the play, but we did come back to win the game. The thing is, nobody else bunted on Pepper that day.

"Once we played an exhibition game in Metuchen, New Jersey, where they put lights up on ladders. I was young and could see better than some of the others. But I thought it was really hard to see. Pepper was in right field and he had a hard time catching the ball anyway. He had missed one or two balls in the first few innings before someone hit one up toward right. I ran over close to him and all of a sudden Pepper pulled a flashlight out of his hip pocket to look for the ball. Where he got the flashlight I'll never know. You just never knew what to expect out of him.

"And Frankie Frisch was a character too. When we played in New York or Brooklyn, Frisch always wanted to get the game over quick, so he could go home to where he lived in that area. One time it was drizzling rain and we were ahead. Frisch kept hollering at the umpires because it was raining and he wanted the game called off. All of a sudden we look out at Frisch, who was coaching at third, and there he was under an umbrella! The umpire ran him out of the game.

"Another time we were in New York and Bill Klem was the umpire in charge. In the very first inning Frisch started a big fuss with Klem over a pitch that Frisch took and Klem called a strike. Frisch argued and spit on him and everything, but Klem just spit right back and then said, 'I don't give a damn what you call me, Frisch. You're going to stay right here and play nine innings.' "

"But Frisch was a good manager, wasn't he?" I asked.

"Yes, but I don't think he would be any good at managing the players of today."

"Oh, no," I agreed. "Very few of the old managers could. John McGraw would be a disaster today."

"Right," said Terry. "In the old days the manager always made more money than the players. Today the players make so much more than the manager that some of them sort of look down on him. You can't believe how much the players make now, especially when you look at the averages. In the old days you had to hit about .270 or so to stay in the league. Today if they hit .250 they want hundreds of thousands of dollars. And when some of these guys get the fabulous contracts they think they're all-time superstars.

"Yesterday I was in Busch Stadium because those of us still around from the '42 team were being honored. Besides myself, the others who attended were Stan Musial, Enos Slaughter, Marty Marion, and Creepy Crespi. They had us come out on the field and they introduced us, you know, and then while sitting on the bench I couldn't believe the way things are now.

"Speaking of the old-style managers not being able to handle it today, remember that Eddie Stanky found out in one game in 1977 that he wasn't up to it. He took over the Texas Rangers in the middle of the season, and after winning one game he quit and went home."

"Terry, what do you remember most about the 1946 World Series against the Red Sox?"

"Well, I think the thing most people remember best is Enos Slaughter scoring all the way from first on Walker's hit in the bottom of the eighth in the last game. Nobody on the Red Sox seemed to think that Slaughter would try to score and that's why no one helped Johnny Pesky handle the relay, and when he saw what was happening his throw to the plate was too late. That gave us a 5-4 lead and cinched the Series. The Sox scared us in the ninth, though, when the first two batters singled, but

Brecheen held on to retire them without damage. And that was Harry's third win in the Series, you know.

"We really were the underdogs in that Series. We had to beat Brooklyn in a playoff before getting to the Series. So we had good momentum going, while Boston had been sitting around for a number of days. The Red Sox really had a much better team than we did, but we won the Series. It was an experience for us, playing in Fenway."

"What would you call your best game in baseball?"

"I remember that in my rookie year I had a game when I was six-for-six, which tied the record at that time for most hits in a nine-inning game."

"You were on hand for the dedication of the Baseball Hall of Fame in Cooperstown in 1935."

"Right," said Terry. "They had two players from each club, and Medwick and I represented the Cardinals. For the exhibition game Babe Ruth managed one team and Dizzy Dean the other, and they chose up sides after going through the old custom of gripping the bat one hand over the other to see who got first choice. That was really a sight, all of those great old players.

"Cooperstown is a beautiful little town, especially in the summer. It's kind of hard to get there. You can't do it by train, you have to drive there. I've played there two other times in the annual game when they induct new players into the Hall of Fame. They have a pretty little ball park right near downtown."

"Comment on the managers you played under."

"I'll tell you, Frisch was a tough one to work with. Ray Blades was one who helped popularize using relief pitchers a lot. He had good success with it in '39, but we were going bad in '40 so they let him go and brought in Billy Southworth. He was good to play for and managed well, but I would have to say that Eddie Dyer was the best.

"Dyer looked out for the players more, and he played a better percentage game. Until he got there we had to take care of our own luggage. When he came in he got that taken care of. And we used to have to pay our own way to the ball park, and he got buses to take us there and back. That was a big help for us, since we weren't making a lot of money, you know. Little things like that were much appreciated. So we went out and won it all for him in 1946."

"What did you do after you finished your playing days in '46?"

"For six seasons between '47 and '52 I was a coach with the Cardinals. I started scouting for the Phillies in 1953 and they brought me in to manage the team in the last half of the '54 season after they let Steve O'Neill go. Then I had some bowling alleys for a time until I came back as a coach with the Cardinals in 1955. Frank Lane asked me to come back. During my years as a coach I worked under several Cardinal managers—Eddie Dyer, Marty Marion, Eddie Stanky, Fred Hutchinson, and Harry Walker."

"Who was the toughest pitcher for you to hit?"

"You know, all those guys who threw the high fastball that took off were tough. But if I had to choose the toughest guy to hit, it was Hubbell, and he was a lefthander. Whitlow Wyatt was tough on me, and a guy named Bill Swift. You see, I had a hard time in the beginning hitting a high ball, until I finally learned to go to right field with it. I had been trying to pull that high ball and I was popping it up. When I started going to the opposite field they stopped pitching me high and came down with it. And they wouldn't throw me any curveballs because I was a low ball hitter. So that's how I changed in my hitting style as time went on.

"I liked to hit nearly all the lefthanders. Even Vander Meer, as great as he was, I got my hits off him. He had that great curveball and was fast. The only lefthander I didn't like was that doggoned Hubbell. He seemed to know what you were looking for.

"If I had my choice of pitchers for one ball game we had to win, I'd have to take Hubbell. Even if it was a game between him and Dizzy, he'd beat Diz. I'd take Hubbell over any pitcher I've ever seen, that's how good I thought he was. Of course, I never saw pitchers like Walter Johnson and other early great ones, but of the ones I've seen it's Hubbell.

"The trouble with Diz was that you couldn't keep him serious enough. And he was liable to throw a big fat one up there just because he liked you. He was that kind of guy. But, boy, that Hubbell, when he walked out there he was serious.

"The reason Hubbell's style didn't bother me too much when I first came into the league was that in the minors I had hit against a fellow named Garland Braxton. He was the same type of pitcher that Hubbell was, and he had a good screwball but not as fast. So when I first faced Hubbell I knew pretty much what to expect. But still I couldn't hit him much. I hit one home run off him, and I kind of fooled him on that one.

"It was in the Polo Grounds and I decoyed him by leaning way over like I was looking for the screwball. When he threw I stretched way back, and he still got the ball in on my trademark. I got hold of it and just hit the tip of the upper stands that jutted out in right field, and it fell down and I had a home run.

"When Don Gutteridge first came into the league in '36 he was hitting the ball good when we went into New York to play the Giants. We told him that when Hubbell's screwball came in it always looked like a strike but often it wasn't. The first pitch that Hubbell threw him, Don swung and missed it a mile because it was way away outside. Then Hubbell wasted one before coming back with the screwball. Don again swung with all he had and missed it bad. Another waste pitch and then came the third screwball. Don swung straight down trying to hit it, and we all fell off the bench laughing, because it was funny to watch somebody who had never hit at it.

"One day in New York Frisch wasn't playing, and I came up against Hub with the bases loaded. He threw me two pretty good screwballs that I fouled off, and then he wasted a fastball in close. I thought, 'Well, he's setting me up for that scroogie' and so I moved up on the plate a little bit. When the pitch came in it looked bad and I just stood there, and darned if it wasn't a little old curve that broke in right over the corner of the plate. Frisch stormed around because I took the third called strike.

"Late in the game we were one or two runs down and we got men on second and third. So Frisch put himself in as a pinch hitter. And he did exactly the same thing I did. Back in the clubhouse he said, 'I've got a lot of guts getting on you.' He was an old pro, so he admitted that it wasn't so easy after all.

"In my time there were lots of good righthanders. Paul Derringer, Bucky Walters, Lon Warneke, Hal Schumacher, Charlie Root, Freddie Fitzsimmons, Guy Bush. They were all over the league. Boy, we had some tough pitchers, compared to what they have today. They were mean out there, too. And we didn't have those helmets they wear now. Oh, yes, another one we left out was Van Lingle Mungo. He was great too.

"But overall I guess I'd say that the best righthander I saw was Bob Feller. He and Mungo were the same type of pitcher, and both came up with a real good curveball. We played an exhibition game against Cleveland in '35, my first year, in old League Park and Feller pitched. I went up to the plate and Steve O'Neill, who was catching, said, 'Now be a little careful. This kid can throw hard but he's a little wild.' I thought to myself, 'Well, I'm a rookie and he's just trying to scare me.' Boy, when he threw that thing it was hard! No curve or anything. Just speed!

"He pitched three innings and I think he struck out seven. Ogrodowski and I were the only ones who got hits, and mine went to right field. At that time I had never hit a ball to right field, so that tells you how fast he was throwing because I couldn't get around on it. I hit against him later in St. Louis, after he had got that real good curveball, and he struck me out. The third strike was that curve, and when it broke over the plate I was already flat on my back. And I wasn't the only one."

"Who were the best players at each position in the National League during your playing career?"

"Bill Terry would be the first baseman, although Dolf Camilli and Charlie Grimm were probably better in the field. At second base I like Billy Herman, and shortstop either Marty Marion or PeeWee Reese. At third I'd have to go with Pie Traynor, although Travis Jackson played a great third base after he moved over from shortstop. And Paul Waner, Lloyd Waner, Stan Musial, Enos Slaughter, and Mel Ott in the outfield. Medwick was a terrific hitter but not too much in the field. There were several good catchers. Walker Cooper, Gabby Hartnett, Jimmy Wilson, Harry Danning, and Ernie Lombardi. Even if Ernie couldn't run, he was a great hitter. Hubbell for the left-handed pitcher, and any of those righthanders I mentioned a while ago. That would be a pretty tough team to beat."

That's for sure!

TERRY BLUFORD MOORE
BR   TR   5'11"   195 lbs.
Born in Vernon, Alabama on May 27, 1912

YEAR	TEAM	G	AB	R	H	RBI	2B	3B	HR	BB	SO	SB	AVG.
1935	St. Louis NL	119	456	63	131	53	34	3	6	15	40	13	.287
1936	" " "	143	590	85	156	47	39	4	5	37	52	9	.264
1937	" " "	115	461	76	123	43	17	3	5	32	41	13	.267
1938	" " "	94	312	49	85	21	21	3	4	46	19	9	.272
1939	" " "	130	417	65	123	77	25	2	17	43	38	6	.295
1940	" " "	136	537	92	163	64	33	4	17	42	44	18	.304
1941	" " "	122	493	86	145	68	26	4	6	52	31	3	.294
1942	" " "	130	489	80	141	49	26	3	6	56	26	10	.288
1946	" " "	91	278	32	73	28	14	1	3	18	26	0	.263
1947	" " "	127	460	61	130	45	17	1	7	38	39	1	.283
1948	" " "	91	207	30	48	18	11	0	4	27	12	0	.232
	11 yrs.	1298	4700	719	1318	513	263	28	80	406	368	82	.280

WORLD SERIES

YEAR	TEAM	G	AB	R	H	RBI	2B	3B	HR	BB	SO	SB	AVG.
1942	St. Louis NL	5	17	2	5	2	1	0	0	2	3	0	.294
1946	" " "	7	27	1	4	2	0	0	0	2	6	0	.148
	2 yrs.	12	44	3	9	4	1	0	0	4	9	0	.205

Records are made to be broken, but Johnny Vander Meer's feat of pitching two consecutive no-hit games is likely to remain unchallenged. Accomplished against the Boston Braves on June 11, 1938 and the Brooklyn Dodgers on June 15, Vander Meer's amazing magic on the mound thrilled the baseball world. Eleven of his 13 years in the big leagues were spent with Cincinnati. Although his won-lost record was 119-121, his no-hit gems assured him a place of prominence in baseball annals.

15

Johnny Vander Meer

There are books offering compilations of baseball records honoring unusual accomplishments in a single inning, a game, a season, and an entire career. They cover batting, pitching, and fielding records by individuals and by teams.

But baseball's greatest records, the ones least likely to be eclipsed, are few indeed. Close analysts of the game, in terms of the "unbreakable" records, generally think of Joe DiMaggio's 56-game hitting streak, Cy Young's 513 wins, Lou Gehrig's 2,130 consecutive games played, Hack Wilson's 190 RBIs in 1930, Hank Aaron's 755 home runs, Walter Johnson's 113 shutouts, Grover Alexander's 16 shutouts in 1916, Joe Sewell's four strikeouts in 155 games in 1925 or his 115 games without striking out in 1929, and Johnny Vander Meer's two consecutive no-hitters in 1938.

A look at that list tells us that most of these achievements were the fruit of many seasons of superior performance. Others were accomplished during all or a considerable portion of a single season. But Vander Meer's feat is the only "unbreakable" mark established in the span of five short days. This is what stamps it as a unique record.

John Samuel Vander Meer, of Dutch ancestry, was born in New Jersey on November 2, 1914. He reached the majors with the Cincinnati Reds in 1937 when he was still only 22. Johnny was first signed by the Brooklyn Dodgers and spent a few years in the minors before making it to the big time.

"The Dodgers sent me first to Dayton, Ohio," recalls Johnny. "A little later I was in a cover-up deal while I was in

189

Scranton, and I was put before Judge Landis. He awarded me to the Scranton ball club and I played there for another year. I was picked up by the Boston Braves in the fall of '35 and then traded that winter for a bunch of ballplayers that were at Nashville. Nashville optioned me to Durham, where Frank Lane was the business manager. It was a Reds' farm and from there I was bought by the Reds."

In his first season with Cincinnati Vander Meer posted a 3-5 record but allowed just 63 hits in 84 innings. He was optioned to Syracuse after the All-Star game and then recalled before season's end.

The '38 season started well for Johnny and on Saturday afternoon, June 11, he went to the mound to face the Boston Braves. Nine innings later he had entered the record book by hurling a 3-0 no-hit game in Cincinnati's old Crosley Field.

"I had a pretty good sinker that day," he says. "I wasn't real quick, didn't have my real good stuff, but it was one of my few days I had control. I think there were only about five fly-balls in that game. They were hitting the ball into the ground.

"I didn't go for a no-hitter till the ninth inning. In that way I didn't put pressure on myself. And I had a bit of philosophy about the last inning. I liked to finish anything I started, and I'd get to the ninth inning and say to myself, 'You've got 20 good pitches left.' I'd start counting with 20, then 19, and so on. Waite Hoyt did this and that's how I picked it up. That gave me a bit of incentive in the last inning that I pushed myself with."

Vander Meer's next start was against the Brooklyn Dodgers on June 15. As it happened, it was the first night game ever played in Ebbets Field. He shut out the Dodgers, 6-0, and again—amazingly—allowed no hits. Recently he was asked if any Dodger came close to getting a hit.

"The only close call, I'd say, in both ball games was when Buddy Hassett of the Dodgers hit a line drive back through the box that I knocked down, and I had to scurry a little bit to pick it up and throw him out. That was probably the toughest ball to handle in either of the two ball games."

The baseball world, properly excited when he hurled his first no-hitter, was positively electrified when he duplicated the feat in his very next start. And why not? Consider the astronomical odds.

Since the beginning of the so-called modern period of baseball in 1901, the majors have seen fewer than 200 no-hit games, for an average of less than three per season. In that time thousands of pitchers have taken the mound, ranging from only one appearance to nearly 700 starts, but barely 130 have ever recorded a no-hitter. While a small number can point to two no-hit games, there are only four who have gone beyond that: Nolan Ryan with five, Sandy Koufax with four, and Bob Feller and Jim Maloney with three each. Other than Vander Meer, the only hurlers to notch two no-hitters in the same year are Allie Reynolds (1951), Virgil Trucks (1952), Maloney (1965), and Ryan (1973).

Vander Meer even started his next game as if he meant to go for a third straight no-hitter. He went along for three and two thirds innings in spotless fashion before Debs Garms of the Braves broke it up with a single. Asked if his string of 21⅔ hitless innings in a row is a record, Johnny said:

"For successive innings it is. I think Cy Young has the record of 23, but they came in four or five relief appearances. Incidentally in the game prior to my first no-hitter I had a three-hitter. I gave up two hits in the first inning to the Giants and shut 'em out. In the ninth inning Hank Lieber came up to pinch hit. I jammed him inside and he blooped the ball just behind Lonnie Frey at second for a base hit. If it hadn't been for that sloppy hit of Hank's I would have had over three full games without giving up a hit.

"Well, records are made to be broken. I look at my record as not likely to be broken, because I don't think anyone is going to pitch three no-hit games in a row or pitch three and two thirds innings beyond a second no-hitter."

Vander Meer finished the 1938 season with a 15-10 record. "I could have had a lot better year than 15-10," he says, "had I not been lying in the hospital for a month. I had seven boils in one ear and six in the other. I was out for a month and lost about 15 pounds. They didn't know much about treating boils inside the ear then, and all I could do was put heat lamps on them. Today they have antibiotics. But there weren't any anti-biotics before the War."

Nineteen thirty eight saw the Reds move up to a strong fourth place finish following their dismal effort of the previous season in which they landed in the basement, 40 games off the pace. The '38 resurgence was the prelude to two straight pennants and was triggered by the arrival of Bill McKecknie as manager.

"Bill came to us in '38," recalls Vander Meer. "He was a great manager. The greatest—well, in my era I guess I'd have to pick McCarthy, Terry, and McKechnie. Bill was an outstanding defensive manager. He wasn't much of an offensive manager because he never had a club where he could be one.

"Bill got Lonny Frey and Wally Berger, and Frank McCormick became a regular in '38. And of course Bucky Walters joined us on the day of my·second no-hitter. It was June 15, the trading deadline. All of that changed our club. And by the next year Bill Werber took over at third base.

"McKechnie was the best manager I played for. He was a great handler of pitchers, and he loved pitchers to give him nine innings. He would put you on a system of starting every so many days, and we started regardless of who we were playing. He got you on that rotation, he got your system going, and he stayed with it."

In 1939 and 1940 the Cincinnati Reds were the National League champions, losing to the Yankees in four games in '39 and beating the Tigers in seven the next year. But Johnny Vander Meer played little part in those heroics. He was 5-9 in '39 and 3-1 in '40, the victim once again of tough luck.

"I pulled my arm just before the 4th of July in 1939 in Pittsburgh on a wet field. The game was held up and I went back to the mound after the rain. My front foot slipped and I tore my back up. I was very fortunate that I didn't tear a throwing muscle, a power muscle, so to speak. I tore up a follow-through muscle and I could probably pitch with about two and a half weeks of rest. That follow-through muscle would then relax. If I threw too much it would act up again. So I was fortunate and was able to pitch for years afterward.

"That's why I went to Indianapolis. It's been said that I went over there because I was wild, but that wasn't the reason, for I had a couple of options left on me. In fact, I could have been optioned out of the big leagues when I left there. So I went to Indianapolis to get my arm straightened out. I threw a one-hitter over there. Would have been a no-hitter but for a freak. A left-handed hitter hit the third base bag and the ball bounced up in the air for a base hit.

"I came back to be eligible for the '40 Series, and that's when I won my three ball games. In fact, I won the game that clinched the pennant in Philadelphia. I had to go 13 innings to win it. I beat Hugh Mulcahy. In the 13th I hit a double, tagged up and went to third on a fly, and came in on a squeeze play. Then McKechnie took me out and Joe Beggs finished the ball game.

"That was one of the highlights of my career, because I went 12 innings and I was just as strong in the 12th as I was in the first. At that point I knew my shoulder was fully restored, and that meant as much to me as a World Series."

In 1941 Vander Meer had a good season at 16-13, with six shutouts and a 2.82 ERA, but the Reds finished third in the standings behind the Dodgers and the Cardinals.

"After those two pennant-winning years," says Johnny, "the Reds went down. I was never on a good ball club again. Actually, I never pitched on a really good ball club. In '39 the Reds won 51 games by one run and came back with 49 one-run wins in '40. We were a one-run ball club. As Joe Beggs would say if we got a run in the first inning, 'Brother, there's your lead and go hold 'em.' We lacked one more good hitter to win games by two or three runs, for they could pitch around Ernie Lombardi."

Johnny's career was further interrupted by military service in 1944 and 1945. He went into the Navy and served at Sampson Naval Training Center in New York and in different places in the Pacific. One of his disappointments is that he lost two years because of a pulled muscle and two more due to the War, though he says he never regretted serving his country.

"I wanted to go to Great Lakes Naval Training Station when I entered the service," he says. "But they stopped that stuff of everybody going to Great Lakes. So I ended up at Sampson. I managed the ball club there. I booked all the games and brought big league clubs in there. Until then they had only played minor league clubs.

"And then I went to Honolulu and played in the Army-Navy World Series. After that Series was over we went on tour of the Pacific for about a month. Then they split us up and scattered us all over the Pacific. I stayed at Guam.

"We played in dungarees and heavy shirts to sweat, and we played everybody who wanted to play us. We didn't care who they were—Sea Bees or maybe a team off a ship. We did this the year around and on Sunday afternoons we'd mostly play the base hospitals."

Vander Meer's best year after the war was 1948 when he logged a 17-14 record. In 1950 he went to the Chicago Cubs and then finished up a brief stay with the Cleveland Indians, with Al Lopez as his manager.

"They had a great pitching staff in Cleveland at that time," Johnny remembers. "That was the greatest staff I ever saw. We had quite a staff at Cincinnati, you know, when Walters and Derringer and I got together. But Cleveland had four—Feller, Wynn, Lemon, and Garcia. They threw great pitches and had a great winning attitude. With them, after two hits in a row, any one of the four would deck the next guy. Great pitching."

After his playing career ended in 1951, Vander Meer managed teams for a number of years in the Reds' farm system. This took him to such places as Douglas, Georgia; Daytona, Florida; Burlington, Iowa; Topeka, Kansas; Tampa; and Syracuse.

In the meantime he had established his home in Tampa, and in the off-season he worked for Joseph Schlitz Brewing Company. By the mid 1960s he left baseball and went with Schlitz full-time, retiring finally 10 years ago.

"Baseball was good to me," says Vander Meer. "It gave me my start, and I got my second start basically through baseball. So I'll never knock it. But I want to see the day that Ernie Lombardi gets in the Hall of Fame."

This is a very sore point with Johnny. "If there's anything in baseball that I don't understand" he says, "it's why isn't Ernie Lombardi in the Hall of Fame? He's the only catcher in the history of the game that led the league twice in hitting. And another thing. Lombardi goes down with Black Mike Cochrane in throwing. And that's the best there is. And Lombardi never let anybody run without his throwing the ball.

"Another thing that Lombardi was great for was that he was a sidearm thrower. I saw a lot of good catchers sit back there and call for fastballs if they knew somebody was running. I don't care who was running or what the game situation was, Lom was just as apt to call for a curveball because he came out of there throwing. If he was down low, he came out throwing sidearm. And he would pick about five to seven guys a year off first throwing sidearm behind left-handed hitters. Great thrower. Like I say, I want to see the day that he gets in the Hall of Fame. And I'll be there in person when he does."

Vander Meer feels strongly that one of the weaknesses in baseball today is that so few catchers can really throw well. "Carter's a good one," he admits. "But I saw Cochrane throw, I saw Hartnett and he was a good one, Dickey was a good thrower, and Ferrell too. There were several. Walker Cooper was a good thrower. Campanella was another one. But Ernie Lombardi was a great one. There weren't any better than Lombardi.

"A great throwing catcher has got to come out of there firing. He's got to have a good arm and he's got to have accuracy. I watch games on TV now and the catcher's throw is over here one time and over there the next, and somewhere else the time after that. Of course, it helps a lot to have a good tagger down there. Lonnie Frey was a great tagger and so was Billy Herman. Now they just swipe that ball in there and half the time they don't touch 'em. If the throw beats you, you're out. Should be. But the throws aren't there."

Asked to identify the best all-around ballplayer he saw, Johnny had to ponder a bit before picking his man, that is, Stan the Man.

"I would say that in my day I'd lean toward Musial. One reason I do is the fact that he could play two positions. Not too many great ballplayers can play two positions. Joe DiMaggio couldn't. He tried it. Ted Williams couldn't do it. But Stan came in from left field to play just as well at first base.

"And Stan was never given credit for his ability to score from first base. He was a great base runner. He didn't steal bases, but when he took off he could run those bases, from second to home, from first to third, first to home. So he did a few other things besides hit that ball."

Vander Meer willingly gave his recollections of a few other well-known major leaguers of his day.

"Ewell Blackwell was the greatest right-handed pitcher I ever saw. I'm not kidding. You ask any right-handed hitter that played against Blackwell and they'll tell you they wanted no part of him. He had motion, he'd look one way and throw the other way. Fantastic stuff.

"He was 6'6" and cross-fired, and that's what caught up with Blacky. He did too much cross-firing and threw against the body. He didn't have to do this but he delighted in doing it. And he wasn't a bull. He had a long, tall, thin type of build. But I'll say this. If Ewell Blackwell could have pitched at his best for 12 to 14 years there would have been some new records in the book.

"Hank Sauer played for us at Syracuse. He was out of our farm system. He had a fantastic year at Syracuse but he couldn't get going with us. We traded him to the Cubs and he had some good years with them.

"When Ted Kluzewski came up he was not a good ballplayer. He was a big fellow and he couldn't pull the ball. He was a left-field hitter, but he worked at it and got to where he could pull. After about three years Ted became a good hitter, though he left a good bit to be desired in fielding, particularly when he first came up.

"Ken Raffensberger had about the best velocity that any pitcher ever had in the big leagues. You had to get to him in the first inning or he would go all nine innings. He didn't get knocked out in the fifth or the seventh or the eighth. He was a spot pitcher, and if he couldn't hit that spot he was in trouble.

"The year I was with Cleveland Al Rosen had a real good year. Basically, he was the real threat on our ball club, as far as consistency goes. Al was an aggressive player who was with them six or seven years, and he was a good one.

"Larry Doby was there, but he was up and down. Sometimes Doby was probably outhustling himself, even in the outfield. He would run past flyballs. Even with his great speed he wasn't a good outfielder.

"You already know how much I thought of Lombardi. But there was a funny incident one day involving him and me. I was pitching a game one day in St. Louis. Pepper Martin was on third base with two out. He was a great base runner and hustler. A Pete Rose type of ballplayer. He was prancing up and down as I cut one loose to the plate. I was known to be a little wild. The ball was outside and Lombardi just reached out there with that big hand of his and caught it barehanded and threw it back to me. On the next pitch the batter popped up and the inning was over.

"I came back to the bench and said to Lombardi, 'Listen, Lom, if you don't start rubbing after catching me barehanded, the manager's going to think I'm losing my stuff and take me out of there. So at least rub your hand a little bit.' "

"Johnny," I said, "it seems you hit only one home run in

the majors, in 1948 when Bucky Walters was managing the Reds. Tell me about it."

"Well, there's a little story to that. Bucky and I were very close. And he was a good hitter. I saw him win 27 games in '39 and he won a number of them with his own bat. I was a good base runner and now and then was used as a pinch runner.

"After Bucky became manager he said to me, 'You may run for me, but you'll never hit for me. If you ever hit a home run I'll leave the ball park. So I hit one over the scoreboard, which was 385 feet to the base of it, off of pitcher Red Barrett. I came around third base and Bucky said he'd leave the ball park and he'd buy the champagne. And that night he did."

Asked about travel by train in his day, Vander Meer had some definite opinions.

"I think that's where we had an edge in my time. When we went on the road, we'd normally pull out at midnight, get a good night's sleep, pull in about 8 A.M. and go to the hotel and have breakfast. Of course, we didn't travel in those days to the West Coast, for that was before expansion.

"Today they play the game usually at night and leave the airport anywhere from 1 to 2 A.M., and arrive anywhere from 3 to 6. They try to rest during the day, and that's not easy. I think we got more rest.

"And we were together more. We always ran around together. You ran with your roommate. You stayed with your roommate, you knew where he was and he knew where you were. And the manager knew. Aw, we had a few guys who didn't, you know, you have a few like Hack Wilson or somebody. There's always a couple of them. And we had a lot of fun playing ball."

With regard to baseball today, Vander Meer doesn't like the designated hitter rule, he has no strong feelings either way about artificial surfaces, and he believes that night games and night travel make it harder on the players today as compared with the day ball and train travel of his time. Free agency he blames largely on the owners themselves. "I don't blame anybody for getting as much as they can get," he says, "whether he's working in an automobile factory or anywhere else."

But concerning expansion and the 25-player limit, Johnny has some very definite ideas. "I don't agree with the 25-player limit," he asserts. "In my day the limit was 21. And most clubs carried 20. I think that's the burden of the big leagues and of the owners today. They've got tremendously high prices with utility ballplayers getting $400,000 or $500,000 sitting there on the bench and hitting .165. Left-handed and right-handed pinch hitters, specialty base runners, McKechnie kept two catchers and we stayed at 20 players most of the season, because if someone got hurt we could bring up a key player from the Triple A club overnight."

Vander Meer is persuaded that expansion from 16 to 26 clubs in the majors has lowered the overall quality. It wouldn't have been possible at all, he is convinced, without the influx of black and Hispanic players in the past few decades. He feels that any further expansion can be done only by a return to the 21-player limit and letting the new franchise take four players from each ball club to create an experienced nucleus for the new teams.

When asked if the two no-hitters were his biggest thrill in baseball, Vander Meer offers a bit of a surprise.

"I think my biggest thrill was having the right skills to get to be a big league ballplayer. When I finally got to Cincinnati after about five years, I got my own locker with my own name over the top of it, and my name on the uniform. I was in the big leagues, and I realized a boy's dream. If I had to pick an individual thrill, that was it.

"The 13-inning game in Philadelphia was a thrill and, you know, I participated in the longest scoreless game in the major leagues. That was right after the war. I think I pitched either 15 or 17 innings in Brooklyn in that 19-inning ball game. Harry Gumpert finished it. It ended 0-0 on account of darkness, because they weren't allowed to turn the lights on at that time to finish a game. I think that was probably the greatest game I ever pitched."

Here we have the case of a man who has performed the unique feat of hurling two successive no-hitters which likely assures him a prominent spot in the record books forever, and still he feels his arrival in the majors was his greatest thrill and thinks the greatest game he ever pitched wasn't a no-hitter but the 15 or 17 innings he worked in a 19-inning scoreless tie. All of this says something about the modesty and level-headedness of a fine southpaw and person named Johnny Vander Meer.

In 1986 the Committee on Veterans elected the late Ernie Lombardi to the Hall of Fame, and on August 3 of that year

Ernie's sister accepted his plaque at the annual ceremonies in Cooperstown. True to his word, Vander Meer came from Tampa to be on hand, even though he had suffered a stroke only six weeks previously.

JOHN SAMUEL VANDER MEER
BR TL 6'1" 190 lbs.
Born in Prospect Park, New Jersey on November 2, 1914

YEAR	TEAM	W	L	PCT.	ERA	G	GS	CG	IP	H	BB	SO	ShO
1937	Cincinnati NL	3	5	.375	3.84	19	9	4	84.1	63	69	52	0
1938	" "	15	10	.600	3.12	32	29	16	225.1	177	103	125	3
1939	" "	5	9	.357	4.67	30	21	8	129	128	95	102	0
1940	" "	3	1	.750	3.75	10	7	2	48	38	41	41	0
1941	" "	16	13	.552	2.82	33	32	18	226.1	172	126	202	6
1942	" "	18	12	.600	2.43	33	33	21	244	188	102	186	4
1943	" "	15	16	.484	2.87	36	36	21	289	228	162	174	3
1946	" "	10	12	.455	3.17	29	25	11	204.1	175	78	94	5
1947	" "	9	14	.391	4.40	30	29	9	186	186	87	79	3
1948	" "	17	14	.548	3.41	33	33	14	232	204	124	120	3
1949	" "	5	10	.333	4.90	28	24	7	159.2	172	85	76	3
1950	Chicago NL	3	4	.429	3.79	32	6	0	73.2	60	59	41	0
1951	Cleveland AL	0	1	.000	18.00	1	1	0	3	8	1	2	0
	13 yrs.	119	121	.496	3.44	346	285	131	2104.2	1799	1132	1294	30

WORLD SERIES

YEAR	TEAM	W	L	PCT.	ERA	G	GS	CG	IP	H	BB	SO	ShO
1940	Cincinnati NL	0	0	—	0.00	1	0	0	3	2	3	2	0

A kingpin of the St. Louis Cardinals of the 1940s, Marty Marion was one in a long line of superlative shortstops for the Redbirds. In 1940, his first season with the Cardinals, the team finished third, with Marion hitting .278. In the nine years to follow, St. Louis would finish either first or second every time—and no one played a more important part in making St. Louis a constant contender than "Slats" Marion. A .263 career hitter, Marion played in four World Series with the Cardinals, later managed them as well as the St. Louis Browns and the Chicago White Sox.

16

Marty Marion

Superlatives galore have been spoken or penned in recent years to extol the defensive skills of Ozzie Smith, the outstanding shortstop of the baseball Cardinals. All who have witnessed his spectacular exploits recognize that he isn't called the Wizard of Oz for nothing.

But it must be kept in mind that the Cardinals have long been blessed with standout shortstops. The list extends back from Garry Templeton, Dal Maxvill, Dick Groat, Alvin Dark, and Marty Marion to Leo Durocher, Charlie Gelbert, Tommy Thevenow, Specs Toporcer, and even to Rogers Hornsby (since he played short mostly in his first few seasons in the majors).

While only Hornsby of those named above has made it into the Hall of Fame, all were outstanding in their time, mostly as defensive stars. And none was a more valuable cog in the Cardinal machine than Marty Marion, the glue that held the St. Louis infield together during the decade of the '40s.

The Cardinals started that 10-year span by finishing third in 1940. Through the following nine years they were either first or second every time. They won the National League title in '42, '43, '44, and '46, going on to take the World Series each time except in 1943.

Terry Moore, great Redbird centerfielder of that era, is convinced that the Cards would have won six or seven pennants in a row had not World War II come along to break up their juggernaut. Marty Marion agrees. "Definitely," he says. "We had the greatest nucleus, and they were all young, too."

A St. Louis newspaper polled its readers in the spring of 1986 to determine their choices for the best players at each position in Cardinal history. Ozzie Smith was the choice at short-stop, with Marty Marion second. Of course, most of the voters never saw Marion in action, and the suspicion here is that those who did favored Marty or at the very least put him in a tie with Ozzie.

At 6' 2" Marion was tall for a shortstop in his day. And he played at 170 pounds. It's no wonder he was soon given the nickname of "Slats." It stayed with him throughout his career. Players and other baseball people from that era agree that Slats Marion was a powerful force in making St. Louis a perennial contender in the National League in those years. In 1944 Marion was voted the MVP in the National League.

"I was born," Marty says, "in a little town called Richburg, South Carolina. Just a little wide spot in the road. My family moved to Atlanta when I was nine months old. I lived there until I came to St. Louis. And I've been in St. Louis since 1940. I played ball in high school, played a lot of American Legion baseball, and signed a major league contract with the Cardinals. Played four years in the minor leagues and came to St. Louis in 1940.

"My first game in the majors was against Pittsburgh. A guy named Bob Klinger was the pitcher for the Pirates. My first major league hit was a swinging bunt down the third-base line and I beat it out."

In his first season Marion played in 125 games and hit .278, just two points shy of the best mark he ever reached in the majors. That season the Cards had three managers—Ray Blades for the first 39 games, then Mike Gonzalez as a fill-in for five contests, and Billy Southworth for the remaining 114 games. How did Marty react to this shuffling of managers?

"Well, I'll tell you, I didn't think there was such a thing as a best manager. One is as good as another. In certain years we had better players than in other years, and that's what makes the manager, not the manager himself."

Nineteen forty was a transitional season for the Cards. The era of the famed Gas House gang had ended, with the likes of Dizzy and Paul Dean, Frankie Frisch, Wild Bill Hallahan, Ripper Collins, Leo Durocher, Joe Medwick, Pepper Martin, and others. Terry Moore was the bridge between the old gang and the juggernaut of the '40s.

Enos Slaughter had come aboard in '38, Mort Cooper in '39, Marion in '40, Johnny Hopp and Walker Cooper in '41. Branch Rickey's innovative farm system came into full bloom in 1942, when Stan Musial and Whitey Kurowski became regulars, Harry the Hat Walker a valuable reserve outfielder, and Johnny Beazley, a 21-game winner as a rookie.

The Redbirds surprised the Yankees—and nearly everyone else—in the 1942 World Series with four straight wins after dropping the first game, Beazley hurling two complete-game victories. The new Cardinal dynasty was in place and rolling. And Marty Marion was a crucial cog in the machine.

Of the decade of the '40s Marty says: "If the good Lord had not taken our boys away to the army and if this hadn't happened and that hadn't happened, we would have won a lot of pennants. We won a lot as it was, but we would have won a lot more.

"In '42 we had a great Series, because that was our first one, at least my first one and the first one the Cardinals had won in a long time. The Yankees were a great ball club. Nobody gave us a chance to beat the mighty Yankees. But we were a cocky bunch and we didn't think they could beat us. History proves we were right. But in '43 it wasn't the same setting. The excitement wasn't there. I don't know why. The Yankees beat us easily.

"In '44 I'll tell you one thing. We took the Browns too lightly. Then when we got on the field with them, they almost beat us. A break here or there and they easily could have won the Series.

"A funny thing about that '44 Series with the Browns. I had a 104° fever for the whole time. I'd go up to my room and I only had orange juice for about a week there. I had an uncle who came up from Thomaston, Georgia. Old Dr. Garner, and he stayed with me. My wife had gone home because we were expecting a baby at that time. So Dr. Garner roomed at the hotel here. And he took care of me. He'd go out at night to get me aspirin and things like that. I was as sick as a dog. But I had a good Series. You used to play as good sometimes when you were sick as when you were well.

"Nineteen forty-six was Eddie Dyer's first year as our manager. Dyer and Walker Cooper had had words in the minors and they didn't like each other. Cooper said he wouldn't play for

Dyer, and so they had to trade Cooper. Joe Garagiola and Del Rice did the catching for us. That was the year we beat Brooklyn two straight in a playoff.

"Durocher was the Dodger manager that year, and he decided to have the first game here and then get two in Brooklyn. We beat him in the first game here and also in the first game in Brooklyn.

"The '46 Series with the Red Sox was a funny one. There again, we were the underdogs and nobody thought we could beat Ted Williams and the Red Sox. But we didn't think we were that bad a ball club ourselves. We figured if we could split with them here, which we did, and win one of three games in Boston, which we did, then we'd come back to St. Louis and beat them. And we did.

"That's the year Brecheen won three games. And Enos Slaughter scored from first on a single to win the last game. I don't really know why everybody was so excited about that. I was the next hitter and I was going to drive him in anyway, so it didn't make any difference.

"Everybody always blamed Johnny Pesky for that play. But it really wasn't his fault. Slaughter was running on the pitch and Harry Walker hit the ball to left-center. Culberson, I think it was, was in center field. Dom DiMaggio wasn't in there at the time. Pesky went out to take the relay, and he didn't have that strong an arm anyway. But nobody was close to Pesky to tell him where to throw the ball. Normally you would think that Enos would go to third and stop. But when Pesky took that second hitch when he saw that Enos was going, it was too late."

Marty Marion was one of Branch Rickey's prizes from the farm system who came up to the big club to become a star. But their relationship wasn't always smooth and happy.

"Branch and I were always fighting. He didn't want to pay any money. And, you know, it's kind of ridiculous to talk about money, compared with what they pay today. But we had a heck of a time making $5,000, so you can see what money meant. I can remember that Mr. Rickey would always say, 'Marty, you just do what I want done and we'll take care of you.' I always told him, 'Mr. Rickey, you pay me and I'll take care of myself.' But he was a great baseball man, one of the greatest of all time. Everybody says that, so it must be true.

"I remember my first meeting with him. In '35, I believe it was. Mr. Rickey had invited me to come from Atlanta, be-

cause they wanted to sign me to a contract. So I came up to
St. Louis to try out with the Cardinals with the big team in
Sportsman's Park. And I sat in the stands and watched a game
that day with the Cubs. Phil Cavarretta hit a home run to beat
Paul Dean, 1-0. That was the year when the Cubs won 21
straight to take the pennant."

In 1945 some Mexican League owners enticed a number
of major leaguers to go south of the border for a lot more bucks
than they were making in the States. Marty remembers those
days:

"I guess it was tempting for those kids because they
weren't making any money. I didn't have that problem. Nobody
offered me any money to go anywhere. But Freddie Martin went,
and Lou Klein and Max Lanier. Off of our club here. Two good
pitchers and a second baseman. I guess it was Rickey or Breadon
who gave Terry Moore a thousand for persuading Musial and
Slaughter not to be tempted too much."

In 1951 Marty Marion was named manager of the Car-
dinals. Because of a back problem he wasn't a playing manager.
The Redbirds came in third, well behind the Giants and the
Dodgers, who put on the torrid race that ended only with Bobby
Thomson's "shot heard around the world" in the third playoff
game. Marty dismisses that season with few words.

"We had some unfortunate luck that year. For a whole
month the whole club was down with the flu, then Musial came
up with appendicitis. We had some problems and we didn't have
the best ball club, but we weren't the worst, either. Anyway,
a guy named Mr. Fred Saigh owned the ball club at that particular time and we didn't get along very well, so he got rid
of me quick."

Before mid-season of '52 Marion was called on to replace
Hornsby as manager of the St. Louis Browns in the American
League.

"After I was fired from the Cardinals I went to play for
the Browns. But I was an old has-been by then. I was a coach
and a player and had a very bad back and everything. I played
a few games, and not too badly. Then when they fired Hornsby
I took the managing over, and I was worse than Hornsby. That
was a very bad ball club."

The '54 season found Marty serving as a coach under Paul
Richards with the Chicago White Sox. Just before the end of
the season Richards resigned to become manager of the Balti-

more Orioles (the former Browns), and Marion became the Sox manager. His 1955 team won 91 games but finished third behind the Yankees and Cleveland. The same teams wound up the '56 campaign in the same order, and thus ended Marty's major league days as player and manager. "I got fired in Chicago," he says, "because I always wanted to come home to St. Louis. I didn't want to live away from my family. That was the toughest thing in baseball."

But he was still to be connected with the game for a while longer. "After '56," he explains, "some of us bought the Houston ball club of the Texas League. The Houston Buffs. We bought them, kept them three years, lost a lot of money, then when we sold out to the people who got the major league franchise we made some money.

"You see, the Cardinals owned the Buffs at that time, and we paid $100,000 for the team and got some ragtag ballplayers. We knew that Houston was going to be a major league city. But we had to ride out the wait, and we didn't have enough money to get the major league franchise. Mr. Hofheinz kicked us out. Nowadays we could have taken it to court, but back in those days they could do what they wanted to."

As would be expected, Marty Marion possesses a treasure of memories from his baseball days. He recalls one that was both exciting and scary.

"I'll tell you the most exciting thing that happened to me. It was when I was managing the Browns. We weren't making any money with the Browns. We didn't have any fans in the stands and we hardly had enough baseballs to take batting practice. Well, on our last trip east we had an exhibition game in Providence, Rhode Island. And everything was Satchel Paige, Satchel Paige. We advertised Satchel Paige. Anyway, they had about 15,000 people out there. We made more money in that exhibition game than we made in the regular season.

"But no Satchel Paige. He didn't show up. So I'm sitting on the bench and, boy, they're all over me. Thousands all around me and they're screaming and hollering. I said, 'I'll tell you what to do. You find him and I'll pitch him.'

"Anyway, Bill Drain was our secretary and I said to him, 'Bill, you go upstairs and get our share of the money; there's going to be a riot here. They're mad. They came to see Satchel Paige. They didn't come to see the Browns play.'

"Satchel almost got us killed. We just got out of there in time. They were stoning the bus and everything.

"The next morning we walked into the Kendall Hotel in Boston and there's old Satchel, sitting in the lobby. I said, 'Satchel, you know you almost got us killed last night. That'll cost you $5,000, buddy.' But Bill Veeck wouldn't take the money from him. So that was my biggest scare in baseball."

And the moment in baseball that Marty remembers best? "Oh," he says, "my first World Series in 1942. A World Series is a big thing, plus the fact, you know, we were poor kids back in those days, and that was big money for us. My check for the winner's share in the '42 Series was $6,192—and my season salary was $5,000. Things have changed, and for the better. I can't say I made a great deal of money in baseball, but I sure made some good contacts."

Naturally, Marty remembers his teammates and the players he managed, and he enjoys recalling some of them.

"Mickey Owen was a great defensive ballplayer, and a real holler guy. I remember the first year I went to spring training with the Cardinals, Mickey was a highly touted rookie coming up from Columbus, Ohio. Boy, he had a lot of ballyhoo about him. But he never made it big with the Cardinals, and they traded him to the Brooklyn Dodgers. He had his better years later, despite the unfortunate incident."

The "unfortunate incident" Marion mentions was, of course, one of baseball's most remembered plays. It came in 1941, during the first of seven World Series between the Yankees and the old Brooklyn Dodgers. In the fourth game Brooklyn led, 4-3, going into the ninth inning. Hugh Casey, stalwart Dodger reliever, had come on in the fifth to throttle the Yankees.

He retired the first two batters in the ninth and then fanned Tommy Henrich, apparently winning the game and tying the Series at two games apiece. But it was not to be. The third strike on Henrich eluded Mickey Owen and then the bottom fell out. Before it ended New York had scored four times to win and closed out the Series the following day. From that day to this no one has let Owen forget the "unfortunate incident."

Of Ted Wilks, who had a 17-4 record for the Cards in 1944, Marty recalls: "We used to ask Ted how he pitched a certain guy, and he'd say, 'I don't know, I just throw it down the middle.' He was a kind of Polish old boy, you know, a straight-talking kid. Nothing fancy about big Ted."

Asked about George Munger, Marion says, "George, yeah. He was from Houston, Texas. We always thought he would be a better pitcher than he really was. If he'd been meaner, he would have been a great pitcher. Red was too easy-going."

And Johnny Hopp? "John was the type of ballplayer that if you played him for two weeks he was the best ballplayer in the league, but if you played him longer than that he would give out. Rest him a few days, put him back in the lineup, he was great. A very good utility ball player."

How about Red Schoendienst? "Well, Red could play anywhere. The reason he didn't play shortstop or second base when he first came up in '45 is that we had two pretty good guys there." The two pretty good guys were Emil Verban at second and Marty Marion at short. But Red took over second base the following year and stayed there almost exclusively in the remainder of his long active career.

And Enos Slaughter? "A lot of guys didn't think Enos had the kind of career to get into the Hall of Fame. Enos, he was a good ballplayer, not a great, great player, but a real good one. One of the famous New York writers called me awhile back and said, 'Marty, I don't know what to do about this Hall of Fame voting. What the hell would you do?' I told him, 'Why don't you put Enos in the Hall of Fame? He wants to be in there. Put him in. He'd be so happy.' And I'm glad they voted him in."

Besides the episode already narrated when Satchel Paige failed to show up for an exhibition game, Marion has more memories about Satchel.

"Satchel was the hardest guy I managed. Satchel was the kind of guy who did what he wanted to. You didn't manage Satchel, he managed you. You know, I had Satchel there and he'd do what he wanted to, and Veeck would back him up. I fined him all kinds of money that year (1953), but Veeck never took a nickel. I didn't see Satchel when he was great. When I saw him he was just an ordinary pitcher. But a great storyteller."

Marty recalls that during his managing days he had some pitchers who were also good pinch hitters.

"You know, the best thing about Gene Bearden when he was with us on the Browns, other than being a fairly good pitcher, was that he was my best pinch hitter. He was a good hitter. I'd send him up there all the time and he'd get a hit for me pretty often. And with the White Sox I had three pitchers who were good hitters—Dixie Howell, Dick Donovan, and Jack Harshman. But you can see we weren't very strong on the bench when we had pitchers pinch hitting for us."

And Billy Pierce? "I'd only pitch Billy Pierce on Sunday. Billy wasn't a very strong kid, and if you pitched him in rotation every fourth day he'd get murdered. But if you'd give him his rest he'd beat the opposition regularly. I never got booed so much in my life as one day when we were playing the Yankees a doubleheader in Comiskey Park. In the first game Billy was pitching and we were leading, 3-2, in the seventh inning. Bases were loaded and Billy was hot, and I went to take him out. I'll tell you one thing. Sixty thousand people all stood up and booed me. I brought Dixie Howell in and Hank Bauer hit a screaming shot to left field right at Minoso, who caught it and we won the game."

When asked to compare Chico Carrasquel and Luis Aparicio, Marty commented with enthusiasm:

"You know, Chico was a good ballplayer, but he didn't have enough desire and we traded him while I was manager of the Sox. We had this kid named Looie Aparicio playing with Memphis, so we brought him up and I taught him everything I knew. And the kid was a good little ballplayer even then. We started the season with him and we were playing Kansas City. He wasn't doing worth a nickel. He was scared to death and couldn't talk English very well.

"I said to him, 'Looie, come over here. I want you to sit right down. You're not going to play today.' And he was pouting, you know. I kept him on the bench a couple of days. But when I put him back in there he was a different ballplayer. And he was never out of his depth. You can see what his career was after that. He was a great kid and turned out to be one of the best."

Jungle Jim Rivera? Marty laughed, and said: "Jim was colorful. He wasn't a very good player. Greatest old boy in the world, though. Give you the shirt off his back. He was just a good-hearted old boy. I loved Jim."

Dick Donovan was another player Marion admired. "He stayed in the minors an awfully long time. We got him in the draft from Atlanta of the Southern Association when he was 28, and that's old to be coming up. I'll never forget the time he was being shellacked out there one day when he first came up. He'd been up and down so many times with different ball clubs. And I went to take him out because he was getting shellacked, and he wouldn't give me the ball. He said, 'No, you're not going to get this ball. I'm going to make this team.' Anyway, I assured him he'd get another chance. And so he did, and had a good year from then on. In 1955 he was our best pitcher. We had a pretty good ball club and might have won the pennant. We were in front about September 1 and then Donovan came down with an appendicitis operation. And boy we went downhill from then on."

Not surprisingly, Marty has some pretty definite ideas about certain aspects of baseball today. Things like free agency, arbitration, the designated hitter, expansion, the type of club owners these days, and the long-term, no-cut, guaranteed contracts.

"Free agency is great for the players. Bad for the owners. But you can't blame the players for anything. The owners are just like a . . . if you can't run your business any better than that, you deserve it. And arbitration is a one-sided street, all in favor of the player.

"I'll tell you, in our day it wasn't like it is now with rules that say you can't do this and can't do that, because of the strong players' union they have. Back in our day, if you didn't want to play for the Cardinals, they'd just say. 'Hey, we'll give you a one-way ticket back to Rochester or Columbus.' They didn't fool with you. Back then it was one-sided in favor of the owners.

"But I think the long-term, no-cut, guaranteed contract absolutely ruins the player's desire. I would never sign a player for over one year. I can tell you from experience, the richer I got from playing baseball, the worse player I was. I didn't put out as much as when I was starving.

"The owners now are business types who want to make money off it. And some of them do but a lot of them don't. In the old days you had owners who bought clubs because they were great baseball fans. Yawkey and Breadon and the Yankee owners. And Wrigley, particularly Wrigley.

"I like the designated hitter. It burns me up to see an old pitcher walk up there and swing at the air three times and go back and sit down. There must be a better way. I like the DH. I think it's good for baseball because it gives you more offense, it gives players a job, and things like that. Those against the DH talk about strategy. Well, that's overblown.

"As for the artificial surface, I never played on it. But I don't see how you could ever miss a ball, because it's like playing on this rug here. I think I would like it. There are no bad hops."

"How about the expansion in the majors from 16 to 26 teams? Has it affected the quality of play?"

"Well, it has weakened the quality of play, no question about it. But if you take most of the big leaguers who are around today, they could have played any time. And the growing number of blacks and Hispanics in the majors have kept the quality almost the same."

"Any comments on the great importance of relief pitchers today?"

"Well, it used to be that if a guy couldn't go nine innings, he wasn't very much of a pitcher. Back in our day we used to relieve with the starters. At the end of my career the relief pitcher had just started to come into being. Now if a guy gives you six or seven innings, man, he's great.

"I used to have a theory, when I was managing, that I never wanted to lose with a tired pitcher. If I lost one with a tired pitcher, I thought it was my fault. Maybe if I made the decision to bring in a fresh pitcher I would still lose, but I always held that theory."

"Didn't you have a brother named Johnny who played in the majors?"

"Yeah, Johnny 'Red' Marion, an older brother. He came up for a cup of coffee, as they say, with Washington but never made it in the big leagues. Good outfielder, never could hit. Later he worked for the Red Sox for a long time in their farm system, and died in California in '75."

"Did you have any connection with baseball after your group sold the Houston club?"

"After we sold the Houston ball club in '61 I came back to St. Louis. For a while I had my own business and was out of baseball for a time. The only connection I had was a radio show I did here. Then they opened the new stadium downtown, and me and some other guys put the Stadium Club in, and I ran it for 18 years. I own some farms and I'm a big duck hunter. More than that, I've got 11 grandkids, and that's fun. I don't like to travel any more. Guess I traveled too much in my day."

As he says, Marty traveled a lot off the field in his day. More than that, he covered many a mile in patrolling the wide domain of the shortstop. And he did it with such consummate grace and elegance that nearly all oldtime Redbird fans give him their vote as perhaps the finest shortstop in Cardinal history— and that's saying something.

Marty Marion also was a key figure, along with Cards' trainer Doc Weaver and centerfielder Terry Moore, in launching the ballplayers' pension fund which today is overflowing with funds. When they were rained out one day in New York in August 1946, they sat around in their hotel and came up with a proposal that soon gained everybody's approval.

Their plan called for funds to be raised from All-Star Game profits, the radio income from the World Series and contributions of $100 per player and $2,500 per team. Later, of course, through aggressive pressure by the players' union and Marvin Miller, a large portion of the annual TV revenues is added to the fund. Thus, today's players will receive pensions so large they ought to be embarrassing, while the old-timers who ended their careers prior to 1946 qualify only for a mere pittance, an inequity which calls out for redress.

MARTIN WHITFORD MARION
BR   TR   6'2"   170 lbs.
Born in Richburg, South Carolina on December 1, 1917

YEAR	TEAM	G	AB	R	H	RBI	2B	3B	HR	BB	SO	SB	AVG.
1940	St. Louis NL	125	435	44	121	46	18	1	3	21	34	9	.278
1941	" " "	155	547	50	138	58	22	3	3	42	48	8	.252
1942	" " "	147	485	66	134	54	38	5	0	48	50	8	.276
1943	" " "	129	418	38	117	52	15	3	1	32	37	1	.280
1944	" " "	144	506	50	135	63	26	2	6	43	50	1	.267
1945	" " "	123	430	63	119	59	27	5	1	39	39	2	.277
1946	" " "	146	498	51	116	46	29	4	3	59	53	1	.233
1947	" " "	149	540	57	147	74	19	6	4	49	58	3	.272
1948	" " "	144	567	70	143	43	26	4	4	37	54	1	.252
1949	" " "	134	515	61	140	70	31	2	5	37	42	0	.272
1950	" " "	106	372	36	92	40	10	2	4	44	55	1	.247
1952	St. Louis AL	67	186	16	46	19	11	0	2	19	17	0	.247
1953	" " "	3	7	0	0	0	0	0	0	0	0	0	.000
	13 yrs.	1572	5506	602	1448	624	272	37	36	470	537	35	.263

WORLD SERIES

YEAR	TEAM	G	AB	R	H	RBI	2B	3B	HR	BB	SO	SB	AVG.
1942	St. Louis NL	5	18	2	2	3	0	1	0	1	2	0	.111
1943	" " "	5	14	1	5	2	2	0	1	3	1	1	.357
1944	" " "	6	22	1	5	2	3	0	0	2	3	0	.227
1946	" " "	7	24	1	6	4	2	0	0	1	1	0	.250
	4 yrs.	23	78	5	18	11	7	1	1	7	7	1	.231

MARTY MARION AS MANAGER

YEAR	TEAM	G	W	L	PCT.	FINISH
1951	St. Louis NL	156	81	73	.526	3
1952	" " AL	105	42	62	.404	7
1953	" " "	154	54	100	.351	8
1954	Chicago AL	9	3	6	.333	3
1955	" "	155	91	63	.591	3
1956	" "	154	85	69	.552	3
	6 yrs.	733	356	373	.488	

Al Lopez, best known as a 17-year manager who twice (1954, Cleveland, and 1959, Chicago) broke Yankee pennant streaks, was a durable defensive catcher. A native of Tampa's Spanish section, Ybor City, the "Señor" was a young Brooklyn Dodger when shown here. His 1,950 games were a record for a catcher. His managerial won-lost record, .581, is the ninth highest in major league history. Lopez was enshrined at Cooperstown in 1977.

17

Al Lopez

Al Lopez, the seventh son of a seventh son from the Asturias region of Spain, was born in 1908 in the Ybor City section of Tampa. He grew up playing ball wherever he could, especially around old Plant Field in Tampa, the spot where Al Lopez Stadium now stands.

The Washington Senators trained in Tampa in those years, and Al got to catch the legendary Walter Johnson in batting practice. Johnson gave the young Lopez an example of hard work and all-out effort that was to become Al's guide in his own career.

"One of my dreams," Al reminisces, "was to become a professional ballplayer. But I never thought I would be one. I played ball in school and sandlot ball around Ybor City. Luckily, I was picked up by the local team. I signed a contract when I was 16 years old. Then to be bought by Brooklyn, a major league club, was a dream I never thought could happen. I was the only Tampa boy who had ever gotten to the majors."

Not only the first Tampa boy, we may add, but at that point one of a mere handful of players of Hispanic descent. Dolf Luque, a really fine pitcher from Cuba, was about the only Latin star to shine in the majors up to that time. No one could even imagine then the wave of Hispanic players dotting big league rosters nowadays.

Lopez first appeared in a Brooklyn box score in 1928, seeing action in three games. In 1930 he became their regular catcher. He played in 128 games, hit for a .309 average, and drove home 57 runs. It was to be his best offensive effort in 19 active seasons.

But the real value of a catcher lies in other things—handling pitchers, throwing out base runners, exerting leadership, etc. It was here that Lopez gained his reputation as one of the premier catchers in the game. To all of that must be added his durability. Al caught 1,918 games in the majors, still a record although present-day receivers like Bob Boone and Jim Sundberg are inching toward his mark.

Al Lopez wasn't through with baseball, however, when he ended his active career. He followed up with 17 years as a manager with Cleveland and the Chicago White Sox. He took the Indians to the World Series in '54 and the Sox in '59, the only interruptions which kept the New York Yankees from rolling up the mind-boggling total of 16 AL pennants in a row. In 1977 came the icing on the cake when Al Lopez was inducted into the Baseball Hall of Fame.

Of all the teams he played on, Lopez is sure which was the best. "The 1930 Brooklyn team was the best I played on. We finished fourth but we led the league most of the year. Injuries caught us toward the end. Johnny Frederick pulled a hamstring and Rube Bressler broke a finger. That hurt us a lot.

"We had Del Bissonette at first, Glenn Wright at short, Babe Herman in the outfield with Frederick and Bressler, and some good pitchers—Dazzy Vance, Dolf Luque, Jumbo Jim Elliott, Ray Phelps, Watty Clark, and Sloppy Thurston. To me old Dolf was a great pitcher. I learned a lot from catching him. And our team batting average for the whole season was .304.

"The next season Lefty O'Doul and Van Lingle Mungo joined us. O'Doul was a great hitter, a smart hitter too. Then Hack Wilson was with us for a couple of years. A great guy, but on his way down. The ball was not as lively as when he had his great years with the Cubs.

"Of all the pitchers I caught, I believe the fastest was Mungo. The trouble was that Mungo's ball didn't move. It came in straight as a string. So, when he got a little tired in the late innings, the batters would catch up with him and knock him out."

After six seasons with Brooklyn, Lopez was traded to the Boston Braves. He was with the Braves for over four years. During his time there he suffered a broken finger, which limited him to just 71 games in the '38 season. It wasn't the only time he was out with that kind of injury. In 1946 he had a broken bone in his throwing hand.

Early in the 1940 season Al was traded to the Pittsburgh Pirates for Ray Berres. In Pittsburgh he caught, among others, Rip Sewell, best remembered for his blooper ball or "eephus" pitch. "Yeah, he came up with that thing while I was there," recalls Lopez. "He said he got the idea in the bullpen. I would be warming him up out there and on the last ball he threw me he would just lob it. That was the start of it. The amazing thing was that he had such good control of it. That blooper would come right down over the plate for a strike."

Al Lopez wasn't really a big, strong catcher. He stood 5'11" and weighed 165 pounds in his playing days. But he was agile, had a mighty quick release on his throws to the bases, and always was in good condition. He didn't smoke and didn't drink, nor was he a carouser at night. He kept himself in fine condition. Moreover, he was an intelligent catcher and no one was more in the game than he was.

One example will surely confirm the above. One day, while he was with Boston, with a 3 and 0 count on the batter Lopez called for a pitchout and picked a runner off third base. "I was sure I could catch the guy off third," says Al. "And it was better to let the batter go to first than to have the runner on third."

Lopez once picked his own All-Star team. It had Bill Terry at first, either Rogers Hornsby or Frankie Frisch at second, Glenn Wright at short, Pie Traynor at third, with Joe DiMaggio, Ted Williams, and Stan Musial in the outfield, and Gabby Hartnett behind the plate. Regarding Hartnett he says, "Maybe even better than Bill Dickey or Mickey Cochrane." He also chooses Hornsby as the best right-handed hitter he ever saw, and Williams as the best from the left side of the plate.

Al offered some special comments about Glenn Wright: "At shortstop, a position where you sacrifice everything for defense, Wright could hit for average and enough power that he batted clean-up at Pittsburgh. He had good running speed and a shotgun arm until he hurt it. Glenn was such a strong right-handed hitter that I remember Dazzy Vance pitching around him, preferring to face a good left-handed hitter coming up next.

"Glenn and Pie Traynor formed probably the finest left side of an infield anyone ever saw. Wright hit 22 homers one year and drove in 100 runs or more four times. How many shortstops have you seen do that and hit at or over .300 too?"

Elaborating on his choice of Williams for his outfield, Lopez commented: "Williams was as good a hitter as any from the left side. More compact and more of a swinger. But I've seen a lot of good ones. Paul Waner, not a lot of power but a great hitter."

The best defensive play Al ever saw was made by Terry Moore. "And it was against me," adds Al. "I hit a blooper off the handle with three men on and two out in St. Louis. Terry came in on the dead run and just dove at the ball with his bare hand. And he caught that ball barehanded!"

As for the great pitchers of his time, Lopez had several thoughts: "There were a lot of good right-handed ones. Dizzy Dean and Dazzy Vance. I saw Alexander when he was about through, and he was a great one. As for lefthanders, I didn't play against Grove, but he was great, and so was Carl Hubbell.

"Hubbell was a shade better even than Dean among the pitchers I caught or hit against. The thing that made Hub was a change in the National League ball in 1933. Two years earlier they had taken some of the jackrabbit out of the ball, but in '33 they raised the seams on the ball. This let Hubbell get a better grip to turn the ball over and get a better snap with that long wrist he had. That's when his screwball faded away into a real butterfly and he became a big winner. For a few years in the mid-1930s he was the best pitcher I ever saw. I don't think any lefthander was ever more effective against right-handed batters.

"Dizzy was a great one too, but he was a happy-go-lucky guy who might loaf with a lead and give you a few runs. Yet in a low-scoring game or a tense situation, you'd see the tough competitor in him. He threw with a three-quarter sidearm delivery, but his fast one had the rise of such overhanded fastball throwers as Lefty Grove, Waite Hoyt, Mel Harder, and Dazzy Vance.

"Another hurler I'll never forget was Dolf Luque. He was perfect in his pitching pattern. Nobody was better at setting up a hitter with a couple of big sharp curves and then getting him with a fastball at the knee for a called strike three."

Al Lopez finished his playing days with the Cleveland Indians in 1947. Bill Veeck then controlled the Indians and intended to install Lopez as his manager in 1948. It was his plan to trade Lou Boudreau, who had been the playing manager at Cleveland since 1942. When word spread about Veeck's intentions, it created such a furor among the fans that Bill backed off.

It was probably just as well, despite the outstanding record Lopez put together when he did become manager later on. In 1948 Boudreau had a sensational season, hitting .355 and winning the American League MVP as he led the Indians to their first pennant since 1920. In doing so he almost single-handedly carried the Tribe past the Red Sox in a one-game playoff, smashing two homers in the 8-3 rout. Next, he guided Cleveland to a triumph over the Boston Braves in the World Series, four games to two.

Lopez meanwhile went to Indianapolis, where he managed his team to the American Association flag with 100 wins. The following two seasons he brought his team in second.

In 1951 Lopez came back to Cleveland as manager, with Boudreau moving on to Boston. In six seasons at the helm of the Indians, Lopez and his teams finished second to the Yankees five times. But in 1954 Al's Indians beat back the New Yorkers and everybody else, setting an American League mark of 111 wins in the process. Favored in the World Series, Cleveland fell victims to the New York Giants in four straight games.

Nineteen fifty-seven saw Lopez take over as manager of the Chicago White Sox, where he remained through 1965 (plus brief stints in '68 and '69). In '59 the Sox gave their fans the first pennant since the Black Sox days of 1919, but the Los Angeles Dodgers whipped them in the Series in six games. Six other times in Chicago Al's teams came in second, each time trailing the Yankees except in '65 when they were outdistanced by the Minnesota Twins.

The various teams piloted by Al Lopez won 1,422 games and lost 1,026, for a percentage of .581. In all of major league history 15 managers have led clubs which won more than 1,422 games, but only Joe McCarthy, Earl Weaver, John McGraw, and Casey Stengel compiled a better average.

As a catcher Lopez was known to be an intelligent student of the game. It was no surprise, then, to see him be successful as a manager, especially since he had played under several smart managers.

"An interesting thing," Al remarked, "is that every manager I played under is now in the Hall of Fame. Wilbert Robinson, my first manager, was a great guy to play for. Max Carey took over in Brooklyn in 1932, and Casey Stengel came on in '34. Bill McKechnie was the Boston manager when I went there in 1937.

"I learned an awful lot from McKechnie. When he went to Cincinnati in 1938, Stengel came over to manage the Braves. When I got to Pittsburgh Frankie Frisch was the manager, and Boudreau was managing in Cleveland when I went there.

"And then there was another manager I admired, and he was John McGraw. I think he's the one who brought in more things like the hit-and-run and going to the opposite field and stuff like that. I played against him and admired him a lot. He knew what he needed to make his club good, and he went out and got it."

"Al, nearly everyone thought your Cleveland team would beat the Giants in the '54 Series. What happened?"

"Well, I think we would have had a good chance to take the Series if we had won that first game. You see, sports are funny. You have streaks where everything you do is right. That year we won 111 ball games, still an American League record. Everything was going just perfect. And then in the Series everything we did went wrong.

"If we had started the Series in Cleveland I think we would have won the first two games. We certainly would have taken the first game, because the 460-foot drive that Wertz hit and Mays caught would have been a three-run homer. And Dusty Rhodes' 260-foot home run that won it in the 10th wouldn't even have happened. And if it did it would have been an easy out in Cleveland. Rhodes really ruined us in that Series.

"Then, in '59, the Dodgers' relief pitcher, Larry Sherry, did the same thing to the White Sox. He got in four games and won two and saved two."

I ventured the thought that Lopez must have felt some frustration over finishing second to the Yankees so many times.

"No," Al replied, "it was no frustration. Actually, I was very fortunate. If you have people who really want to play the game and go out and give you all they've got, I think that's the main thing. I had winning ball clubs, good players to work with, and good management too. So, no frustration.

"Both the '54 Indians and the '59 White Sox were good teams. The Cleveland pitching staff was the best I've ever seen on any club. They were entirely different types of ball clubs. Cleveland had great pitching, hard hitting, power hitting, while Chicago had real good pitching and speedy defense."

"How good was Larry Doby?"

"You know, Larry was the second black player to appear

in the majors. He was a fine player, but he should have been better yet. He had so much pride that he wanted to do better than he could. And he fought himself a lot. He had power, he had everything. He was a very proud man, and his feelings were hurt easily. He tried too hard and hurt himself by doing so."

"How about some of your White Sox stars?"

"Well, Minnie Minoso was a great guy on the club. Everybody liked him and he was a good, hustling ballplayer. He played every day, hurt or not. And Billy Pierce was a fine pitcher and real nice guy. I used to wish I had 25 guys like Billy. He didn't drink, didn't smoke, and you never had to worry a bit about him.

"Gerry Staley was a very good relief pitcher. He had a good sinkerball and made batters hit that ball on the ground. Gary Peters and Joe Horlen and Tommy John all pitched good ball for me. Tommy ought to thank Ray Berres, for Ray really helped him a lot.

"Juan Pizarro was another guy like Doby. He had tremendous ability but was a moody fellow. With his ability he should have been a lot better than he was."

"What was the most interesting game you ever witnessed?"

"One of the great games while I was managing Cleveland was in Yankee Stadium. This was when the Yankees were a powerhouse and Allie Reynolds, then one of the best in the league, was pitching against us. They scored seven runs in the first inning against either Early Wynn or Bob Lemon. Of course, I had to change pitchers in the very first inning.

"I started bringing in bullpen pitchers and pinch hitting, and the first thing you know we're creeping up on 'em, and finally we ended up beating them in the 10th inning, 8-7. That was one of the best games I can ever remember."

"Was there any one umpire you recall as the best?"

"Yes, Bill Klem. Definitely."

"And what was your own best game in the majors?"

"I think my best game was once in the Polo Grounds. It was the first game I played there against the Giants. If I remember right, I was five-for-six that day and drove in a number of runs."

"How do you rate Judge Landis with the later baseball commissioners?"

"Well, that's about like trying to compare some later players with Babe Ruth. But I think Judge Landis was the greatest. He didn't need the job. So, he could afford to rule the game the way he did. Once there was an owner complaining about the way Landis handled something. Landis called a meeting of the owners, took his contract and tore it up in front of them, and said, 'If you're not satisfied with the way I'm doing things, just get somebody else.' And everybody voted for him to stay. He could foresee trouble and would call a player or an owner to his office and settle the matter before anything wrong could happen."

As a manager, Al Lopez wasn't known to panic. On the outside, at least, he was calm, yet it's evident he wasn't all that cool on the inside, for he developed a nervous stomach that gave him a lot of trouble. And he admits he didn't sleep well while managing, though when he was a player he slept like a baby. He was patient with his players, especially the younger ones, but he wouldn't tolerate a player repeating the same mistakes.

One of his players once described Al as "the nicest guy in the world, but he rules with an iron hand." He expected his players to give him their very best, and also their respect. It's a tribute to him that they always did.

Al couldn't have been a rah-rah type if he tried. He didn't believe in clubhouse meetings or in fines. "Nobody can get a club up for 162 games," he said. And if someone wouldn't play Al's way, Al let him play his own way—but for some other team. Lopez felt his contribuitons to the club lay in getting the players to give their best and in handling pitchers.

Bob Lemon, a great pitcher for Al in Cleveland, was quoted as saying that Lopez could write the book on pitching. When to use a certain pitch, and why. And which pitch should follow another, and why, etc.

Lopez insisted in particular on three things from his players. A batter should never hesitate in rounding first base on a single if a runner is trying to score from second. An outfielder always has to throw to the cut-off man instead of to a specific base. And every player has to observe the curfew.

In addition to a tight defense and good pitching, Lopez loved speed in his players. Yet he was reluctant to use the bunt in the early innings. Good speed on the bases lessened the likelihood of hitting into double plays, and he was partial to the hit-and-run. He felt, however, that really good hit-and-run men are few and far between. "I've only seen four or five," he admits. "Alvin Dark, Dick Groat, Tony Cuccinello, and Billy Herman."

One thing that mystifies Al to this day is the drastic decline in the number of .300 hitters in the majors. He points out that the players now are bigger and better coordinated than in the '30s and '40s, yet they don't hit as well. He offers two reasonable explanations: night baseball and the predominant urge to swing from the heels in search of home runs. He is somewhat appalled by the huge number of strikeouts now recorded each season. He sees no chance of anyone hitting .400 again unless the batters change their tactics and concentrate on making contact.

It's no surprise that Lopez, being an old catcher himself, should have some thoughts about today's catchers. First he says, "I think the number of passed balls these days is ridiculous." For someone who went through the '41 season with no passed balls, the high count of passed balls nowadays must loom as a cardinal sin.

Al also has some opinions on base stealing. "They didn't try to steal as much in my day. The increased base stealing is a composite of three things. There's more speed now in baseball, and also there's more emphasis on base stealing. The other thing is that the pitchers are taller and it takes a little longer to deliver the ball. So, I don't think stolen bases are the catcher's fault in most cases. And there are still some catchers who throw a lot of those guys out. The quick release is a big thing in throwing runners out. I was lucky enough to have a quick release myself."

Asked about such modern developments in baseball as the designated hitter, artificial surfaces, free agency, astronomical salaries, and expansion, Al ventured these opinions:

"Personally, I think the designated hitter takes a lot away from managing. I would like to be able to maneuver a little more than you can with the DH.

"The artificial surface is a great advantage to the hitters, and it gives the infielders a truer bounce. There's no question about that. Management likes it because it reduces the number of rainouts. I'd rather see just a regular turf, and I think a lot of the players would too.

"Free agency, I think, is a terrible thing. When that judge made the decision, I guess he knew the law, but I think it hurt baseball. As for the big salaries, I don't blame the players for getting all they can. But the owners are the cause of it, and they have nobody to blame but themselves. And the players, once they sign a contract, should honor it and not try to re-negotiate all the time. Also, there's no question in my mind that the long-term, guaranteed, no-cut, no-trade contracts are a bad thing for baseball.

"Sooner or later they'll have to expand both in baseball and in football. There are large cities that want teams. One thing they have to straighten out is that the American League has two more teams than the National League. The American League schedule is all screwed up on account of that. They have to do something about it. To expand so that each league would have 16 clubs would be asking too much, because where are you going to get the players for six new teams? I think they should get two more teams in the National League and then play interleague baseball."

For the past several years Lopez has been a member of the 18-man Veterans Committee which selects old-time ballplayers for admission into the Hall of Fame. He was asked why a size-able number of former players who apparently have Hall of Fame credentials haven't been elected, players such as Phil Riz-zuto, Glenn Wright, Riggs Stephenson, Babe Herman, Wes Fer-rell, Hal Newhouser, and various others.

"Well," Al responded, "you'd be surprised that a lot of players that many think ought to be elected have been voted on and didn't get in, because you have to have a two-thirds ma-jority of the votes. You'd be surprised at how many are in that situation."

And so ended a pleasant conversation with the affable Señor, Al Lopez, in his very comfortable home in Tampa in January 1985. Al is definitely one who always did honor to baseball in his long active association with the sport, and he still does honor to it in retirement.

ALFONSO RAYMOND LOPEZ

BR TR   5'11" 165 lbs.

Born on August 20, 1908 in Tampa, Florida

Hall of Fame, 1977

YEAR	TEAM	G	AB	R	H	RBI	2B	3B	HR	BB	SO	SB	AVG.
1928	Brooklyn NL	3	12	0	0	0	0	0	0	0	0	0	.000
1930	" "	128	421	60	130	57	20	4	6	33	35	3	.309
1931	" "	111	360	38	97	40	13	4	0	28	33	1	.269
1932	" "	126	404	44	111	43	18	6	1	34	35	3	.275
1933	" "	126	372	39	112	41	11	4	3	21	39	10	.301
1934	" "	140	439	58	120	54	23	2	7	49	44	2	.273
1935	" "	128	379	50	95	39	12	4	3	35	36	2	.251
1936	Boston NL	128	426	46	103	50	12	4	8	41	41	1	.242
1937	" "	105	334	31	68	38	11	1	3	35	57	3	.204
1938	" "	71	236	19	63	14	6	1	1	11	24	5	.267
1939	" "	131	412	32	104	49	22	1	8	40	45	1	.252
1940	2 teams	Boston NL (36G — .294)				Pittsburgh NL (59G — .259)							
	total	95	293	35	80	41	9	3	3	19	21	6	.273
1941	Pittsburgh NL	114	317	33	84	43	9	1	5	31	23	0	.265
1942	" "	103	289	17	74	26	8	2	1	34	17	0	.256
1943	" "	118	372	40	98	39	9	4	1	49	25	2	.263
1944	" "	115	331	27	76	34	12	1	1	34	24	4	.230
1945	" "	91	243	22	53	18	8	0	0	35	12	1	.218
1946	" "	56	150	13	46	12	2	0	1	23	14	1	.307
1947	Cleveland AL	61	126	9	33	14	1	0	0	9	13	1	.262
	19 yrs.	1950	5916	613	1547	652	206	42	52	561	538	46	.261

AL LOPEZ AS MANAGER

YEAR	TEAM	G	W	L	PCT.	FINISH
1951	Cleveland AL	155	93	61	.604	2
1952	" "	155	93	61	.604	2
1953	" "	155	92	62	.597	2
1954	" "	156	111	43	.721	1
1955	" "	154	93	61	.604	2
1956	" "	155	88	66	.571	2
1957	Chicago AL	155	90	64	.584	2
1958	" "	155	82	72	.532	2
1959	" "	156	94	60	.610	1
1960	" "	154	87	67	.565	2
1961	" "	163	86	76	.531	4
1962	" "	162	85	77	.525	5
1963	" "	162	94	68	.580	2
1964	" "	162	98	64	.605	2
1965	" "	162	95	67	.586	2
1968	" "	81	33	48	.407	8 (tie)
1969	" "	17	8	9	.471	4
	17 yrs.	2459	1422	1026	.581	

WORLD SERIES

YEAR	TEAM	G	W	L	PCT.
1954	Cleveland AL	4	0	4	.000
1959	Chicago AL	6	2	4	.333
	2 yrs.	10	2	8	.200

About the Author

Walter Langford is a former Professor of Modern Languages at the University of Notre Dame, where he also compiled an impressive record as tennis and fencing coach. He has published *The Padre Fan's Calendar* and numerous articles on baseball history for major sports publications. His love of baseball was nurtured as a high school, college and semi-pro player. The curve dashed his major league dreams but not his devotion to The Game.